CHARACTER EDUCATION
IN AMERICA'S BLUE RIBBON SCHOOLS

Character Education
in America's Blue Ribbon Schools

Best Practices for
Meeting the Challenge

Madonna M. Murphy, Ph.D.
College of St. Francis
Joliet, Illinois

TECHNOMIC
PUBLISHING CO., INC.
LANCASTER · BASEL

Character Education in America's Blue Ribbon Schools
a TECHNOMIC® publication

Published in the Western Hemisphere by
Technomic Publishing Company, Inc.
851 New Holland Avenue, Box 3535
Lancaster, Pennsylvania 17604 U.S.A.

Distributed in the Rest of the World by
Technomic Publishing AG
Missionsstrasse 44
CH-4055 Basel, Switzerland

Printed in the United States of America
10 9 8 7 6 5 4 3 2

Main entry under title:
   Character Education in America's Blue Ribbon Schools: Best Practices for
      Meeting the Challenge

A Technomic Publishing Company book
Bibliography: p.
Includes index p. 243

Library of Congress Catalog Card No. 97-62359
ISBN No. 1-56676-593-5

To my mother, Dorothy Murphy,
the Blue Ribbon teacher in my life.

To Tom Lickona,
America's Blue Ribbon character educator.

To my niece, Cara Murphy.
Your smiling face in your difficult condition
has given me the fortitude and perseverance I needed
in order to see this book through its many revisions.

Contents

Foreword xiii

Preface xvii

Introduction xxi

Acknowledgements xxix

1. CAN GOOD CHARACTER BE TAUGHT?   1

Can Values and Virtues be Taught? 1
What is a Virtue? 2
Moral Values 2
What is Good Character? 5
A Construct For Understanding Good Character 6
How Do the Blue Ribbon Schools Foster the
    Development of Sound Character? 7
The Blue Ribbon Schools Comprehensive
    Model of Character Education 8
Summary 11
References 11

2. A BRIEF HISTORY OF CHARACTER EDUCATION IN THE U.S. SCHOOLS   13

Should Our Public Schools Teach Virtues
    and Values? 13

A Nation at Risk 14
Character Education in the Colonial Schools 15
Character Education at the Turn of the Century 16
John Dewey's Criticism of Character Education 17
Character Education Under Fire 18
The Value-Free Society 19
The Cognitive Moral Development Approach 19
As We Approach the 21st Century 21
Summary 23
References 23

3. CHARACTER EDUCATION PROGRAMS IN THE BLUE RIBBON SCHOOLS   27

Moral Education Required for Nomination as a
   Blue Ribbon School 27
Good Character as Defined by the Blue
   Ribbon Schools 29
Good Character Defined by a Catholic School 30
Importance of the School's Mission 31
Character Education in Private Schools 32
Identifying Core Values and Key Human Virtues 32
Blue Ribbon Schools' Lists of Key Character Traits 34
Curricular Ideas 38
The Teacher's Role in Character Development 46
Role of the Principal as Moral Leader 50
The School Counselor as Character Developer 52
Advisor/Advisee Programs 53
The Key Role of Parents in Character Education 53
Summary 55
References 55

4. DARE WE COUNT DRUG PREVENTION PROGRAMS AS CHARACTER EDUCATION?   59

Drug-Free Schools 59
A Reactive Approach to Character Development 60

Are Drug Education Programs Character
   Education Programs? 61
What Drug Education Programs are Used in the
   Blue Ribbon Schools? 62
Research Results 72
What Does Work? 73
Sex Education 75
Health Curriculum 78
Child Abuse Awareness 80
Research Results on Health/Sex
   Education Curricula 80
Summary 81
References 82

5. MOTIVATING STUDENTS   85

Will Knowing the Good Lead to Doing the Good? 85
Developing the Affective Side of Character 86
Motivation Programs 87
Guidance Programs 96
Self-Esteem Programs 104
Summary 112
References 113

6. TEACHING TECHNIQUES THAT
   PROMOTE CHARACTER   117

The Role of Academics in Promoting Character
   Development 119
The Value of Work and of a Students's Work 119
Academic Work in the Blue Ribbon Schools 120
Learning that Promotes "Achievement Self-Esteem".... 121
Cooperative Learning 122
Learning Styles 124
Integrated Language Arts or "Whole Language"
   Instruction 126

Thematic Instruction 128
Portfolios and Authentic Assessment 129
Summary 130
References 131

7. **HOW DO DISCIPLINE PROGRAMS DEVELOP
   GOOD CHARACTER?**   133

Discipline as Moral Education 133
Discipline Programs that Emphasize
   Character Traits 134
Discipline that Develops Character 136
True Discipline is Self-Discipline 136
Discipline as Part of the Educational Process 136
Role of the Teacher in Promoting Good Discipline ... 137
High Expectations 137
The Proactive Approach to Discipline 138
Creating Safe Schools 139
Assertive Discipline and "Modified"
   Assertive Discipline 139
Behavior Modification Techniques that Promote
   Character Development 141
Catch Students Doing Something Right 142
The Class Meeting 142
Conflict Resolution and Peer Mediation 143
Resolving Conflicts Peacefully 144
Cooperative Discipline 145
Developing Good Decision-Making Skills 146
Discipline with Love and Logic 146
Judicious Discipline 147
Moral Discipline 148
Positive Discipline 148
Quality Schools 149
School Handbooks and Daily Planners That
   Promote Character 150
School Rules That Promote Character 151
School-Wide Discipline Programs 152
Teaching Respect in Schools 153
Teaching Responsibility in Schools 153

Summary 155
References 155

8. **HOW DOES GOOD CITIZENSHIP CONTRIBUTE
   TO GOOD CHARACTER?** 157

Education for Citizenship as the Goal of Universal
    Education 157
Civic Education Versus Character Education 158
Democratic Traits of Character 159
School Mission to Promote Citizenship 160
Promoting Citizenship in the Social Studies Class 161
CIVITAS 161
Current Events 163
Developing Decision-Making Skills................... 163
Citizenship Programs Found in the
    Blue Ribbon Schools 164
Caring as a Moral Value 164
Caring within the Classroom 165
Caring beyond the Classroom 173
Global Concerns 176
Summary 178
References 179

9. **EVALUATING THE EFFECTIVENESS OF CHARACTER
   EDUCATION IN THE BLUE RIBBON SCHOOLS** 181

Evaluating These Research Findings 181
The Blue Ribbon School Evaluation Process 182
An Evaluation Model for Character
    Education Programs 184
Evaluation of Character Education in the Blue
    Ribbon School Applications 187
Evaluation of Character Education by U.S.
    Department of Education Site Visitors 188
Evaluations of Character Education Programs 190
Evaluation of Blue Ribbon Schools' Character
    Development Programs 192

Components of Effective Character
Education Schools 199
Summary 200
References 200

Appendix A... 203

Appendix B... 217

Appendix C... 235

Index 243

About the Author..................................... 253

Item: In a recent survey reported by the *Boston Globe,* more than half of ninth-graders in an affluent suburb said they saw nothing wrong with stealing a compact disc or keeping money found in a lost wallet.

Item: Fifty percent of U.S. high school seniors say they are currently sexually active; half of these say they have had four or more partners: and the United States has the highest teen pregnancy rate and teen abortion rate in the industrialized world, according to the federal government's 1995 National Survey of Family Growth.

Item: In June, 1997, during her high school prom, a New Jersey 18-year-old girl gave birth to a baby boy in the school bathroom, then strangled the child and disposed of it in a waste receptacle. In the first half of 1997 there were six such reported cases of "dumpster babies."

Item: Among leading industrialized nations, the United States has by far the highest murder rate for 15- to 24-year-old males—seven times higher than Canada's and 40 times higher than Japan's.

Reports like these give us pause. Children hold up a mirror to society; in it, we see ourselves. Disturbed by that image, increasing numbers of schools and their communities are coming together to return American schooling to its most important historical mission: the formation of good character.

The premise of character education is straightforward: Uncivil, irresponsible, and destructive youth behaviors such as disrespect, dishonesty, violence, drug abuse, sexual promiscuity, and a poor work ethic have a common core, namely, the absence of good character. Character education, unlike piecemeal reforms, offers the hope of improvement in all these areas. It reminds us that we shouldn't wait for kids to do something wrong before teaching them what's right. It invokes the wisdom expressed in Donald DeMarco's book *The Heart of Virtue*: "Trying to become virtuous merely by excluding vice is as unrealistic as trying to cultivate roses simply by excluding weeds."

In response to the moral crisis of our culture, character education has become what is perhaps the fastest growing educational movement in the country today. The 1990s have seen a spate of books on the subject; the emergence of three national organizations—the Character Education Partnership, the Character Counts Coalition, and the Communitarian Network—dedicated to promoting character education; federal funding of character education projects; four White House Conferences on Character-Building for a Democratic and Civil Society; state mandates requiring that schools spend time on character education; the creation of university-based centers and training programs in character education; and grassroots initiatives by schools that are reportedly having a positive impact on school climate and student behavior.

Madonna Murphy's book, *Character Education in America's Blue-Ribbon Schools,* is a major contribution to the growing literature on character education. It will, I believe, be of great value to both college educators and school practitioners. I plan to use it in my own graduate course on character education and to recommend it to the schools working with our College's Center for the 4th and 5th Rs. Her book shows how character education was central to the mission of early American schools, why it declined in this century, and how its renewal has been spurred by the U. S. Department of Education's Blue Ribbon Awards program. It offers a rich compendium of character education practices drawn from more than 100 Blue Ribbon winners all across America—schools large and small, affluent and poor, homogeneous and diverse. It distills these many practices into six that seem to represent the "best practice" of character-building schools. It provides conceptual criteria to help the reader understand why not every values-related practice in a Blue Ribbon School necessarily qualifies as true character education. Throughout the book, we are told where to get more information about the programs cited so we can judge them for ourselves. For all these reasons, Madonna Murphy's book provides, in my judgment, the most complete and detailed picture available of what is happening in character education today.

As character education has mushroomed into a movement, skeptics and critics have emerged to raise challenges. Does character education develop better people — including people capable of critical moral judgment — or does it merely train students to do what they're told? Does it develop students' intrinsic motivation to be good or undermine it through reliance on external incentives? Is there research on the effectiveness of character education practices, and, if so, what does it show? Is character education something a school can evaluate? To questions like these, Dr. Murphy's book offers thoughtful answers that should elevate the level of national debate.

"The character education movement is a mile wide and an inch deep," said a skeptical middle school principal recently. "Everybody's talking about it, but nobody really knows what it is." *Character Education in America's Blue Ribbon Schools* makes it clear that "character education" is not one thing but many; that not all schools define it in the same way; and that not all approaches are equally sound. But contrary to what the middle school principal says, anyone interested in character education has a significant knowledge base to build on. And we are all indebted to Madonna Murphy's book for expanding that knowledge base in important ways.

TOM LICKONA
Author, *Educating for Character*
Director, Center for the 4th and 5th Rs,
State University of New York at Cortland

I was first introduced to Aristotle while in college at the University of Chicago. The study of his *Nichomachean Ethics* gave me the moral compass I needed in order to realize that what my classmates were doing was not always good or right, even if they were of a different religion than I. Moral values do exist, and they transcend religious, cultural, and social differences.

I first began to teach philosophy, ethics, and character education in the 1980s while at Lexington Institute of Hospitality Careers (now Lexington College). These students were preparing for a career in the business world, but they came into my course imbued with relativism, having very little background in the area of ethics and moral virtues. Through the course curriculum, I tried to teach the students key virtues that would be desirable for them to develop in their chosen fields, while teaching them the philosophic principles required for ethical decision making and moral integrity in business endeavors.

Since 1990, I have been teaching philosophy of education, ethics, and character education to undergraduates preparing to be teachers in the public schools. These students also lack an understanding of the difference between personal values and moral values. However, in this situation the challenge is not only to teach these students character education but to teach them in such a way that they will then be able to teach others. These future teachers need to be able to teach character to young students through the elementary or secondary curriculum.

My experience in the 1970s as a Chicago public school teacher and my volunteer work at the Metro Achievement Center in Chicago put me in close contact with elementary, middle school, and high school students from the inner-city schools. I saw that if the teacher had high expectations, students could be taught demanding academics and learn to develop their characters by meeting these challenges. At Metro, for instance, girls from inner-city schools were taught academics and character education in an afternoon and weekend program. Some graduates went on to college and returned to help change their inner-city neighborhoods. My experiences confirmed by convictions: Character education could be taught to students, and it did make a difference in their lives when they were taught about living a life of virtue.

The year 1990 was a significant turning point in my professional career. I graduated with my doctorate in education from Loyola University, I met Tom Lickona at a preconference workshop of the Association for Moral Education's annual meeting and was introduced to his model of character education, and I began my postdoctoral work in values and character education by participating in the Hyde School Research Project.

The Hyde School Project was initiated by Lawrence Baer, the parent of a child in the small K–5 public school in Washington, D.C. The purpose of the project was to establish a national model of an elementary school based on a composite of the best examples from elementary schools that had been recognized through the U.S. Department of Education's School Recognition Program.

In July of 1990, I was invited by Mr. Baer to participate in the Hyde School Project with a group of eight other researchers from across the nation. The research group consisted of three Ph.D.'s, two doctoral candidates, three graduate students, and one college student. After five weeks of intensive work together and one year of correspondence from our respective cities, we completed our research. It had soon become clear to the group that a "national model" of an elementary school was not going to emerge, but that many models of different exemplary practices were emerging. We presented this research at the American Educational Research Association's annual conference in San Francisco on April 18, 1992. In addition, individual members of the group have made other presentations and published articles on the area(s) that they researched (Kletzien, 1993; Murphy, 1991, 1995a, 1995b, 1995c, 1996).

Although the original plan was to publish a book summarizing all of the researchers' findings in the areas they reviewed, the final decision was for each to publish his or her own area of investigation. I therefore returned to Washington, D.C., in 1994 to update my data, adding information from the applications of the 1991–92 and 1993–94 award-winning schools. During 1995 and 1996, I visited a stratified sample of these schools. This book, *Character Education in America's Blue Ribbon Schools* is the result of these six years of research. It is my hope that this book will assist teachers, administrators, and teachers-in-training. It attempts to present a framework in which to understand the philosophic foundations of character education and to give a plethora of teaching ideas that will help those who wish to include character education in their classes.

REFERENCES

Kletzien, S. 1993. "Reading Programs in Nationally Recognized Elementary Schools," *National Reading Conference,* Charleston, S.C.

Kletzien, S., Bas-Isaac, E., Brown, R., Carter, D. Gilbert, A., McGree, K., Murphy, M., Russo, R. 1992. "Models of Excellent Practices in the U.S. Department of Education Blue Ribbon Schools". *American Educational Research Association Annual Conference.* San Francisco, CA.

Murphy, M. 1991. "Models of Moral Education That Work: Values Education Programs in the U.S. Department of Education Award Winning Schools." Association of Moral Education Annual Conference. Atlanta, GA.

Murphy, M. 1995a. "Character Education Programs in the U.S. Department of Education Blue Ribbon Schools". *Character Education Partnership 2nd Annual Forum.* Washington, D.C.

Murphy, M. 1995b. "Character Education Programs in the U.S. Department of Education Blue Ribbon Schools". *Character Educator,* 1(3):1–7.

Murphy, M. 1995c. "Good Discipline Programs Create Safe Schools and Help Develop Character," *Illinois School Research and Development Journal.* 32(1):3–6.

Murphy, M. 1996. "Character Education Programs in the U.S. Blue Ribbon Schools". *National Character Education Conference.* St. Louis, MO.

"I challenge all our schools to teach character education, to teach good values, and to teach good citizenship," the President told the nation on January 23, 1996, during his State of the Union message. He thus focused national attention on one of the fastest growing needs in public education. School principals might ask where they can find examples of schools that are teaching good values and good citizenship successfully to students. The President would refer these administrators to the Blue Ribbon Schools, the schools that have won the National Award for Excellence. For in the words of the president in an earlier speech, "The winners of the Blue Ribbon Awards . . . represent what is best in American education. These are schools producing world-class results by any rigorous measure. The challenge for us . . . is to figure out how to replicate them" (Clinton, 1993).

Character Education in America's Blue Ribbon Schools is based on descriptive, documentary, and qualitative research conducted on the award-winning school applications submitted under the U.S. Department of Education's Elementary School Recognition Program. The Elementary School Recognition Program, also known as the Blue Ribbon Award Program, was begun in 1985 by William Bennett, Secretary of Education. The program was modeled after its successful predecessor, the Secondary School Recognition Program, which was initiated three years previously as a positive response to the criticisms in the report *A Nation at Risk* prepared by the National Commission on Excellence in Education. The purpose of the Blue Ribbon Award Program was to identify and give public recognition to outstanding public and private elementary schools across the United States. It focused national attention on schools that were doing an exceptional job with all of their students in developing a solid foundation of basic skills and knowledge of subject matter and *fostering the development of character, values, and ethical judgement.*

Every other year, elementary and middle schools participated in the award program. Thus, there were five "award years" during the first decade of the program, 1985–1994. The total number of elementary schools that won the Blue Ribbon Award during this period was 1224. Table 1 shows the number of schools recognized in each award year.

This book reports on the first decade of the Elementary School Recognition Program, from 1985 to 1994. A random sample of 350 applications was chosen from the total database of 1224 Blue Ribbon School reports submitted during the five award years of that decade. The data were qualitatively validated through personal visits to these schools from 1994–1996. The programs in these award-winning schools that related in any way to character development and fostering good behavior in students were identified and categorized. Close attention was given in particular to the answers found in the section of the applications referring to "Student Environment"; however, the whole application form was studied.

The categories showed the many different ways in which the schools promote character development. They showed that the majority of the schools use some kind of curricular program or unit of study devoted particularly to character development. However, they also showed the importance of a schoolwide effort to promote character in all that the school does. An important consideration for national recog-

TABLE 1
Number of Blue Ribbon elementary schools.
(1985–1994).

Years	Number of Schools
1985–86	212 Schools
1986–87	287 Schools
1989–90	221 Schools
1991–92	228 Schools
1993–94	276 Schools
Total	1224 Schools

nition is the school's success in furthering the intellectual, social, and *moral* growth of all its students. In fact, all schools selected as Blue Ribbon Schools must show evidence "that school policies, programs, and practices foster the development of sound character, a sense of self-worth, democratic values, ethical judgment and self-discipline" in some way. This book reports on how these schools say that they do this and also attempts to assess the effectiveness of the programs mentioned by these schools.

Percentages of responses quoted throughout the book refer to the answers given by the schools to the questions asked on the application form. Quotes from schools are from direct conversations with the principal, teachers, and/or counselors when the school was visited and/or are taken directly from the school's application to the School Recognition Program.

It should be noted, however, that the existence of a particular character education program in a Blue Ribbon School does not necessarily mean that this program itself is of Blue Ribbon caliber. Whenever research data was available, it has been presented in an attempt to evaluate the desirability and effectiveness of the programs in the particular Blue Ribbon Schools. As often as possible, complete information on the different programs and methods has been given, so that the readers will have as much information as possible if they want to start a program.

The demographics of the random sample accurately represent the general Blue Ribbon School demographics. In particular, these schools are from all 50 states and the District of Columbia, with the largest percentage of award-winning schools coming from the states of New York (7%), California (6%), Ohio (5%), Illinois (4%), and Texas (4%). With the exception of Ohio, this corresponds directly to the states with the largest populations and therefore the greatest number of schools. Public and private schools can participate in this award program; 83% of the winners in this sample were public schools, whereas 17% were private.

Twenty percent of the schools were from large central cities, 22% from medium cities, 18% from towns, and 18% from rural areas, with the majority (42%) of the award-winning schools coming from suburban locations. The socioeconomic status of the students in the schools was measured by the number of students who qualified for free lunch. Ten percent of the schools could be characterized as having more than half of their students from lower-income families, and 15% had 25%

of their students from lower-income families. The student bodies of
the Blue Ribbon Schools were commonly a little more than 10% ethnically diverse; however, 20% of the schools had student bodies that
were 20% to 60% ethnic minorities. In the description of each school
cited in the book, the former are referred to as "ethnically diverse"; the
latter are referred to as a "heterogeneous" population," an "integrated"
school, or a "very diverse" student body. Schools with less than 10%
of the population from diverse backgrounds are referred to as having a
"homogeneous" student body.

The most common school organization in the Blue Ribbon Schools
is K–5 found in 68% of the schools, with 16% of the schools having
the common private school K–8 organization. The organization of the
schools cited in this book is assumed to be K–5, unless otherwise
noted. Variations of middle school configurations were found in 8% of
the schools. Half of the schools had a student body of 500–750 students, and 40% of the schools had 250–500 students. Schools falling
in the first category are referred to in the book as "large," the latter as
"small," and over 750 students as "very large." Eighty-eight percent of
the schools had between 26 and 55 full-time staff members for their
students. These statistics show that although almost half of the schools
were suburban, middle- to upper-class and not ethnically diverse, there
were inner-city schools with students of poor socioeconomic status
and ethnically-diverse schools among the Blue Ribbon Award winners.
Wherever possible, the success stories of these inner-city schools in
teaching character education will be highlighted in this book.

As mentioned earlier, for each of the Blue Ribbon Schools in the
sample, the school application report and the U.S. Department of Education site-visits report were read, with special attention to the programs mentioned that referred in any way to character development
and fostering good behavior in students. Close attention was given in
particular to the answers found in the applications referring to "Student Environment." (A sample application form can be found in Appendix A.) Particular note was made of the answers to the following
questions illustrated with significant quotes when appropriate:

- D2   What specific programs, procedures or instructional
  strategies do you employ to develop students' interest in
  learning and to motivate them to study?

- D6   What is your school's discipline policy?
- D7   By what means does the school prevent the sale, possession and use of drugs, including alcohol and tobacco, by its students on and off school premises?
- D9   How do school programs, practices, policies, and staff foster the development of sound character, democratic values, ethical judgment, good behavior, and the ability to work in a self-disciplined and purposeful manner? In 1987–88, this question was, "What are your schools' expectations in the area of character development, and how are these expectations communicated? What in the school contributes to the development of the attributes of sound character, such as a sense of fair play, a concern for others, a commitment to truthful and virtuous behavior, and the availability and willingness to assume responsibility for one's own behavior? How do school policies, programs, and practices foster the development of a child's self-discipline and self-confidence?"
- D11   (beginning in 1991–92): How is your school preparing students to live effectively in a society that is culturally and ethnically diverse and in an economy that is globally competitive?

Frequencies of responses were tabulated using the computer program, "The Statistical Package for the Social Studies" (SPSS). Categories emerged through statistical analysis of the answers. The categories showed the many different ways in which the schools promoted character development. A stratified sample of these schools was then visited in order to garner further information on their character education programs. Schools were chosen to be visited if their answers to the questions in Section D were significant; some elaborated on specific programs that seemed to be effective in promoting character education, and others proposed more creative, unique, or innovative ways of promoting character in their schools. In total, twenty schools were visited from eight different states (California, Illinois, Indiana, Maryland, Minnesota, Missouri, New York, Ohio, and Texas). The content of this book has been selected from the most interesting examples and programs found in the Blue Ribbon School applications. In total, 150 schools have been cited. The Blue Ribbon Schools speak for themselves through direct quotes taken from the applications and from the teachers, administrators, and counselors visited at the schools.

The chapters of the book have been organized around the categories that emerged from the statistical analysis of the responses. The tables found in each chapter represent a tabulation of the methods and programs reported by the schools in their application forms under the different question headings. These frequencies can be seen as indicators of promising practices (Isacc & Michael, 1984) but should not be considered as statistically significant nor rigorously valid, as they are the result of self-reporting by the applicants. Some applicants may have omitted some of the ways in which they promote character in their schools because either (1) they did these things on a schoolwide basis as effective teaching and did not consider them as character education, or (2) they did not consider these activities as a valid answer to the question. For example, only a small percentage of the schools report that their scouting program helps promote the formation of good character in their students; however, visits to the schools revealed that almost every school has a scouting program. Principals interviewed explained that they did not include this as part of their answer because the scouting program is not sponsored by the school but uses the school facilities for its meetings.

This book is a research report with a practical purpose. It can be considered "action" research as it seeks to find out what the best schools in America are doing to teach character education, in order to allow others to use this information and these ideas to start programs "that work" in their schools. Each chapter begins with a report of the research findings, analyzes their validity, and then synthesizes the best ideas for possible implementation by school practitioners. The goal is to use the emerging theoretical research findings on character education programs to inform practices. When available, research reports on the effectiveness of various of these programs have been cited in order to provide the reader with further criteria to weigh when deciding whether or not to implement a given program.

Chapter 1 provides an introduction to character education with a philosophic explanation of the terms used throughout the book; Chapter 2 provides a brief historical background of character education; Chapter 3 presents the most common answers regarding the programs used to promote character development; Chapter 4 highlights the drug education programs used in these schools; Chapter 5 focuses on motivation, self-esteem, and guidance programs; Chapter 6 examines teaching techniques that promote character development; Chapter 7 shows how discipline programs are used to promote character development; Chapter 8 explains citizenship programs in the Blue Ribbon Schools; and Chapter 9 focuses on the evaluation of character development programs. There is overlap among these programs; this categorization is not meant to be definitive but of assistance to those looking for specific programs to meet their school's needs in character education.

Appendix A provides a thorough explanation of the Blue Ribbon Award program and a sample application form. Appendix B lists each of the Blue Ribbon Schools cited in this book with its address, phone number, and contact name. Appendix C is a list of the character education books found in the Plano School District library.

This book attempts to show what the best schools in America are doing to train students in moral values and ethics. Using their own words, it documents the innovations in teaching and learning that they have implemented to foster the development of character. It can be seen as a compendium of programs found within these schools. It is a practical book that will guide school administrators, teachers, parents, board members, and concerned citizens interested in having their school implement the President's challenge to teach character education—a challenge reiterated a year later in the 1997 State of the Union message: "Character education must be taught in our schools. We must teach students to be good citizens" (Clinton, 1997).

REFERENCES

Clinton, W. 1993. "Awards Ceremony." May 13–14, 1993. Washington, D.C.

Clinton, W. 1996. "State of the Union Message." [On line] Available URL: http://www1.whitehouse.gov/WH/news/other/sotu.html

Clinton, W. 1997. "State of the Union Message." [On line] Available URL: http://www1.whitehouse.gov/WH/news/other/sotu.html

Isaac, S. and W. Michael. 1984. *Handbook in Research and Evaluation*. San Diego, CA: Edits Publishing. pp. 188–189.

Acknowledgements

This book has been in the making for several years, and many people have assisted me in making it a reality. It only exists today because Dr. Joseph Eckenrode from Technomic Publishing Company responded so positively to my book proposal. I wish to thank him for his editorial comments and for his patience and understanding as I extended the deadline for submission of the final manuscript.

I would also like to thank the following people:

- Jean Narayanan, Diane Jones, and Lois Weber from the U.S. Department of Education for facilitating the original and subsequent research on the Blue Ribbon Schools
- Lawrence Baer for initiating the Hyde School Research Project and Rosario Jimenez for facilitating my participation in the original research project in 1990
- Sharon Kletzien for serving as the coordinator of the Hyde School Research Project and for her encouragement and insight regarding the realization of our publication desires
- the Faculty Development Committee at the College of St. Francis for the faculty scholarship in spring of 1996 that allowed me to work on this book
- Amanda and Meghan Murphy for their organizational assistance helping to find the school reports needed for each chapter
- Dorothy Murphy and Arlene Packley for their assistance in typing the appendices and index

- Joan Koran at the College of St. Francis and Sara Thomas at the University of Illinois for their research assistance
- all my faculty colleagues at the College of St. Francis and Lexington College for their encouragement as I wrote this book
- Sharon Banas, Thomas Lickona, Joy Reiner, and Lori Wiley for their helpful editing and comments on reading the manuscript
- Karen Johnson, Carolyn Manalo, Linda Motz, Holly Salls and Eileen Sheu for help in editing the page proofs

Finally, a very special thank-you is extended to Tom Lickona for writing the Foreword, for his very careful reading of this manuscript, his extensive editorial comments, which challenged my thinking, and his very insightful additions to this book.

Chapter 1

CAN GOOD CHARACTER BE TAUGHT?

Character is what we say and do when no one else is looking. It is not what we have done, but who we are.—Anonymous

Only a virtuous people are capable of freedom.—Benjamin Franklin

Character building begins in our infancy and continues until death.
—Eleanor Roosevelt

CAN VALUES AND VIRTUES BE TAUGHT?

"Can virtue be taught?" Meno asked Socrates over 2000 years ago in the *Meno* dialogue written by Plato. It is a question that is still of great interest today. Can we teach virtues, values, and character to students in today's schools? Some of these young people will be our leaders in the twenty-first century. Will they be ethical, moral, and virtuous leaders who promote peace and justice and show through their actions that they care for others? Or will they be hypocritical leaders who lie, steal, and cheat as long as no one catches them?

This first chapter tries to answer Meno's question regarding the teachability of virtue. The philosophic foundations of character education are explained. Some key terms such as virtues, values, and character are defined in order to clarify the use of this terminology throughout the book. This chapter concludes with a paradigm which summarizes the main ways in which character education is taught in America's best schools, the Blue Ribbon Schools. Chapter 1 seeks to answer the following questions:

1

- What are virtues and moral values, and can they be taught in the public schools of America's pluralistic society?
- What is a definition of good character?
- Must a school have a character education program in order to be nominated as a Blue Ribbon School?
- What are the components of the Blue Ribbon Schools' Comprehensive Model for Character Development?

WHAT IS A VIRTUE?

Aristotle gives a helpful definition of "virtue" in his work *Nichomachean Ethics*: "Virtue is a state of character concerned with choice, lying in a mean between two vices, one involving excess, the other deficiency . . . with regard to what is best and right." (1107a1-7). He tells us that virtue is of two kinds, intellectual and moral. Intellectual virtue can be taught, while moral virtue comes about as a result of habit. Children need to be taught in order to *know* what virtue is, and then they need to be guided in order to reason well and choose the correct action in a given situation. It is no easy task to be good, according to Aristotle. This is because in everything we need to find the middle road of virtue: "To do this [the good] to the right person, to the right extent, at the right time, with the right motive, and in the right way is no easy task" (1109a27). According to Aristotle, we must also develop the *desire* and *love* for the good in order to be virtuous. Finally, we must have the opportunity for *action* in order to *live* virtuously: "The moral virtues we get by first exercising them. . . . We become just by doing just acts, temperate by doing temperate acts, brave by doing brave acts" (1103b).

Aristotle stresses the importance of developing moral habits from the earliest years: "It makes no small difference, then, whether we form habits of one kind or another from our very youth; it makes a very great difference, or rather all the difference" (1103b10-25). Educators today might ask Aristotle, "What values and virtues should schools teach youth given America's pluralistic society?"

MORAL VALUES

Thomas Lickona, author of *Educating for Character: How Our Schools Can Teach Respect and Responsibility* (1991) and director of

The Center for the 4th & 5th R's, defines moral values as "values that tell us what we ought or ought not to do." Among moral values there are two categories: (1) universal, which are those that have to do with fundamental human worth and dignity and which we have a duty to practice and enforce, and (2) non-universal—values that do not carry universal obligation but to which an individual may feel a serious personal obligation.

Larry Nucci, director of the Center for the Study of Moral Development and Character Education and editor of *Moral Development and Character Education: A Dialogue* (1989b), provides us with a helpful paradigm for understanding the difference between moral and non-moral values. In interviews with young children, he found that they were able to distinguish between those rules or values which were set up merely out of convention, such as "not talking in line," or "not eating certain foods for religious reasons," and those values which were of a moral nature and should be followed whether or not there was a convention regarding them, such as "not deliberately hurting another," "not killing another," and "telling the truth" (Nucci, 1989a). This distinction is nicely illustrated by an example taken from an interview with a four-year-old girl regarding her perceptions of spontaneously occurring transgressions at her preschool.

MORAL ISSUE

Did you see what happened? *Yes. They were playing and John hit him too hard.* Is that something you are supposed to do or not supposed to do? *Not so hard to hurt.* Is there a rule about that? *Yes.* What if there were no rule about hitting, would it be all right to do then? *No.* Why not? *Because you could get hurt and start to cry.*

CONVENTIONAL ISSUE

Did you see what just happened? *Yes. They were noisy.* Is that something you are supposed to or not supposed to do? *Not do.* Is there a rule about that? *Yes. We have to be quiet.* What if there were no rule, would it be all right to do then? *Yes.* Why? *Yes, because there is no rule.* (Nucci 1991, p. 23)

A Venn diagram can perhaps illustrate these domains for us (see Figure 1). Among social values, there are those that change, such as what clothes or jewelry are proper for a man or a woman to wear, and those that never change, for instance, one's obligation to treat others with respect, civility, and politeness.

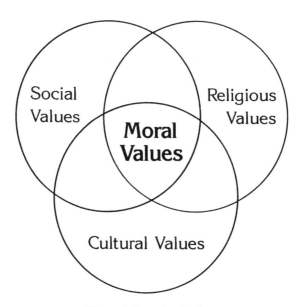

Figure 1 *Domain of values.*

There are cultural values that change, such as whether or not a woman changes her name upon marrying, and those values that do not change, for example, the belief that the education and upbringing of children is primarily the responsibility of the parents.

Likewise, there are personal values that change, such as whether one prefers the color blue or the color yellow, and those that never change, such as ensuring one's word is always truthful.

In addition, there are religious values that change, for instance, whether one should go to church services on Wednesday, Saturday, or Sunday, and those that never change, such as the belief that one should respect the life of another.

Each of these domains intersects with the others in an area called the "moral values"—those values that all human beings should uphold no matter what their society, culture, personal preferences, or religion. These are the core values that define how human beings should or should not act toward themselves and others. These moral values can also be referred to as Aristotle's human virtues, and they are the qualities that define a person's character.

WHAT IS GOOD CHARACTER?

Character comes from the Greek work *charakter*, which means "enduring mark." The *charakter* on a coin gives its worth. The *charakter* of a person is considered to be the distinguishing qualities or principles to which the person subscribes as a guide for his or her behavior. Character influences how someone makes decisions or chooses to act or not to act; it summarizes the general way in which a person deals with others. Aristotle says, "Each man speaks and acts and lives in accordance with his character" (1127a27); the virtue of a man will be "the state of character which makes him good and makes him do his own work well" (1106a23). Aristotle tells us that there are three steps necessary in order to form one's character: "In the first place, he must have knowledge; secondly, he must choose the acts, and choose them for their own sake; and thirdly, his action must proceed from a firm and unchangeable character" (1105a31).

Others have similar definitions. Character is "engaging in morally relevant conduct or words, or refraining from certain conduct or words" (Wynne & Walberg, 1989, p. 38). Moral character includes "those enduring aspects of the expression of personhood to which we are inclined to give moral evaluation across different attitudinal and behavioral contexts" (Boyd 1989, p. 99). According to Kevin Ryan (1993), Professor at Boston University and Director of the Center for the Advancement of Ethics and Character: "To have good character means to be a person who has the capacity to know the good, love the good and do the good" (p. 16). Character therefore is a holistic term, concerning the whole person. It means to have a good head, good heart, and good hands.

"Good character," according to the traditional perspective, needs to be taught, imparted; that is, children must be directly instructed in virtuous behavior. The premise of character education is that there are virtues—objectively good human qualities—that should be taught to all. These virtues are held to transcend religious and cultural differences (Traiger, 1995). "Character education" usually involves explicit teaching of what each of these different virtues is, how to distinguish "right" from "wrong," and the provision of examples of virtuous and morally correct behavior through the use of either literature or real-life models (Watson et al., 1989). Virtues such as honesty, tolerance, respect, hard work, and kindness are taught, modeled, and reinforced by the significant adults in children's lives. Students also need the opportunity to practice virtuous actions, for, as Aristotle pointed out, one becomes virtuous by practicing virtuous actions. In order to promote this aspect of character education, schools need to provide students with opportunities in which they can perform virtuous acts and acts of service for others. For instance, schools might promote clubs or offer opportunities to volunteer.

A CONSTRUCT FOR
UNDERSTANDING GOOD CHARACTER

Lickona's model of character development, found in *Educating for Character,* defines good character as a combination of moral knowing, moral feeling, and moral action (Lickona, 1991). It is helpful to visualize good character as the point where all three of these aspects intersect (see Figure 2). This is also a useful construct for organizing the many different ways in which a school can promote character development. First, schools must make an effort to teach specific values and virtues directly, so that students have the "moral knowing" of what they should do. This can be done through a mission statement that identifies the

Figure 2 *A model of good character (adapted from Lickona, 1991).*

virtues that a school professes to promote. It can also be accomplished through the use of curricular programs that teach what specific virtues and moral values mean or by teachers who take advantage of specific "character moments," that is, incidents or situations in school or society that they use as content for a class on moral decision making. Second, through assemblies, school mottos, awards, and other special programs, schools can instill moral desire in students by encouraging students to *want* to live a life of good character values. This "moral feeling" aspect of character education is the way in which a school motivates students and guides them in the development of a sense of positive self-esteem based on human dignity. Third, schools wishing to foster character must encourage students' "moral actions" through high academic standards, good discipline, citizenship, and community service.

HOW DO THE BLUE RIBBON SCHOOLS FOSTER THE DEVELOPMENT OF SOUND CHARACTER?

As stated in the introduction, this book is based on descriptive, documentary, and qualitative research conducted on the award-winning school applications in the U.S. Department of Education's Elementary School Recognition Program, the "Blue Ribbon Award Program." A total of 350 applications were chosen from the total database of 1282 submitted during the five award years in the decade from 1984 to 1994. Some of these schools were personally visited to garner further information on their character education programs.

The programs mentioned in these award-winning schools that referred in any way to character development and fostering good behavior in students have been identified and categorized. As noted above, close attention was given in particular to the answers found in the section of the applications referring to "Student Environment"; however the whole application form was studied.

Categories emerged through the statistical analysis of the answers to these questions on the award-winning applications (Table 2). These categories show the many different ways in which schools promote character development. They showed that the majority of the schools use some kind of curricular program or unit of study to promote character development; however, they also show the importance of a schoolwide effort to promote character in all that the school does.

TABLE 2 How do the Blue Ribbon Schools
promote character development?

Category Label	Count	Percent of Cases
Assemblies, PA announcements	22	7
Community service	9	3
Curriculum programs/units	128	39
Discipline plans	45	14
Integrated throughout	78	24
School awards, mottos	91	27
Staff models good behavior	84	25

Schools may be counted in more than one category. Valid cases, 330; missing cases, 20; This means that 20 of the schools did not report an answer that could be counted in this category.

THE BLUE RIBBON SCHOOLS COMPREHENSIVE MODEL OF CHARACTER EDUCATION

Thomas Lickona (1991), in *Educating for Character*, describes a comprehensive model of character education. He lists twelve strategies for promoting character education in the school, including the role of the teacher, the importance of discipline, the curriculum, the class-room/school environment, and the community. Analysis of the categories of programs that Blue Ribbon Schools use to promote character development (see Table 3) leads to a similar model, the "Blue Ribbon Schools' Comprehensive Model for Character Education."

This Blue Ribbon model gives importance to all areas of the curriculum: the formal, the informal, and the hidden. The formal curriculum is the intended or explicit curriculum, that is, the stated objectives, content, and organization of instruction as approved by the state and local boards. It is instituted through the formal adoption of character education programs or school-wide character traits. The informal curriculum deals with the interactions among students and teachers, that is, how they should behave and act towards one another. It is found in discipline codes and citizenship programs. The hidden curriculum is taught implicitly by the school experience; for example, the effect of architecture and environment, the use of time during school, and the ways students are rewarded both in and outside of the classroom (Orn-

TABLE 3 What programs in the Blue Ribbon Schools
promote character development?

Category	Count	Percent of Responses
Character education program	27	11
Citizenship	31	13
Conflict management	19	3
Discipline program	44	18
Drug education program	81	33
Guidance program	45	19
Motivation program	8	3
School developed program	30	12
Self-esteem program	47	19
Other	22	7

Valid cases, 240; missing cases 110

stein & Hunkin, 1988; Schubert, 1986). It is expressed by school awards programs and by the presence of—or absence of—drug education and sex education programs.

The Blue Ribbon Schools' Comprehensive Model for Character Development (Figure 3) emphasizes the importance of parents, teachers, counselors, and principals working together to promote character in youth. The model also shows how each subject in the curriculum can be used to promote character and how extracurricular activities can give students opportunities to manifest good character qualities and do good actions. The model recognizes that students should be helped to develop their character in such a way that they naturally do good deeds out in their neighborhood and community, on the playground, on the sports field, and in their families. The Blue Ribbon Schools' model for character education is comprehensive because it gives students opportunities for developing all the areas of their character: moral knowing, moral feeling, and moral action.

The Blue Ribbon Schools' responses to the question, "How do school programs foster the development of sound character?" is used as the organizing framework for the chapters in this book on character development, drug education, motivation, guidance, and self-esteem programs, teaching techniques that promote character, discipline programs, and citizenship development.

Figure 3 *Blue Ribbon Schools' comprehensive model of character education (adapted from Lickona, 1991).*

The purpose of this book is to present the "best practices" in character and moral education programs as found in the Blue Ribbon Schools. It can be seen as a compendium of programs found within schools that have been designated among the best schools in the United States. However, as stated in the introduction, the existence of a particular program in a Blue Ribbon School does not necessarily mean that this is a "Blue Ribbon Character Education Program," so data is presented, wherever it is available, that will assist the reader in evaluating the desirability of implementing a particular program found in the Blue Ribbon Schools.

One could ask, are Blue Ribbon Schools more likely to have a character education program than other schools? To answer this conclusively, data from other schools, not nominated as Blue Ribbon Schools, would have to be compared to the data of our sample. Nevertheless, an analysis of the findings in this research, which will be elaborated in subsequent chapters, show that although each school had to answer this question, many of the Blue Ribbon Schools do *not* have a character education program *per se* in place. Schools included in their answer to this question a large range of other types of programs. These programs are mentioned in Table 3 above and are discussed in subsequent chapters. Some schools said that they foster the development of character in their students through their drug education program or their discipline program. Although these are important components of a moral education program, they are not sufficient in themselves. One could conclude that character education and moral education in schools is still a new area that needs to be further developed. This book, by highlighting the ethics, moral development, and character education programs found in America's best schools, provides much-needed guidance as schools tread once again a path that has not been followed for a long time in our schools.

SUMMARY

This chapter provides the rationale behind the book. The philosophic foundations of character education have been outlined. Terms have been defined, as they have been presented, in order to provide readers with a common conceptual basis. The National Award Winning Elementary Schools, the Blue Ribbon Schools, have been chosen to show the reader what the best schools in America are doing to promote character education. The information found in these schools has been categorized to construct a comprehensive model for character education. These categories form the basis upon which this book is organized.

REFERENCES

Boyd, D. 1989. "The Character of Moral Development," in *Moral Development and Character Education*. L. Nucci, ed. Berkeley, CA: McCutchan Publishing Corp.

Lickona, T. 1991. *Educating for Character: How Our Schools Can Teach Respect and Responsibility*. New York: Bantam.

McKeon, R. 1941. *The Basic Works of Aristotle*. New York: Random House.

Nucci, L. 1989a. "Challenging Conventional Wisdom About Morality: The Domain Approach to Values Education," in *Moral Development and Character Education: A Dialogue*. Berkeley, CA: McCutchan Publishing Corp., pp. 183–203.

Nucci, L. ed. 1989b. *Moral Development and Character Education: A Dialogue.* Berkeley, CA: McCutchan Publishing Corp.

Nucci, L. 1991. "Doing Justice to Morality in Contemporary Values Education" in Benninga, J. editor, *Moral, Character and Civic Education in the Elementary School.* New York: Teachers College Press, p. 23.

Ornstein, A. and F. Hunkins. 1988. *Curriculum: Foundations, Principles, and Issues.* New Jersey: Prentice Hall.

Plato. 1949. *Meno.* translated by Benjamin Jowett. New York: Macmillan Publishing Co.

Ryan, K. 1993. "Mining the Values in the Curriculum," *Educational Leadership,* 51(3), p. 16.

Schubert, W. 1986. *Curriculum: Perspective, Paradigm, and Possibility.* New York: Macmillan, pp. 104–107.

Traiger, J. "The Time Is Now: Reflections on Moral Education," *Education* 115(3): 432–434.

Watson, M., D. Solomon, V. Battistich, E. Schaps, and J. Solomon. 1989. "The Child Development Projects: Combining Traditional and Developmental Approaches to Values Education," in *Moral Development and Character Education.* L. Nucci, ed. Berkeley, CA: McCutchan Publishing Corp., pp. 51–92.

Wynne, E. and H. Walberg, eds. 1989. "Character Education: Toward a Preliminary Consensus" in *Moral Development and Character Education: A Dialogue.* Berkeley, CA: McCutchan Publishing Corp., p. 38.

A BRIEF HISTORY OF CHARACTER EDUCATION IN THE U.S. SCHOOLS

America is great because she is good; but if America ever ceases to be good, she will cease to be great.—Alexis de Tocqueville

People of character are the conscience of society.
—Ralph Waldo Emerson

To educate a person in mind and not in morals is to educate a menace to society.—Theodore Roosevelt

SHOULD OUR PUBLIC SCHOOLS TEACH VIRTUES AND VALUES?

Just a decade ago some people still debated whether our public schools *should* teach virtues or values. In 1985, the *New York Times* quoted educators who said that "they deliberately avoid telling students what is ethically right or wrong" (Bennett, 1988, p. 133). But today people are debating *what* values to teach and *how* to teach them in the most effective way. In 1995, the same *New York Times* was quoting educators as saying, "A whole generation has grown up in a moral vacuum. . . . Character education is a great hope for our future" (Rosenblatt, 1995, pp. 36, 40).

This chapter highlights the main historical events that have precipitated this dramatic change in attitude. It presents a short history of character education as taught in our nation's schools from the colonial times to the current day. It shows how a national movement has begun promoting the vital importance of once again teaching character education in our schools. It shows the reader what the best schools in

13

America, the National Award Winning Elementary Schools or Blue Ribbon Schools, are doing to promote character education.

Chapter 2 seeks to answer the following questions:

- Why was character education an aim of American schools in the colonial times?
- Why did the teaching of character education decline and values clarification and cognitive moral development approaches take its place?
- What events have led to the renewed national interest in character education?
- Why will this book *Character Education in America's Blue Ribbon Schools* make an important contribution to the character education movement?

A NATION AT RISK

Although the reform document *A Nation at Risk* (National Commission on Excellence in Education, 1983) focused mostly on academics, it did catch the public's attention through its statement that our nation was at risk, and it went beyond matters such as industry and commerce. "It [our concern] also includes the intellectual, moral, and spiritual strengths of our people, which knit together the very fabric of our society" (p. 7). The public did not need a national document to tell them what they already knew. There had been a substantial long-term decline in the conduct of young Americans (e.g., rising youth homicides, suicides, teenage pregnancies, and school vandalism), along with declining academic performance in school. In addition to these indicators were statistics that showed the effect that the breakdown of the traditional family and the lack of traditional socialization for the youth had had on school performance (Wynne & Ryan, 1993; Kilpatrick, 1992; Lickona, 1991).

These societal problems fueled the re-evaluation of moral education in America. The school reform movements that followed upon the release of *A Nation at Risk* looked at the important role character development in schools played in promoting academic excellence. Students in schools that promoted character and moral values had better test scores and had lower incidents of vandalism, absenteeism, and dishonesty on tests (Wynne & Walberg, 1985).

The most broad-based efforts to revitalize moral education came from a variety of individuals who favored traditional, virtue-centered approaches that sought to cultivate good conduct, now labeled "character education." The most articulate of the group was William J. Bennett, director of the National Endowment for the Humanities in the early Reagan years, then secretary of the U.S. Department of Education and initiator of the National School Recognition Program, also known as the Blue Ribbon School Award program (McClellan, 1992).

Currently, politicians from both parties, concerned citizens, business leaders, educational researchers, and parents are urging the schools to return to a deeper and more conscientious involvement in the moral life of their students. The recognition that schools inevitably teach values has become widespread through a realization that the very act of educating another is a moral act (Goodlad et al., 1990; Tom, 1984). Possibilities for moral education lie in every part of the curriculum. There is a general consensus that we need a comprehensive approach for teaching character education and moral values: one that begins in the early grades and continues through the college years. Teachers and schools, like parents and families, cannot avoid teaching values. In fact, one might ask, why did American schools ever stop teaching students about good character, human virtues, and moral values?

CHARACTER EDUCATION
IN THE COLONIAL SCHOOLS

Historically, character education was one of the missions of the American public schools from the first formation of the New England Town School in Boston during the Colonial period. Using the *Hornbook* and *The New England Primer* students learned the close relationship among reading, religion, and character education; the integration of these was the hallmark of elementary education in this period (Gutek, 1970). The child learned "An Alphabet of Lessons for Youth," "The Dutiful Child's Promises," and "The Duty of Children toward their Parents."

THE DUTIFUL CHILD'S PROMISES

I will fear GOD and honour the King
I will honour my Father & Mother
I will obey my Superiours
I will submit to my Elders
I will love my friends
I will hate no man
I will forgive my enemies and pray to
God for the will as much as in me lies to
keep all God's Holy Commandments
                                        Gutek, 1970, p. 25

The Founding Fathers, especially Thomas Jefferson, were advocates of character education for all in order to train students in democratic citizenship. The Declaration of Independence and the Preamble to the Constitution are clear statements of the moral values and virtues we hold sacred in our democracy. "We hold these truths to be self-evident, that all men are created equal, that they are endowed by their Creator with certain unalienable Rights, that among these are Life, Liberty and the pursuit of Happiness." Educators continued to foster these values in the nineteenth century. For instance, the McGuffey Readers (Vail, 1909) were the primary character education curriculum in the 1800s. Students read stories about children their own age who successfully learned to live good virtues in their everyday life.

McGUFFEY'S PRIMER LESSON XIV

This old man cannot see. He is blind.
Mary holds him by the hand.
She is kind to the old blind man.
                                        Vail, 1909, p. 20

CHARACTER EDUCATION AT
THE TURN OF THE CENTURY

During the opening decades of this century, interest in character education and citizenship training flourished (Pietig, 1977). There were national contests for the best morality codes and the best methodologies for teaching character education. These were sponsored by the Character Education Association, a private organization created in 1911 and headed by Milton Fairchild. The "Children's Morality Code" outlined "ten laws of right living": self-control, good health, kindness, sportsmanship, self-reliance, duty, reliability, truth, good workman-ship, and teamwork (McClellan, 1992). Youth organizations that pro-moted moral education were founded. The character education move-ment identified a body of activities and principles by which moral education could be transmitted in a secular institution (ASCD Panel 1988a).

Character education programs then, as now, used either the direct or the indirect method of moral instruction. The direct method viewed character development as the acquisition of desirable traits or virtues. This method centered on learning creeds, slogans, and pledges and reading classical texts with heroes and noteworthy actions. The indi-rect method, by contrast, did not explicitly teach the desirable virtues but created the situations in which these virtues could be developed and practiced. All the processes of school life—classroom activities, disciplinary procedures, personal contacts, and extracurricular func-tions—were scrutinized for their character-training potential. Each of these methods was explained in detail in the classic textbook of the era, *Character Education*, written by Harry McKown (1935), which was used by all teachers-in-training who wanted to know how to teach character education.

JOHN DEWEY'S CRITICISM OF CHARACTER EDUCATION

John Dewey, America's chief philosopher of education at the turn of the century, could be considered singly responsible for the dramatic change in the character-promoting mission of American education. On the surface, it may seem that Dewey was merely a proponent of indirect instead of direct moral instruction, because he focused on the moral or-ganization of the schools rather than instruction in virtue formation (Dewey, 1909). However, Dewey based his educational ideas on his pragmatic, philosophic ideas, that is, an instrumentalist's view of truth: something was true "if it worked" as a solution to a practical problem. Dewey therefore was a moral relativist who believed that values arose as outcomes of human responses to varying environmental situations (Gutek, 1988). To ask if something was a value was for Dewey to ask whether it was "something to be prized and cherished, to be enjoyed"

(Dewey, 1929, p. 260). He wrote: "A moral agent is one who proposes for himself an end to be achieved by action and does what is necessary to obtain that end" (Dewey, 1891, cited in Copleston, 1967, p. 124).

According to Dewey, moral education was not a matter of teaching students what to do or not to do, but it was a method to help them decide what to do: "Moral education in school is practically hopeless when we set up the development of character as its supreme end" (Dewey, 1916). Dewey articulated a theory of moral development that emphasized reflective thinking rather than moral lessons (ASCD Panel, 1988a). His writings focused moral education for the next fifty years on a process-oriented approach rather than the content-oriented approach of character education. Dewey promoted logical positivism and pragmatism. His philosophy formed the basis for values clarification and Kohlberg's developmental approach to moral education (Carlin, 1981; Harrison, 1980; Kohlberg, 1975). Dewey's ideas on education and his philosophy still influence American thinking and schooling today.

CHARACTER EDUCATION UNDER FIRE

The research of Hartshorne and May in 1930 added support to Dewey's contention that character education was ineffective. Hartshorne and May assessed the character-related behavior of almost 11,000 youth in grades five through eight by administering 33 different behavioral tests of altruism (service), self-control, and honesty versus deceit. Analysis of the results of each individual test showed that there was little evidence that classrooms that had character education produced a lower incidence of deceit or a higher incidence of service behavior in their students. The researchers concluded that the character education techniques then in use in the schools bore little or no significant relationship to pupils' general patterns of moral conduct (Leming, 1993a). These findings resulted in a general decline in interest in character education research and/or policy proposals. It should be noted that recent and more sophisticated research has used the principle of aggregation to combine the multiple test measures into aggregate sets. These batteries of scores have thus revealed a much higher correlation between participation in character education classes and the students' likelihood to continue to practice these virtues in other contexts (Rushton et al., 1983; Wynne, 1989).

THE VALUE-FREE SOCIETY

The protests of the 1960s led to the fall of many established American values such as respect for authority and rules, hard work, sexual restraint, and patriotism. Educational institutions were told to become value-free. The values clarification movement of the 1970s taught students that the process of valuing is value-free, that is, there are no better or worse answers. Values clarification helps students to clarify their own values, choose their beliefs and then be willing to act on their beliefs (Raths et al., 1966). As a natural application of Dewey's value theory, values clarification does not stress true and right behavior. It is a relativistic approach. Today, many one-time proponents of this approach have admitted that they made a mistake in devaluing and taking for granted traditional values (Harmin, 1988; Kirschenbaum, 1995). However, many teachers in the field today are still trying to teach in a value-free way using values clarification activities, since this is the way that they were taught to teach when they were in college.

THE COGNITIVE MORAL DEVELOPMENT APPROACH

In the 1970s, Lawrence Kohlberg proposed a cognitive-developmental approach to moral education based on the work of Dewey and Piaget (Kohlberg, 1978, 1984; ASCD Panel, 1988a). His doctoral dissertation findings led to a resurgence of research interest in moral education in the United States. Kohlberg's research validated the Dewey-Piaget levels and added to their model; his theory asserted that a person developmentally progresses through a series of moral stages or, more specifically, three levels with two stages in each level (Kohlberg, 1975).

Kohlberg's Stages of Moral Development

(*1*) Preconventional level
- Stage 1: punishment-and-obedience orientation
- Stage 2: instrumental-relativist orientation

(*2*) Conventional level
- Stage 3: interpersonal concordance or "good boy-nice girl" orientation.
- Stage 4: "law and order" orientation.

(*3*) Postconventional, autonomous, or principled level
- Stage 5: social contract, legalistic orientation
- Stage 6: universal-ethical-principle orientation

Kohlberg asserted that cognitive development was important for moral development; that is, logical reasoning is necessary for moral judgment, and moral judgment is necessary for moral action, but neither is sufficient in itself. Kohlberg found, similar to the research of Hartshorne and May, that there are additional factors necessary for principled moral reasoning to be translated into moral action. Kohlberg emphasized the development of moral reasoning toward increasingly complex concepts of justice (Kohlberg, 1975).

Research has been supportive of the teacher's ability to foster the development of higher cognitive levels of moral reasoning through the use of dilemma discussions in the classroom (Nucci, 1987). The "just community" approach to moral education evolved out of a practical application of Kohlberg's theory in prisons and then in schools. In the just community, students develop the basic elements of morality by democratically deciding all of the rules and norms of their school by the application of certain "master virtues of the community" such as caring, trust, collective responsibility, concern for fairness, and community (Power et al., 1989).

Although values clarification and moral reasoning classroom methods are different in many ways, the theoretical premises upon which they are based are similar. They both avoid the virtue-centered approaches to character education, emphasizing instead the *process* of moral decision-making and the importance of individual freedom and autonomy. Both believed that their open-ended approaches offered a moral education consistent with contemporary American lifestyles. In both of these systems, teachers are not to moralize; teachers are facilitators of student-generated discussion, creators of cognitive conflict, and/or stimulators of social perspective-taking in students (Reimer et al., 1983; McClellan, 1992). Research on the effectiveness of these two approaches has shown that the moral discussion approach is effective, that is, one can measure increases in cognitive reasoning levels through the use of moral dilemma discussions; but values clarification research findings are inconclusive; it does not seem "to work." However, it is also hard to define exactly what it would do effectively if it did work (Leming, 1993b). Values clarification and moral reasoning can be classified as process-oriented approaches to moral education that lack a contextual base.

AS WE APPROACH THE 21ST CENTURY

Today, the escalating problems in society, such as crimes of violence by young people, make it imperative that schools once again directly address the subject of values and character (Traiger, 1995). Research cited above, and to be cited throughout this book, helps us to understand that it is difficult, no matter what method is used, to shape moral conduct, because the process of moral shaping is enormously incremental, cumulative, and complex (Wynne, 1989). However, it is possible. We can answer Socrates's question, "Can virtue be taught?" affirmatively.

The teaching of human virtues and the subsequent shaping of "good character" needs to be restored to its historical place as the central desirable outcome of the school's moral enterprise (Lickona, 1993). The school reform movement precipitated by the report *A Nation at Risk* has engendered many reports on what makes for excellence in education; included within these reports are many discussions of the need to return to the moral purpose of teaching (Fenstermacher, 1990).

In 1988, the Association for Supervision and Curriculum Development (ASCD) brought together eleven experts in moral education to form a panel. The panel drafted the document *Moral Education in the Life of the School* (1988b) in which they listed the six characteristics of a "morally mature person." The morally mature person habitually

(*1*) Respects human dignity
(*2*) Cares about the welfare of others
(*3*) Integrates individual interest and social responsibilities
(*4*) Demonstrates integrity
(*5*) Reflects on moral choices
(*6*) Seeks peaceful resolution of conflict

The panel also gave eight recommendations for moral education.

Four years later, in March of 1992, the ASCD, the Princeton Project 55, and the Johnson Foundation convened a Wingspread Conference in

Racine, Wisconsin, around the question, "How to provide effective K–12 character education?" The goal of the conference was to encourage leaders of national education associations to give greater attention and priority to character education. The conference participants recommended the formation of a new national coalition to support and facilitate efforts to disseminate information about the need for K–12 character education and to provide assistance to schools and communities across the country as they became interested in initiating character education activities (Character Education Partnership, 1996).

In July of that same year, twenty-eight leaders of diverse backgrounds met for four days in Aspen, Colorado, at a summit hosted by the Josephson Institute. The conference was entitled "Teaching Ethics and Character: What Should Be Done? What Can Be Done? What Will Be Done?" It looked at ways in which character and values could be instilled in young people in all areas of their lives. After hours of debate and discussion, the twenty-eight participants signed a declaration that defined six core ethical values that "form the foundation of democratic society" and called for character education programs to implement them. "People do not automatically develop good moral character; therefore, conscientious efforts must be made to help young people develop the values and abilities necessary for moral decision making and conduct" (Aspen Declaration, 1992). The Character Counts Coalition was founded as a result of this conference. It is "a national partnership of organizations and individuals involved in the education, training, or care of youth, joined together in a collaborative effort to improve the character of America's young people based on six core ethical values, the Six Pillars of Character: trustworthiness, respect, responsibility, fairness, caring and citizenship" (Josephson Institute, 1993, p. 1).

The Character Education Partnership was founded on February 5, 1993, by a number of individuals and organizations, many of whom had actively participated in the Wingspread and/or Aspen meeting. The group defines itself as "a national, non-profit, non-partisan coalition dedicated to developing good character and civic virtue in young people as one way of promoting a more compassionate and responsible society" (Character Education Partnership, 1996, p. 6).

Through the joint work of the Character Counts Coalition and the Character Education Partnership, bipartisan support for character education was garnered from the federal government. In 1994, both the House and Senate unanimously adopted a joint resolution supporting character education and designating October 16–22, as National

Character Counts Week. In July of 1994, Congress reauthorized the Elementary and Secondary Education Act (ESEA) and added to the statute two sources of funding for character education (see ESEA: Section 10103 "Partnerships in Character Education Pilot Project").

The White House sponsored conferences on Character Building for a Civil and Democratic Society in July of 1994, May of 1995, and in June of 1996 and 1997. The conferences brought together educators, community leaders, and representatives of national organizations to exchange ideas on how character education can be provided most effectively and how it can be spread to more U.S. school districts (Character Education Partnership, 1996). All of the senators, representatives, and political leaders who addressed this group reiterated that character education was a national priority.

It is with this historical momentum that this book is presented to parents, teachers, school administrators, and concerned citizens. It outlines what the Blue Ribbon Schools, the best schools in America, are doing to promote character education and train students in ethics and moral values. It provides a plethora of ideas that can be analyzed, assessed, and perhaps adopted in particular schools and school districts that are interested in joining the national movement by adding character education to their program.

SUMMARY

As this chapter has shown, character education was one of the original purposes of the colonial and American schools until the beginning of the twentieth century. John Dewey's instrumental, relativistic philosophy promoted a decline in the direct teaching of character education in the schools and inspired values clarification and cognitive moral development approaches. As these methods did not prove effective in teaching moral content to students, a renewed national interest has grown in character education. The Blue Ribbon Schools provide examples of what the best schools in American are doing to promote character education.

REFERENCES

"Aspen Declaration on Character Education." 1992. *Ethics in Action*. Marina del Rey, CA: Joseph & Edna Josephson Institute of Ethics, insert.

ASCD Panel on Moral Education. 1988a. "Moral Education in the Life of the School," *Educational Leadership*, 45(8):4–8.

ASCD Panel on Moral Education. 1988b. *Moral Education in the Life of the School.* VA: Association for Supervision and Curriculum Development.

Bennett, W. 1988. "Moral Literacy and the Formation of Character," from *Our Children and Our Country* New York: Simon and Schuster, reprinted in *Moral, Character, and Civic Education.* J. S. Benninga, ed. New York: Teachers College Press, p. 133.

Carlin, D. 1981. "Is Kohlberg a Disciple of Dewey?" *Educational Theory*, Summer/Fall: 31 (3&4), 251–257.

"Character Counts Coalition." 1993. *Ethics in Action*. Marina del Rey, CA: Joseph & Edna Josephson Institute of Ethics, May/June, p. 1.

Character Education Partnership. 1996. *Character Education in U.S. Schools: The New Consensus*. VA: The Character Education Partnership, Inc., pp. 3–6, 23–26.

Dewey, J. 1891. *Outlines of a Critical Theory of Ethics*, Ann Arbor: University of Michigan, p. 3 as cited by Copelston, F. 1967. *A History of Philosophy, Vol. 8*, New York: Image Books, p. 124.

Dewey, J. 1909. *Moral Principles in Education*. Carbondale, IL: Southern Illinois University Press, p. 4.

Dewey, J. 1916. *Democracy and Education*. New York: Macmillan.

Dewey, J. 1929. *The Quest for Certainty*. New York: Macmillan.

Fenstermacher, G. 1990. "Some Moral Considerations on Teaching as a Profession," in *The Moral Dimensions of Teaching*. J. Goodlad, R. Soder and K. Sirotnik, eds. CA: Jossey Bass, pp. 130–151.

Goodlad, J., R. Soder, and K. Sirotnik, eds. 1990. *The Moral Dimensions of Teaching*. CA: Jossey-Bass.

Gutek, G. 1970. *An Historical Introduction to American Education*. New York: Thomas Crowell Co.

Gutek, G. 1988. *Philosophical and Ideological Perspectives on Education*. Boston: Allyn & Bacon.

Harmin, M. 1988. "Value Clarity, High Morality—Let's Go for Both." *Educational Leadership*, 45(8):24–30.

Harrison, G. 1980. "Values Clarification and the Construction of the Good." *Educational Theory*. 30(3):185–191.

Josephson Institute. 1993. "Character Counts Coalition," *Ethics in Action*. Marina del Rey, CA: Joseph & Edna Josephson Institute of Ethics, May/June, p. 1.

Kilpatrick, W. 1992. *Why Johnny Can't Tell Right from Wrong*. New York: Simon and Schuster.

Kirschenbaum, H. 1995. *100 Ways to Enhance Values and Morality in Schools and Youth Settings*. Boston, MA: Allyn & Bacon.

Kohlberg, L. 1975. "Moral Education for a Society in Moral Transition." *Educational Leadership*, 33(2):46–54.

Kohlberg, L. 1978. "The Cognitive-Developmental Approach to Moral Education." in Peter Scharf, ed. *Readings in Moral Education*. Winston Press.

Kohlberg, L. 1984. *Essays on Moral Development, Vol. 2: The Psychology of Moral Development*. San Francisco, CA: Harper and Row.

Leming, J. 1993a. "Synthesis of Research: In Search of Effective Character Education," *Educational Leadership*, 51(3),63–71.

Leming, J. 1993b. *Character Education: Lessons from the Past, Models for the Future*. Camden, Maine: Institute for Global Ethics.

Lickona, T. 1993. "The Return of Character Education," *Educational Leadership*, 5(3),6–11.

Lickona, T. 1991. *Educating for Character: How Our Schools Can Teach Respect and Responsibility*. New York: Bantam.

McKown, Harry. 1935. *Character Education*. New York: McGraw-Hill.

McClellan, B.E. 1992. *Schools and the Shaping of Character: Moral Education in America, 1607–Present*. Bloomington, IN.: ERIC Clearinghouse for Social Studies.

National Commission on Excellence in Education. 1983. *A Nation at Risk: The Imperative for Educational Reform*. Washington, D.C.: U.S. Government Printing Office. April.

Nucci, L. 1987. "Synthesis of Research on Moral Development," *Educational Leadership*, 44(5):86–92.

Pietig, J. 1977. "John Dewey and Character Education," *Journal of Moral Education*, 6(3):170–180.

Power, C., A. Higgins and L. Kohlberg. 1989. "The Habit of the Common Life: Building Character Through Democratic Community Schools," in *Moral Development and Character Education: A Dialogue*. L. Nucci, ed. Berkeley, Calif.: McCutchan Publishing Corp., pp. 125–143.

Raths, L., M. Harmin and S. Simon. 1966. *Values and Teaching*. Ohio: Charles Merrill Publishing Co.

Reimer, J., D.P. Paolitto and R.H. Hersh. 1983. *Promoting Moral Growth: From Piaget to Kohlberg*. Prospect Heights, Ill.: Waveland Press.

Rosenblatt, R. 1995. "Who'll Teach Kids Right from Wrong?" *New York Times Magazine*, April 30, pp. 36–65.

Rushton, J., C. Brainerd, and M. Pressley. 1983. "Behavioral Development and Construct Validity: The Principle of Aggregation," *Psychological Bulletin*, 94(1),18–38.

Tom, A. R. 1984. *Teaching as a Moral Craft*. New York: Longman.

Traiger, J. 1995. "The Time Is Now: Reflections on Moral Education," *Education*, 115(3):432–434.

U.S. Department of Education. "Partnerships in Character Education Pilot Project," Elementary and Secondary Education Act: Section 10103 on-line: URL: www.ed.gov/offices/OERI/charactr.html.

Vail, H. 1909. *McGuffey's Eclectic Primer, Revised Edition*. New York: Van Nostrand Reinhold.

Wynne, E. 1989. "Transmitting Traditional Values in Contemporary Schools," in *Moral Development and Character Education: A Dialogue*. L. Nucci, ed., Berkeley, CA: McCutchan Publishing Corporation, 19–36.

Wynne, E. and K. Ryan. 1993. *Reclaiming Our Schools: A Handbook on Teaching Character, Academics and Discipline*. New York: Macmillan Publishing Company.

Wynne, E. and Walberg, H. 1985. "The Complementary Goals of Character Development and Academic Excellence," *Educational Leadership*, 43(4):15–18.

Chapter 3

CHARACTER EDUCATION PROGRAMS IN THE BLUE RIBBON SCHOOLS

Education worthy of its name is essentially education of character.
—Martin Buber

We must remember that intelligence is not enough. Intelligence plus character—that is the goal of true education.—Martin Luther King, Jr.

In matters of opinion, swim with the fish; but in matters of principle, stand firm like a rock.—Mark Twain

MORAL EDUCATION REQUIRED FOR NOMINATION AS A BLUE RIBBON SCHOOL

Even today some people still debate whether public schools should teach values or virtues. However, judging by the application form for the Elementary School Recognition Program, this question is not an issue for the Department of Education. In order to be recognized for Blue Ribbon achievement, a school must already be successfully furthering the intellectual, social and *moral* growth of all its students. One of the purposes of the recognition program is to "identify and give public recognition to outstanding public and private elementary schools across the United States . . . that are doing an exceptional job in this area of values education and character development." Specifically, the application asks, "How do school programs, practices, and policies foster the development of sound character, democratic values, ethical judgment, and the ability to work in a self-disciplined

27

and purposeful manner?" In fact, in order to clarify even more what was meant by character education, the 1987–88 application asks: "What are your schools' expectations in the area of character development, and how are these expectations communicated? What in the school contributes to the development of the attributes of sound character, such as a sense of fair play, a concern for others, a commitment to truthful and virtuous behavior, and the availability and willingness to assume responsibility for one's own behavior? How do school policies, programs, and practices foster the development of a child's self-discipline and self-confidence?"

This chapter reports on the ways in which character education is taught in the Blue Ribbon Schools (see Table 4). Specifically, it seeks to answer the following questions:

- Why are a school's mission statement and school motto important for character development?
- What value do district/schoolwide character traits have for promoting character in students?
- How are the principal, teachers, counselors, and parents involved in promoting character development in young people?
- Should character education be a separate class, or is it possible to integrate it into the academic curriculum?

This chapter presents those programs mentioned by the Blue Ribbon Schools that explicitly attempt to teach character education in the

TABLE 4 Ways in which character education is promoted in the Blue Ribbon Schools.

Category	Count	Percent
Assemblies, PA announcements	22	7
Community service	9	3
Curriculum programs/units	128	39
Discipline plans	45	14
Integrated throughout	78	24
School awards, mottos	84	27
Staff models	84	25

Valid cases, 330; missing cases, 20.

school, thus reflecting the more traditional "direct approach" to teaching virtue discussed in Chapter 2. Programs were selected for this chapter if they specifically referred to character development and/or made reference to other programs that were specifically designed to teach students moral values or virtues. Schools also included a large range of other types of programs as they sought to answer this question. These different programs will be mentioned in the tables that summarize the results but will each be dealt with in an appropriate later chapter.

Percentages of responses quoted in this chapter will refer to the answers given by the schools to the above question asked on the application form. Quotes from schools are from direct conversations with the principal, teachers, and/or counselors when the school was visited and/or are taken directly from the school's application to the School Recognition Program.

GOOD CHARACTER AS DEFINED BY THE BLUE RIBBON SCHOOLS

Most interesting are the different ways in which the Blue Ribbon Schools defined "the development of sound character" as they sought to answer this question (Table 5). The most common definition (32%) was "teaching ethics, moral virtues, and character development," but a surprising close second response (22%) was learning "good discipline and good behavior." Another common definition was practicing "citizenship, patriotism, and leadership."

Chapter 1 presented a construct for understanding character as "moral knowing, moral feeling, and moral doing." From these definitions of good character, the Blue Ribbon Schools each seem to key in on only one aspect of good character, thereby presenting only a partial description of character rather than a complete definition.

The Saddle Rock Elementary School in Great Neck, New York, is a school of 500 children with a growing ethnically and linguistically diverse student body. In addition, over 10% of the students are emotionally or physically challenged. Their staff found it difficult to define good character succinctly. "Although such qualities as character, citizenship and democratic values are intangibles, we make a united concerted effort to make them meaningful for our students. Students learn

TABLE 5 How do Blue Ribbon Schools define "character"?

Category	Count	Percent
Citizenship	52	20
Ethics, moral virtue	84	32
Good decision making	4	14
Good discipline, good behavior	57	22
Leadership, doing one's best	11	4
Respect for others and self	28	11
Responsibility for own actions	17	6
Service to others	10	4

Total valid cases, 250; missing cases 100.

to accept responsibility in student mediation groups. We help students build character by learning to derive satisfaction from intrinsic rewards."

GOOD CHARACTER DEFINED
BY A CATHOLIC SCHOOL

St. Luke's School, a private Catholic school, pre-K to eighth grade in suburban Oak Park, Illinois, began its application with a definition of character which articulates one of the two main goals of the school:

"Character" is defined as the inner strength of an individual that expresses itself in appropriate visible behavior. It is the sum of the attitudes and actions of a person that have become so ingrained through habit that they form part of his/her whole personality. The formation of good character in young people is primarily the responsibility of parents.

The principal, Dr. Judith Wynee, explained that St. Luke's School plays a supportive role in concert with parents in continuing the learning and development of Christian character in its students. St. Luke's students are expected to come to value and exhibit in their daily lives the virtues of respect, generosity, courtesy, integrity, and loyalty, which are manifestations of a person's inner strength.

IMPORTANCE OF THE SCHOOL'S MISSION

Character development, teaching values and virtues, and promoting the ability to make ethical decisions was specifically mentioned in the mission statement of many of these Blue Ribbon schools (Table 6). According to Edward Wynne and Kevin Ryan (1993), noted scholars in character education and authors of *Reclaiming Our Schools: A Handbook on Teaching Character, Academics, and Discipline*, a school's mission statement is very important in making public the specific character-building goals that the administration, teachers, and staff are committed to fostering.

The character-building mission of the Blue Ribbon Schools is reflected in the comments made in many of the reports. For example, the Quailwood Elementary School in the community-oriented suburb of Bakersfield, California, is committed to its mission to "develop students who have sound ethical values, a commitment to academic excellence, and a concern for the betterment of society." This vision is carried throughout the school's programs and in the monthly school-wide goal that focuses on developing positive student attitudes and behavior. Quailwood has almost 500 students, 15% of whom are racially and ethnically diverse.

TABLE 6 Common Words found in Blue Ribbon Schools' Mission Statements.

Category	Count	Percent
Academics, responsibility	18	5
Collaborative, cooperation	2	1
Create positive environment	27	8
Develop citizenship	111	32
Have high expectation of all	5	1
Orderly environment	14	4
Student centered, develop self-esteem	22	6
Teaching decision making, problem solving	66	19
Teach ethics, character development	89	26
Whole child developed	134	39
Missing values	69	20

Valid cases, 337; missing cases 11.

CHARACTER EDUCATION IN PRIVATE SCHOOLS

It is interesting to note that character or moral development was not necessarily evident in all of the mission statements of the private, religion-based Blue Ribbon Schools in the sample. The Christian school community sees education as involving the "whole person" unfolding in an environment of faith, hope, and love and the school as a place for helping students toward a "responsible and coherent way of life" (Travis, 1985). One would think that every religion-based school in its statement of philosophy would mention the students' moral development, but this was not found to be so. Schools develop students "spiritually and doctrinally," but specific efforts also need to be made to develop their character so that students do the good moral actions that their religious training tells them they should do. When a religion-based school teaches character development to its students, there is a clear focus on the promotion of human virtues as a goal of the school.

The Catholic Church has long held that there is a specific set of moral truths based on universal principles that must be handed down, generation to generation (Travis, 1985). One could hypothesize that a denominational school should be more successful in promoting character education since they need to teach only a single, coherent "system" as true, and they can incorporate character education throughout the curriculum as well as into noncurricular functions such as liturgies. Years ago, one could assume that schools with a religious focus also promoted character development in their students. Nevertheless, the long-term decline in the conduct of young Americans cited in Chapter 1 has affected all our youth, those in private as well as public schools, and there is a real need for specific instruction dealing with ethical issues and moral values. To address these challenges, a National Council for the Promotion of Character Education in the Catholic Schools was formed in 1996 by the National Catholic Education Association.

IDENTIFYING CORE VALUES
AND KEY HUMAN VIRTUES

The identification of the moral values and human virtues that particular schools or districts intend to promote is the first step to be undertaken before character education can begin in the schools. Each school or district needs to clarify what its community understands by "good character" and what core values it feels each student should learn.

Character education was studied in both the 25th and 26th Annual Phi Delta Kappa/Gallup Poll of the Public's Attitudes toward the Public Schools. The 25th Gallup Poll (Eliam, 1993) asked if the respondent thought it would be possible for local communities to agree on a set of basic values to be taught in the public schools. A solid majority (69%) said yes and went on to approve strongly the teaching of eight values: honesty, democracy, patriotism, caring for others, moral courage, the golden rule, acceptance of people of different races, and religious tolerance. The 26th Gallup Poll (Eliam, 1994) registered strong approval for a set of personal traits or virtues that could be taught in the public schools. These virtues included respect, industry or hard work, persistence, fairness, compassion, civility or politeness, self-esteem, and high expectations for oneself.

Phi Delta Kappa conducted research on core values by collecting data from 10,000 persons in over 150 communities across the country in 1994. It found high levels of agreement about values young people should learn. Democratic values such as civility, honesty, equality, freedom, nonviolence, responsibility, and respect should be taught by the family, the church, and the school. They found agreement on the understanding of a "person of character" as one who is honest, responsible, dependable, loyal, and having integrity. Their report concluded that schools are not teaching these values as well as most educators think they should be taught (Frymier et al., 1995).

Many of the Blue Ribbon Schools stated that they had developed their own character education curriculum and that the essential organizing framework was a set of core values. The collegial work of teachers, parents, and administrators in drawing up the list of core values was central to their curricular success. All involved then had a sense of ownership for the values chosen (Saterlie, 1988). Henry Huffman (1994) states that at the heart of a district's character education program is the process for deciding the set of core values that the school will promote.

In one sense, it really does not matter which values or virtues are chosen; even learning to live one virtue alone will help to build a student's character. The words of Blessed Josemaria Escriva de Balaguer (1973), the founder of Opus Dei and a person responsible for the foundation of many schools internationally that focus on character development, are particularly helpful in this area:

> I don't know if I could say which is the most important human virtue. It depends on the point of view from which they are considered. In any case, this question doesn't really get us anywhere, for it is not a matter of practicing one or even a number of virtues. We have to try to acquire and practice all of them. Each individual virtue is interwoven with the others and thus, our effort to be sincere will also make us upright, cheerful, prudent and composed. (pp. 6–7)

William Kilpatrick (1992), professor of Education at Boston College and author of *Why Johnny Can't Tell Right from Wrong*, agrees with this idea that the virtues form a unity and that in order to be a person of character you must have several virtues working together. He and most other character education scholars (Wynne & Ryan, 1993; Vincent, 1994) agree that, as a bare minimum, every list of character traits ought to contain the four cardinal virtues that have come down to us from the Greeks: prudence, fortitude, temperance, and justice. They are called cardinal because they are the axis (cardo) on which the moral life turns (Kilpatrick, 1992). A comparison of the Blue Ribbon School's lists of character traits finds these four virtues are usually included, although the schools may use more modern terminology for them: For example, prudence is "good decision making skills," fortitude is "courage," temperance is "self-discipline," and justice is "fairness."

BLUE RIBBON SCHOOLS' LISTS OF KEY CHARACTER TRAITS

Plano School District in Texas

Whole school districts have adopted sets of core values that the particular Blue Ribbon Schools also support. For example, the Plano School District in Texas has adopted a set of citizenship/character traits for its schools. These traits are courtesy, courage, discipline, honesty, human worth and dignity, justice, patriotism, personal obligation for the public good, respect for self and others, respect for authority, tolerance, and responsibility. At the Huffman School in suburban, middle-class Plano, the staff and teachers model these twelve traits of good citizenship and sound character. Each week teachers emphasize a schoolwide specified character trait at teachable moments. This trait is taught through lessons involving discussion, identification of examples and non-examples, and modeling. The teachers expect all of the students to develop each of these character traits over time. The school shares the targeted weekly citizenship trait with parents through newsletters, monthly calendars, and the marquee. These twelve traits are posted in every classroom.

At Hedcoxe School, also in Plano, the twelve district-wide character traits appear on the screen whenever a school computer is turned on. The teachers use these traits as a foundation to their discipline program and for their enrichment activities. They seek to develop a sense of social responsibility and citizenship in the students. Hedcoxe has experienced large increases in student enrollment and has had to divide into two schools. Hedcoxe's student body is 15% ethnically diverse, and over 10% have some physical/learning handicap. By emphasizing the trait of respect for others and tolerance, students have learned to get along well with all of their different schoolmates.

Character education permeates every aspect of academic and extracurricular practice at Wells School, a large school also in Plano, with a more homogeneous student body. The entire staff participates in community service. Custodians, food servers, coaches, teachers, and the principal are mindful of the image they portray—as children are forever watching. The school also uses, in every classroom, the district posters that identify the good character traits, and they have also programmed this list onto their computer screens. One of the teachers concurs on the importance of these posters: "The character posters in the classrooms remind you to try to make a connection between the character topics and whatever you are teaching." Each month one trait is spotlighted, taught, and recognized schoolwide.

When visiting the Plano School District, the author received a Plano "Character Traits Poster." It was learned that these character traits have been in the Plano district for over fifteen years. They were developed by teams of teachers, counselors, and administrators and have been well-accepted by the total community. They have been successfully incorporated in each new district curriculum revision. Plano schools have used them as objectives in district grade level and subject level curriculum guides, in cooperative groups, as a basis for thematic instruction, and, most recently, for the development of their outcomes, goals, and assessment plans. According to the counselor at Wells, "Promoting lifelong learning traits is where the district is heading now and these character traits fit right into the lifelong learning traits as well."

Princeton School District in Ohio

The Princeton City School District in Cincinnati, Ohio has the motto: "Respect yourself and others." It has also adopted a set of character education values for the entire school district. Dr. Richard Denoyer, superintendent at that time, began a districtwide, year-long process in 1987 to identify these core values. Dr. Denoyer believes that Princeton was the first public school district to attempt to integrate a system of values into the curriculum beginning with kindergarten. Its goal was to coordinate the establishment of their character education program with the celebration of the Bicentennial of the U.S. Constitution. He invited all interested instructional leaders, principals, faculty, parents, and students to districtwide discussions to identify these core values. The group then forwarded its ideas on important values to the character education committee. The committee finally came up with its list of twelve values, which consisted of the following:

(*1*) Honesty and integrity—Be truthful and sincere to others and yourself.

(*2*) Trustworthiness—Be true to your own word.

(*3*) Civility and compassion—Be polite and caring to others.

(*4*) Loyalty—Be faithful to lawful ideals and beliefs of country, school, and friends.

(*5*) Wisdom—Search for knowledge and truth—the ultimate realities of life.

(*6*) Freedom—Express yourself responsibly in making choices.

(*7*) Justice—Be fair to others and accept consequences for your own actions.

(*8*) Equality—Support free choice and opportunities for all.

(*9*) Diversity and tolerance—Appreciate differences and variety in people and nature.

(*10*) Responsibility—Maintain personal accountability, exercise rights and exert influences as a citizen in a democratic society.

(*11*) Unity—Support family and group cohesiveness through appropriate interpersonal relationships.

(*12*) Self-Discipline and courage—Demonstrate self-control and be true to your convictions.

The principals and staff were then asked to develop a plan to incorporate these values into all phases of the day-to-day school activities. The twelve values were included in the district curriculum guides, the annual report, and each school's annual goals and objectives. The process, program, and its results have been reported in many newspaper articles.

Visits to the schools in the district show that their effort has been successful. For instance, these values are prominently displayed in each classroom at the Stewart School in the Princeton School district. Stewart School is a racially and socio-economically diverse school. It has experienced large enrollment increases over the past five years, with minority enrollment increasing by almost 200%. Personal responsibility is stressed at Stewart. Students are expected to be prompt and prepared, and they are asked to perform regular jobs within the school environment. Older students model good behavior when reading with kindergartners and first-graders. Students work cooperatively in their classrooms and together on committees and special interest groups.

The Everdale School is a K–6 school, also in the Princeton School District, that is about 10% racially/ethnically diverse. At Everdale, teachers systematically and sequentially teach these twelve character traits as they would any other part of the curriculum. The principal explains their school's philosophy: "Students are taught attributes of sound character in much the same way as any other subject is taught." By all working together on the district core set of values, they showed that they accepted as a tenet that public schools were to teach values: "We believe that the teaching of values has a place in the classroom."

Core Values in School Districts in Georgia

The County Line Elementary School is a beautiful, renovated, well-landscaped school in Widner, Georgia. The school adheres to the Barrow County School System's core values and tries to integrate both implicit and explicit values instruction throughout the curriculum based on the state's list of core values. These values are included in the curriculum manuals and must be included in each teacher's daily lesson plans. The school provides opportunities for practicing these values through such activities as student organizations, team sports, assembly programs, and community service. Good manners, consideration for others, freedom from prejudice, and high ethical and moral values are modeled by faculty and staff. These practices encourage students, as they strive to fulfill the school motto, "Learn Today to Lead Tomorrow."

In line with the renewed interest in values education, both nationally and at the state level, teachers at Elm Street School in Newman, Georgia, incorporate "mini lessons," which they have structured around character development, as opportunities arise. For example, a discussion about accepting difference in others evolved naturally when a kindergarten class observed a wheelchair-bound student's arrival at school. Elm Street's population is one of social and economic extremes. Of the 572 students, approximately one-half are transported from low-socioeconomic, inner-city areas. In sharp contrast, the other 50% of the students came from middle- to upper-income neighborhoods due to system-wide redistricting. Forty percent of the students are from an African-American heritage, and over 25% of the student body are handicapped. Teachers have had extensive staff development training on multiculturalism and seek to integrate intercultural experiences into all areas of the curriculum. For example, a first grade whole-language unit on "Christmas Around the World" now includes a study of African customs, music, art, and literature. To better understand world cultures, the school participates in the International Internship Program and currently hosts a Japanese intern who teaches the students about the culture, food, art, and customs of her country.

CURRICULAR IDEAS

As shown in Table 4, on page 28, about one fourth of the Blue Ribbon Schools reviewed stated that they integrate character development throughout their curriculum. Some school districts have developed curriculum guides that incorporate character education qualities such as honesty, kindness, truthfulness, fairness, responsibility, appreciating differences, and valuing friendships into the social studies, English, and guidance program objectives. Other schools focus on a "Virtue-of-the-Month" or "Virtue-of-the-Week" and include family participation in the character development program by sending home notes outlining the virtue under study and asking parents to encourage specific virtuous actions at home.

For example, character development goals are incorporated into the daily learning activity at the Governor Bent Elementary School in Albuquerque, New Mexico, whenever appropriate. Governor Bent serves a large and diverse population from distinctly different geographic and socioeconomic areas.This population includes middle-income homeowners, professionally educated families and lower-income families that live in government-subsided housing. Almost 40% of the student body is of Hispanic ethnicity. According to Marilyn Davenport, the principal, the school makes a conscious effort to communicate its expectations of children:

> All the adults in the school strive to model an appreciation and respect for others and for children, which we feel is reciprocated by the student body. The students are expected to actively contribute to the overall environment. They are given leadership roles in organizations such as the student council and are helped to be sensitive toward the needs of others through food and clothing drives. We feel children should develop the positive attributes of patriotism, honesty, and empathy for others to become strong citizens of the community. Character development goals are incorporated into all daily activity in the school. We make a conscious effort to communicate our expectations for children.

The students at the Volker Applied Learning Magnet School in Kansas City, Missouri, would be characterized by others as an "at risk" student body. More than half of the student body of this middle school of fourth- and fifth-graders are of African-American origin and are from lower-income families. One-quarter of the students qualify for special education services. According to Dr. Rayna Levine, the principal:

> Knowing right from wrong is taught and reinforced at the school. Honesty is appreciated and commended. We use students' sense of fairness, equality, and justice when discussing incidents. In this way, personal responsibility is built. Our goal is for students to assume personal responsibility for their actions and not blame others when things do not go as envisioned.

Some schools reported a variety of methods used to integrate character education in the curriculum. At the Harrison Elementary School in Harrison, Ohio, core values include honesty, respect, acceptance, and justice. Staff teach these values in classroom activities involving role playing and discussion as well as through the use of literature, films, and other media. Harrison is a very large K–6 suburban school with a middle-class, white student body. Harrison has also instituted a PRIDE Program (Positive Recognition for Individual Discipline and Enthusiasm) that strives to build students' self-esteem and to recognize students who have good conduct and work habits.

Puppets with a Purpose

A unique curricular program designed to develop ethical judgment, manners, and values was found in the Irwin School, a K–5 school in suburban East Brunswick, New Jersey. In this program, Puppets with a Purpose, students supply ideas for the topics of the plays. The puppets act out the situations suggested by the students. Then students in the class comment on the actions of the puppets: "Rudie's being Rude. Betsy is Bossy." Post-play discussions are lively and help students to verbalize their feelings about situations similar to those they personally have experienced. The puppets are able to bridge cultural and linguistic differences and bring their message to the large group of Asian students as well as to the Caucasian students.

Curricular Programs

Almost 40% of the schools answered the question "How do school programs, practices, policies and staff foster the development of good character?" by stating that they promote character development through a specific curricular program or units in the curriculum. The majority of the curricular programs identified by schools answering this question focused more on drug education than "character education." These programs will be described in Chapter 4 on drug education. Nevertheless, approximately 11% of the Blue Ribbon Schools use commercial character education programs, specifically those developed by the Character Education Institute, the Jefferson Center for Character Education, the Child Development Project, and the Heartwood Foundation.

Character Education Institute

The Del Cerro Elementary School, a magnet school in suburban, middle-class Mission Viejo, California, uses the Character Education

Institute curriculum for its character education program. Del Cerro has designed its school program so that staff promote the teaching of positive attitudes and behavior on a regular basis. A word is highlighted each month in every classroom, and the teacher is provided with opportunities in the curriculum to reinforce and use the concept. Words such as friendship, kindness, cooperation, responsibility, honesty, sportsmanship, respect, courage, self-control, and freedom are presented schoolwide. Numerous suggestions are given to the teachers for using written language, literature, science, social studies, reading, art, and oral language classes to promote further understanding of the target values. Each teacher encourages discussions regarding ways in which to apply the values that have been introduced. Cooperative learning groups further help children learn to work together and be more accepting of others' opinions. In addition to assemblies and awards, a banner displays the "Word-of-the-Month, bulletin boards portray the word, and cards and certificates are given during the month by adults when they notice someone exemplifying the month's word.

The Character Education Institute's curriculum focuses on instilling universal values, refining critical thinking skills, clearly teaching right from wrong, and building good self-esteem. Though most of the values taught through the curriculum are overt, additional objectives are reinforced through topic lessons. These include responsibility, self-esteem, conflict resolution, respecting the rights of others, obeying rules and the law, service learning, and cooperative learning. Some of the ancillary concepts taught that further aid in building good character include setting goals, planning ahead, sharing, cliques, patience, perseverance, using time wisely, managing money, and table manners. More information on the curriculum can be obtained by contacting Jay Mulkey at the Character Education Institute, 8919 Tesoro Drive, Suite 220, San Antonio, TX 78217-6253; phone: 210-829-1727; internet address: http://www.charactereducation.org/.

Jefferson Center for Character Education Curriculum

The Bellerive School, with a culturally diverse population of over 500 students in suburban Creve Coeur, Missouri, uses the Jefferson Center for Character Education Curriculum with the STAR system. This curriculum focuses on the systematic teaching of common values that cut across ethnic, cultural, and religious lines. These values include honesty, respect, responsibility, integrity, courage, tolerance,

justice, and politeness. According to Dr. David Brooks, the program director of the Jefferson Center, the Character Education Curriculum is
used in about 6,000 schools and approximately 50,000 classrooms. The
curriculum teaches students the four-step decision-making model for
solving problems and resolving conflicts: The model is known as STAR
or "Stop, Think, Act, Review." It also teaches them to accept the consequences of their actions; develop and improve self-confidence, self-esteem, and positive attitudes; set and achieve realistic goals; and accept
attendance, punctuality, and reliability as part of being personally responsible. STAR also stands for Success Through Accepting Responsibility, a schoolwide systematic program for improving school climate,
attendance, achievement, and self-discipline.

The curriculum includes short and easy-to-follow weekly lessons
that can be infused into the regular curriculum. It encourages the use of
monthly themes that are featured on classroom posters. For example, at
Bellerive the October theme was "Be a Goal Setter." Other monthly
themes are "Be Responsible," "Be Polite," "Be on Time," "Be a Listener," "Be a Risk Taker," "Be a Tough Worker." The personal values of
accountability, honesty, integrity, responsibility, and self-esteem are
taught through the Bellerive Cadet Helper Program. The Cadet Program provides students with the opportunity for providing service to
the school. Teachers ask for assistance in the classroom in such areas as
reading aloud to a student or helping with math facts. Cadets pick the
teacher, job, and time they will be able to assist. In this way, they are
given actual opportunities in which they can live the monthly themes.

More information on the STAR curriculum can be obtained from Dr.
David Brooks at the Jefferson Center for Character Education, 202 S.
Lake Avenue, #240, Pasadena, CA 91101; phone: 1-818-792-8130; internet address: http://www.netspace.org/~zaqix/ jefferson.html. Information
on the multicultural literature that the Jefferson Center has developed
around the STAR process can be obtained from the Young People's Press,
Inc., 1731 Kettner Blvd., San Diego, CA 92101; phone: 800-231-9774.

Child Development Project

Recognized schools from California's San Ramon County were members of the Child Development Project (CDP), which has been implemented in eight schools in the district. This project has now become nationally known as the only character education program included in the

National Diffusion Network of "Educational Programs that Work." The Country Club Elementary School is a model school of the Child Development Project. The families in the Country Club attendance area have the lowest average income in the district and the greatest number of students whose native language is not English. The CDP was conceived after a review of the literature on promoting caring and responsible behavior in students suggested that a long-term, comprehensive school intervention program, delivered primarily by classroom teachers but with considerable parental involvement, was likely to produce widespread and long-lasting changes in children's pro-social attitudes, motives, and behaviors (Kohn, 1990; Watson et al., 1989). The major components of the project include (1) direct teaching of prosocial values through the use of a literature-based reading program, (2) developmental discipline as an approach to classroom management, which involves creating a warm, caring classroom where children help to solve problems through class meetings, (3) cooperative learning, which fosters children working together and practicing pro-social values, and (4) mutual understanding, promoted by allowing students to help one another. The program is designed to increase children's responsibility, helpfulness, cooperation, and social skills. Ongoing evaluation of the project has indicated that it is successful and effective (Developmental Studies Center, 1994). This evaluation model is described in more detail in Chapter 9.

A visit to the school confirms the positive effect of the program. Although the official funding for the program at Country Club Hills ended more than eight years ago, principal Carol Rowley and the faculty who participated in the original program continue to pass on the CDP philosophy to new faculty. A caring environment truly exists in the school. An effort is made to give the students many examples of the character qualities of respect, responsibility, problem solving, and caring throughout the curriculum.

For more information on the Child Development Project and the Literature Based Curriculum that they use, contact Eric Schaps at the Developmental Studies Center, 2000 Embarcadero, Suite 305, Oakland, CA 94606; phone: 800-666-7270 or 510-533-0213.

The Heartwood Curriculum

The Sewickley Academy, a small-town middle school in the Quaker Valley School District in Pennsylvania, uses the Heartwood

Curriculum. Heartwood is a multicultural curriculum that uses stories that convey basic ethical concepts directly and effectively. The stories, from award-winning children's literature, exemplify the concepts of courage, justice, hope, love, loyalty, respect and honesty. The Heartwood Curriculum is a comprehensive program that includes varied materials for teachers such as exercises that encourage student writing, storymaking, and group interaction. The process stimulates the children to grapple thoughtfully with profound concepts, share their own experiences, and make personal connections with ideas. The children apply the concepts in their daily lives and carry home activities to involve their families in the teaching and learning process as well. The manual is organized for classroom use. It outlines the best sequence for teaching the books: preview, reading, discussion, activities, interdisciplinary ideas, wrap-up, resources, and strategies for achieving the objectives of the lessons.

An evaluation conducted by Research for Better Schools reported that the Heartwood materials were highly commended by the field test teachers. Almost all of the teachers emphasized the importance and need for this type of program in their schools. Teachers felt strongly that students were lacking in their ethical development and that this program provided a constructive strategy for initiating discussion with students in this critical area. The Heartwood Curriculum is one of the best character development programs that this researcher has found. It teaches the direct instruction of specific virtues; it uses classical literature to provide models of characters who have lived these virtues; and it includes comprehensive, interdisciplinary lesson plans that allow teachers to integrate character education into literature, social studies, art, and music. The most recent evaluation of the Heartwood Curriculum is summarized in Chapter 9.

Information on the Heartwood Curriculum can be obtained by contacting Eleanor Childs at The Heartwood Institute, 425 North Craig Street, Suite 302, Pittsburgh, PA 15213; phone: 412-688-8570 or 800-432-7810.

Teaching Character Development Through Literature

In addition to these curriculum materials, many of the Blue Ribbon Schools mentioned that their school library had a variety of books on character development relating to honesty, fairness, character, responsibility, dedication, and other virtues. Teachers use the books in various classes. The schools also make a conscious effort to choose textbooks that foster traditional American values. The Joy Wilt books and the Ann Johnson biographies were cited as excellent character-building books to include in the library.

Joy Wilt Berry has written over 200 self-help books for children, from babies to twelve-year-olds. Her goal is to help children become competent, responsible, and happy individuals. There are several series of books that are produced by Living Skills Press, Sebastopol, California, and published by Children's Press, Chicago, that can be purchased for school libraries. One series, called the Living Skills, includes titles such as *Every Kids' Guide to Manners, . . . to Making Friends, . . . to Handling Arguments, . . . to Family Rules and Responsibility.* Another series includes such titles as: *About Divorce, About Change and Moving, About Death.* Finally, for preschoolers there is another series: *Teach Me about Looking, . . . about Smelling, . . . about Pretending, . . . about Tasting.*

Ann Donegan Johnson has written a series of biographies that emphasize specific character qualities. Called the ValueTale Series, they are published by Value Communications, Inc., P.O. Box 101, La Jolla, CA 92038. They include such titles as *The Value of Determination: The Story of Helen Keller, The Value of Courage: The Story of Jackie Robinson, The Value of Respect: The Story of Abraham Lincoln,* and *The Value of Honesty: The Story of Confucius.*

Several schools also noted that the *Weekly Reader* has actual lessons on character development. Robbie the Raccoon is the section in which these citizenship and moral situations are discussed in the primary editions. For example, in the January 1997 Grade Three *Weekly Reader* the students are given the following situation to discuss:

> Hi Girls and Boys!
> It snowed yesterday. My friends and I . . . made some snowballs, and we started tossing them around. I tried to throw one up on the roof of Mrs. Perkin's house. But it didn't make it. The snowball smashed one of the house's upstairs windows. Now what should I do? Have you ever broken something that didn't belong to you? What did you do?
> Your friend,
> Robbie Raccoon

The *Weekly Reader* is one of the most widely read newspapers for children, reaching 40% of the elementary school children in this country. It is published by The Weekly Reader Corporation, 245 Long Hill Road, P.O. Box 2791, Middletown, CT 06457-9291; internet address: http://www.weeklyreader.com.

The character education holdings of the Plano school libraries can be found in Appendix C and include the Joy Wilt and Johnson biographies as well as many other value-rich books.

THE TEACHER'S ROLE
IN CHARACTER DEVELOPMENT

The role of the teacher was found to be very important especially in schools that do not have specific curricular programs for the character development of students. These schools report that their "teachers try to incorporate a strong sense of values in all that they teach." The teachers and staff are expected to be character models for the students: "Each teacher fosters good character and democratic values in the classroom and on the playground. Ethical judgments are fostered by modeling appropriate behaviors through classroom management techniques." Another example: "We believe that students must be taught by word and example the moral principles upon which our nation was founded. Each teacher is expected to teach character education." According to Gary Fenstermacher (1990), the teacher is a key player in promoting character education in the schools. He states: "There are three different ways in which teachers serve as both moral agents and moral educators. They can be quite directive, teaching morality; outright—a form of instruction called didactic instruction. . . . Second, teachers can teach about morality. A third way is to act morally, holding oneself up as a possible model for the students, a model of honesty, fairplay, consideration of others, tolerance and sharing" (p. 134). William Bennett (1991) expands upon this last point:

> To put students in the presence of a morally mature adult who speaks honestly and candidly to them is essential to their moral growth. It seems to me that this is why many teachers entered the profession in the first place—because they thought they could make a positive difference in the lives of students, in the development of their character, i.e., to make them better men and women.

The teachers in the Blue Ribbon Schools try, in the words of one school, to "offer experiences throughout the program which teach the values of character, ethics and democracy." Examples in these schools include English classes that use Aesop's fables and other stories to foster character development and exemplify values which lead to writing assignments such as "How to settle a disagreement" or "How to avoid a fight." Social studies classes teach the values and ideals of famous Americans, and teachers make special efforts to emphasize some of the virtuous qualities of national heroes. Fair play is often developed in physical education classes.

In order to do this effectively, one needs a strong background in character education content and methods. How did these teachers get this preparation and training?

Teaching Character Education to Teachers

Schools and districts wishing to begin a character education program need to provide for staff development. As noted by Henry Huffman (1994) in his book on the development of a character education program in the Mt. Lebanon School district in Pennsylvania, "Most teachers have not received any formal preparation at the undergraduate or graduate level for their role as character educators" (p. 45). In fact, according to Wynne and Ryan (1993), many teachers lack "moral literacy" that is, a framework regarding concepts of character, values and moral behavior; they lack knowledge of the psychological principles of human moral development, and they have not learned methodologies appropriate for developing character. A doctoral dissertation by Alice Lancton (cited in Wynne & Ryan, 1993) found that in a sample of 30 middle school and junior high teachers not a single teacher recalled being told in college or in a district in-service about the teacher's role or responsibility as a moral educator or developer of good character. Of the twenty-nine schools, colleges, or departments of education visited by John Goodlad and Kenneth Sirotnik in 1989, none addressed the moral dimensions of teaching in the foundations courses required of prospective teachers (Goodlad et al., 1990). A survey of 43 heads of teacher education from denominational, state, and private higher education institutions from four distinct regions in the United States (east, west, midwest and south) was conducted by Dara Vernon Wakefield (1996) of Baylor University. She found that although the heads of these teacher education programs supported the notion of instruction in moral education methods, more than half of the programs did not directly teach these methods to any significant extent. This is true today, even though a survey in 1991 by the American Association of School Administrators indicated that moral education programs were a part of the curriculum in more than 10,000 schools nationwide (Wakefield, 1996).

Wynne and Ryan (1993) list specifics of a moral education methodology that should be taught to teachers. These include learning how: (1) to focus students' attention on the ethical dimension of a story, (2) to lead students to thoughtfully consider the ethical principles, (3) to focus students' attention on the moral aspects of a historical event in order to analyze and discuss it, (4) to engage students in the moral of a story and see how it may apply to their own lives, and (5) to build among students the skills of moral discourse, that is, the serious thinking about what is correct and about what "ought to be done."

The author is a professor at a teacher preparation institution and teaches character education to her students. Character education principles and the specific moral education methodology mentioned above could fit well in the following teacher certification courses: History and Philosophy of Education, Educational Psychology, Methods of Teaching Reading/English, Methods of Teaching Social Studies/History, and Classroom Management and Discipline. It could also find its way into other teacher preparation courses, with a little initiative and creativity on the part of the professor. Graduate courses on character education could also be taught to practicing teachers. Titles again could vary, such as Character Education for Teachers, Moral Development, Values Education, and Issues in Education.

Associations of teacher educators, school administrators, and curriculum directors are aware of the challenge and have begun to speak out about the need for teaching ethics and character education to pre-teachers and teachers in-service. Entire journal issues have been dedicated to this topic. The reader is referred to the *Journal of Teacher Education*, Vol. 42, No. 3, May-June 1991; *Journal of Education*, Vol. 175, No. 2, 1993; *Educational Leadership*, Vol. 51, No. 3, Nov. 1993; *The School Administrator*, Vol 52, No. 8, Sept. 1995 and *Journal of Staff Development*, Spring 1996.

As noted in Chapter 2, any educator who has learned about teaching values in schools was probably taught the values clarification philosophy prevalent in the 1970s—a philosophy that purports that the teacher should use morally neutral methods—or the moral dilemma discussion method of Kohlberg that was prevalent in the 1980s. Both methods focus on process, not on moral content. Training in these process approaches does not prepare teachers for their role as character educators, which includes teaching—directly and indirectly—the virtues (moral content) that make up good character.

There is a real need for teachers in schools today to learn how they can foster and develop good character through their teaching. Hopefully, teachers reading this book will find some valuable ideas on how to promote character while teaching their subject area. In the theoretical comments included in each chapter, the author tries to give the reader an intellectual framework for understanding character education and for evaluating the curricular programs that are found in the schools. This author also suggests that teachers read *Education for Character: How Our Schools Can Teach Respect and Responsibility* by Thomas Lickona. This book has been cited extensively here, as it provides an excellent foundation for understanding character education. One can then continue one's formation as a character educator by reading the other books cited by name in the text of this book (e.g., Nucci, 1989; Benniga, 1991; Kilpatrick, 1992; Kohn, 1993; Wynne & Ryan, 1993; Goleman, 1995; Wiley, in press). Also the involvement of teachers in the formulation of a district/school's core values and as key players in the development of the curriculum provides invaluable faculty development experience.

Teachers can receive valuable in-service training on how to promote character if their district adopts a set curriculum. The Character Education Institute, the Thomas Jefferson Center, and the Heartwood Foundation all offer initial in-service training upon adoption of the curriculum. Teachers can augment their knowledge of character education by taking one of the graduate courses listed above at their local teacher training university, by attending a summer institute, or by attending a national conference on character education.

Summer institutes for teachers have begun across the nation. Tom Lickona sponsors a summer institute through the Center for the 4th & 5th R's at the State University College in Cortland, New York. Contact the Center for the 4th & 5th R's, P.O. Box 2000, Cortland, NY 13045; phone: 607-753-2455; internet address: http://www.cortland.edu/www/c4n5rs. Kevin Ryan, from the Center for the Advancement of Ethics and Character, offers a one-week summer institute at Boston University, 605 Commonwealth Ave., Boston, MA 02215; phone: 617-343-3262. These "teacher academies" emphasize the use of the curriculum as the primary vehicle for transmitting moral values to the young. Larry Nucci and Edward Wynne offer summer institutes and classes in Chicago through the Center for Studies in Moral Development and Character Education hosted by the University of Illinois at Chicago. Contact the Center for Studies in Moral Development and Character Education, Chicago, IL 60607; phone: 773-996-5580; internet address: http://www.uic.edu/~lnucci/MoralEd./ Finally, workshops for teachers on character education are provided by Madonna Murphy at the College of St. Francis, 500 Wilcox, Joliet, IL 60435; phone: 815-740-3212, and by Lori Wiley at the Character Development Foundation, P.O. Box 4782, Manchester, NH 03108; phone: 603-472-3063.

Additionally, there are four national conferences on character education and moral development that can provide valuable faculty development. The Character Education Partnership sponsors the Character Education Forum in February of each year. Contact Character Education Partnership, 809 Franklin St., Alexandria, VA 22314-4105; phone: 800-988-8081; internet address: http://web2010.com/cepweb. The Communitarian Network sponsors a White House Conference on Character Education in the summer. Contact Amitai Etzioni, the Communitarian Network, 2130 H Street, NW, Suite 714J, Washington, DC 20052; phone: 202-994-7997. The National Character Education Conference is in July each year in St. Louis, Missouri. Contact Linda McKay at the Cooperating School Districts, 13157 Olive Spur Rd., St. Louis, MO 63141; phone: 800-478-5684. Finally, the Association for Moral Education sponsors a conference in November. Contact Ann Higgins at Fordham University, 411 E. Fordham Road, Bronx, NY 10458; phone: 718-817-3885.

ROLE OF THE PRINCIPAL AS MORAL LEADER

The principal also plays an important part in creating a climate for character development in the schools. According to Lickona (1991), whenever you find a school with a healthy moral environment, you will find a principal—or another person with responsibility delegated from the principal—who is leading the way. How do principals lead? Recurring leadership methods cited in almost half of the Blue Ribbon Schools include character-building assemblies, plays, school mottos or slogans, bulletin board messages, posters, and public address (PA) announcements. In some schools, the Pledge of Allegiance is followed by an inspirational thought, or the principal gives a thought for the week each Monday on the PA. Through these means, principals try to foster individual self-discipline, values, and new understandings of behavior. For example, at the Crest Hill Elementary School, in Casper, Wyoming, the biweekly American Heritage assemblies give students the opportunity to practice good behavior, democratic values, and sound ethical judgment. Assembly programs present such topics as respect, courtesy, getting along with others, friendship, self-reliance, sportsmanship, and sharing. Crest Hill is a K–6 school with almost 500 students, most of whom are white. Students are highly motivated to learn and participate in school activities. A very large proportion have qualified for special education services, from gifted education to instruction tailored to physical and emotional disabilities. Getting along with others and understanding others are key character development goals at Crest Hill.

At the Como Park Elementary School in Lancaster, New York, the sign on the office door of Andrea Stein, the principal, reads: "The answer is yes unless there is a compelling reason to say no." In this way, she conveys confidence in her staff and students. There is a sense of pride that permeates the entire building. Como Park is a large school in a suburban district with two diverse economic groups. Most of the students are white; 17% come from lower-income families.

Miriam Remar, the principal at the Howard Reiche Community School in Portland, Maine, has a "Principal's Corner." In this section of the office she displays the students' quality work and also lists the students who have achieved awards or honors. She tries to send the message that positive attitudes, respect, and quality work go hand in hand. Classrooms at Reiche reflect a unique blend of student backgrounds, cultures, and aspirations. Many students are considered "high risk," while many others are at risk of not reaching their potential due to low motivation and the multiple consequences of poverty and family substance abuse. Expectations are consistently high for each and every child. By giving recognition to students who exhibit good character qualities, the school encourages them to do their best.

James Kolb, the principal at Brumfield Elementary School in Princeton, Indiana, helps build character by talking to students personally about morally significant events. One Brumfield parent who had a very positive regard for Mr. Kolb recounted a key incident: "My son lied in school. Mr. Kolb, the principal, talked to him about responsibility and honesty. He has never had a problem since." Brumfield is a large rural school with almost all white students. However, the Brumfield student body has diverse economic and linguistic backgrounds. Almost 10% of the students are limited English speakers, over 15% are from low-income families, and another 15% qualify for special education services.

THE SCHOOL COUNSELOR
AS CHARACTER DEVELOPER

The counselor is mentioned in several schools as also playing a very important role: In counseling sessions a class explores social responsibility, values, and ethical judgment. The Kilgour Elementary School in Cincinnati, Ohio, explains: "The counselor plays an important role in the development of sound character. Class presentations and discussion are used to explore social responsibility, values, and ethical judgment. The classroom teacher then integrates these discussions appropriately."

Visits to the Blue Ribbon Schools helped the author to realize how important the counselor is to a school's character development program. According to Lori Wiley, author of *Character Education* (in press) and a teacher educator who specializes in early childhood education, guidance counselors realize a key role as character educators:

> Their primary responsibility is helping students who have problems functioning in a school environment. Through individual counseling, small group work, teaching in the regular classroom and other techniques, they work with needy students. They also teach regular students how to make good choices so as to function well in society. Developing character is the essence of the guidance counselor's work.

In subsequent chapters we look at the different programs schools use in the areas of motivation, drug education, and self-esteem building. Many times these programs originate from and/or are supported by the counselor's office. A good principal knows how important a good counselor is for the school. In a small school, many times the counselor acts as an assistant to the principal. One Blue Ribbon

School principal told me that when she was offered the principalship at the school where she is currently employed, she said that she would take the job if she could also bring with her the counselor from her previous school. The important role of the counselor in character development is shown in more detail in Chapter 5 on guidance and self-esteem programs.

ADVISOR/ADVISEE PROGRAMS

Several schools reported having an advisor/advisee program for character development that is organized by the school counselor. Each student picks a faculty member to be his or her advisor. Typically, advisors and advisees meet each day for five minutes and once a week for forty-five minutes. In most of the schools reporting an advisory system, the advisors use a character development curriculum during this period to discuss social and emotional concerns important to children at this age. The goal is that the students learn to respect themselves and others. The advisor makes a special effort to maintain contact with students, greet them, and ask about their progress. The advisor/advisee program helps develop students' self worth, cooperation, and teamwork.

Another method reported by several schools is to sponsor activities and clubs through the counselor's office. Students can participate in these if they demonstrate appropriate character qualities. For instance, students might need to get "letters of recommendation" from teachers and other adults who have noted their character qualities in these areas. Some of these activities include CLASS (Community Leadership Activities for Students), Peer Tutor Program, Safety Patrol, Scouts, and leadership conferences in which selected student leaders meet with leadership groups from other district schools.

THE KEY ROLE OF PARENTS
IN CHARACTER EDUCATION

Parents are the primary educators of their children and their key character educators as well. At the Monte Garden School in Concord, California, the teachers, principal, and parents cooperate to ensure that students achieve academically, while also developing personal values of self-esteem, honesty, and responsibility. As stated by the principal in a letter home to the parents, "You, as parents, are the primary educators of your children. You know your children differently than the school does. It is important that you communicate with the school what you know about your children. Your input can make a difference." Monte Garden is a large school (over 500 students) in suburban Concord, with a diverse student body that is almost 10% Asian-American and 9% Mexican-American.

At the Flanders Elementary School in Connecticut, the parents show that they are interested in learning, and their children understand the importance of school particularly because of their parents' physical presence. Parents are everywhere: the media center, classroom, publishing center, playground and anywhere else their help is needed. Flanders is a large K–5 school, a "microcosm of society" in which students find themselves in heterogeneously-grouped classrooms where they learn to work with different kinds of people. They are active and frequent participants in the school as visitors and volunteers.

Hundreds of parents volunteer at the Blue Ribbon Schools. They are actively involving themselves in their children's learning. Yet, it is true that family life and the basic structure of the family are changing, and schools are asked to do more. Statistics show that approximately one-third of the children in school today come from single-parent families. The presence of other parents in the schools can help those students who have only one parent at home.

According to the research of Robert Chaskin (1995), the family is the most common context in which a human being learns about care and nurturing. Not enough research studies have sought to examine the links between family characteristics and pro-social moral development. Those that have report a positive correlation between an adult family member's involvement in volunteer work and a young adolescent's involvement in the same or like works of caring for others. In addition, special attention should be given to the role that parents (as well as the media and private associations) play in helping children develop into informed and effective citizens who understand and appreciate the fundamental values and principles of American democracy. According to Secretary of Education, Richard Riley (1995), "We know that all families can make a difference in their children's learning, and we also know that linked to academic achievement is the development of standards of character: hard work, discipline, respect for others and good citizenship" (p. ix–x).

SUMMARY

This chapter shows the many ways in which the Blue Ribbon Schools teach moral education and values, using deliberate school-wide efforts to integrate character development throughout the curriculum and school community. All members of the school community are important players in the realization of this goal. Parents, teachers, principals, and students are involved in the writing of mission statements and the identification of core values for schools and school districts. Every subject matter lends itself to providing opportunities for teaching character education. In order to use these opportunities effectively, teachers need training. Some curricular programs are available that provide this guidance through their teacher materials and guides, but in this area, much growth is needed. Not only the teacher, but also the principal, counselor, school staff, and parents, are all important keys in the promotion of character development in students.

This chapter shows that character education is alive and is working well in many of the Blue Ribbon Schools today. There are many different ways in which a school defines its core character qualities and tries to develop character in its students. Indeed, there are different levels toward which a school can strive to become a value-conscious community. As explained by the Regnart Elementary School, a very culturally diverse K–6 school in suburban Cupertino, California:

> The stages of character development can be compared to that of a flower. It begins with a tightly folded bud and then with the nurturing of sun, water, and soil, it blossoms into a cluster of petals. Each petal of that flower represents a different aspect of a child's character development: honesty, integrity, responsibility, consideration of others, respect for self.

REFERENCES

Benninga, J.S., ed. 1991. *Moral, Character, and Civic Education.* New York: Teachers College Press.

Bennett, W. 1991. "Moral Literacy and the Formation of Character," in *Moral, Character, and Civic Education.* J. S. Benninga, ed. New York: Teachers College Press, p. 134.

Chaskin, R. and D. M. Rauner. 1995. "Youth and Caring: An Introduction," *Phi Delta Kappan* 76(9):667–674.

Developmental Studies Center. 1994. *The Child Development Project: Summary of Findings in Two Initial Districts and the First Phase of an Expansion to Six Additional Districts Nationally.* Oakland, CA.: Developmental Studies Center, pp. 3–4.

Eliam, S., L. Rose, and A. Gallup. 1994. "The 26th Annual Phi Delta Kappa/Gallup Poll of the Public's Attitudes Toward the Public Schools," *Phi Delta Kappan,* 76(1):41–56.

Eliam, S., L. Rose, and A. Gallup. 1993. "The 25th Annual Phi Delta Kappa/Gallup Poll of the Public's Attitudes Toward the Public Schools," *Phi Delta Kappan,* 75(2):137–152.

Escriva de Balaguer, J.M. 1973. *Human Virtues.* New York: Scepter Press.

Fenstermacher, G. 1990. "Some Moral Considerations on Teaching as a Profession," in *Moral Dimensions of Teaching.* J. Goodlad, R. Soder, and K. Sirotnik, eds. CA: Jossey Bass, pp. 130–137.

Frymier, J., L. Cunningham, W. Duckett, B. Gansneder, F. Link, J. Rimmer and J. Scholz. 1995. *Values on Which We Agree.* IN: Phi Delta Kappa.

Goleman, D. 1995. *Emotional Intelligence: Why It Can Matter More Than IQ.* New York: Bantam Books.

Goodlad, J., R. Soder and K. Sirotnik, eds. 1990. *The Moral Dimensions of Teaching.* CA: Jossey Bass.

Huffman, H. 1994. *Developing a Character Education Program: One School District's Experience.* Alexandria, VA: ASCD.

Kilpatrick, W. 1992. *Why Johnny Can't Tell Right from Wrong.* New York: Simon & Schuster.

Kohn, A. 1990. "The ABC's of Caring." *Teacher Magazine.* January, 52–58.

Kohn, A. 1993. *Punished by Rewards.* Boston, MA.: Houghton-Mifflin.

Lickona, T. 1991. *Educating for Character: How Our Schools Can Teach Respect and Responsibility.* New York: Bantam Books.

Nucci, L., ed. 1989. *Moral Development and Character Education: A Dialogue.* Berkeley, CA: McCutchan Publishing Corp.

Riley, R. 1995. "Foreword" *Best Ideas from the Blue Ribbon Schools, Vol. II.* CA: Corwin Press, pp. ix–x.

Saterlie, M. E. 1988. "Developing a Community Consensus for Teaching Values," *Educational Leadership,* 45(8):44–47.

Travis, M.P. 1985. *Student Moral Development in the Catholic Schools.* Washington, D.C.: National Catholic Educational Association.

Vincent, P.F. 1994. *A Primer: Developing Character in Students.* Chapel Hill, N.C.: New View Publications.

Wakefield, D. V. 1996. "Moral Education Methods Survey Results." Baylor University, March 16.

Watson, M., D. Solomon, V. Battistich, E. Schaps, and J. Solomon. 1989. "The Child Development Projects: Combining Traditional and Developmental Approaches to Values Education," in *Moral Development and Character Educa-*

tion: A Dialogue. L. Nucci, ed. CA: McCutchan Publishing Corporation, pp. 51–92.

Wiley, Lori. in press. *Character Education*. New Hampshire: Character Development Foundation.

Wynne, E. and K. Ryan. 1993. *Reclaiming Our Schools A Handbook on Teaching Character, Academics and Discipline*. New York: Macmillan Publishing Co.

Chapter 4

DARE WE COUNT DRUG PREVENTION PROGRAMS AS CHARACTER EDUCATION?

What you think of yourself is much more important than what others think of you.—Seneca

Many persons have a wrong idea of what constitutes true happiness. It is not attained through self-gratification but through fidelity to a worthy purpose.—Helen Keller

Better keep yourself clean and bright: you are the window through which you must see the world.—George Bernard Shaw

DRUG-FREE SCHOOLS

The U.S. government has already decided the answer to the values education controversy by funding anti-drug programs. In so doing the government is telling us that no matter what our religious, cultural, or social values are, there is something that *all* of us in this nation can agree is a moral wrong—substance abuse.

The Anti–Drug Abuse Act of 1986 gave the Department of Education authority to carry out federal education and preventive activities in order to work aggressively to combat drug abuse by youth. The Drug Free School Recognition Program was established in 1987 to seek out and honor schools that had developed exemplary programs to combat student drug use and thereby focus national attention on these successful drug prevention efforts. This program was discontinued in 1995 in order to consolidate all school recognitions into one program—the U.S. Department of Education's School Recognition

59

Program. To win this national recognition a school must give a satisfactory answer to the application's question "By what means does the school prevent the sale, possession and use of drugs, including alcohol and tobacco, by its students on and off school premises?"

This chapter reports on the various substance abuse and health programs found in the Blue Ribbon Schools. It seeks to evaluate these programs in order to determine which, if any of them, can be considered valid character education programs. This chapter seeks to answer the following questions:

- Can a substance abuse program alone be considered a school's entire program for fostering the development of character in students?
- What has research shown about the effectiveness of substance abuse and drug education programs in schools?
- How have the Blue Ribbon Schools successfully become "drug-free schools"?
- What kinds of health education/sex education programs are effective for promoting character in students?

A REACTIVE APPROACH TO CHARACTER DEVELOPMENT

Anti-drug programs guide students in making informed moral decisions; but the name itself implies a reactive more than a proactive approach to character development. Substance abuse programs could be considered as contributing to the students' "moral knowing" domain of character education because of their emphasis on decision making based on informed knowledge. The inclusion of drug, sex, and alcohol education in the schools represents a paradigm shift in the public's attitude towards the schools as agents of character education (London, 1987). Before the 1960s the consensus had been to consider these issues the realm of the home, not of the public schools. In fact, prior to the 1960s, cigarettes were probably the only destructive substance brought to schools. Now, because of hard data that shows substantial increases in substance abuse among young Americans, the public has changed its general opinion and is asking the schools to teach traditional values that include the sacredness of life, the value of sex within marriage, and how to say no to drugs and alcohol. (Wynne, 1989) The U.S. Department of Education (1989) handbook, *What Works: Schools without Drugs* states that "In America today, the most serious threat to the well-being of our children is drug use."

ARE DRUG EDUCATION PROGRAMS CHARACTER EDUCATION PROGRAMS?

One third of the Blue Ribbon Schools answered the question, "How do school programs, practices and policies foster the development of sound character, democratic values, ethical judgment and the ability to work in a self-disciplined and purposeful manner?" by mentioning the school's drug education program as its "character development" program (see Table 2). According to Larry Nucci (1991), drug education programs are moral education programs if they induce students to consider how drug use has meaningful consequences for the welfare of self and others. Due to the fact that drugs block, retard, and distort the most crucial human capacities—perception, planning, physical coordination, and moral judgment (Hawley, 1987)—one can conclude that a person of character should not use drugs, and some instruction in this area should be included in any moral or character education program.

Lickona (1991) has argued that for drug education to be effective, it must be part of a broader program of moral values education that helps students value themselves, aspire to worthwhile goals, and reject all forms of self-damaging behavior. He states that a good drug education curriculum helps students make a *moral* judgement about drugs: Doing drugs is wrong because it is self-destructive, it leads to wrongful behavior such as stealing and lying, it causes suffering, and it is against the law.

Character education is much broader and more encompassing than drug education alone, as it addresses *all* moral issues (Wiley, in press). However, learning about drug and substance abuse is important in order to address moral knowing and moral feeling in this area so that a person then chooses to do the right moral action, which in this case is to refrain completely. Drug education can be seen as a subset of character education (see Figure 4).

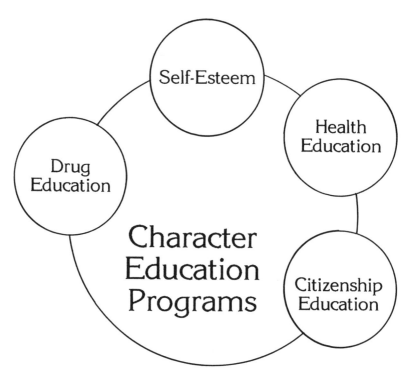

Figure 4 *Subsets of character education.*

WHAT DRUG EDUCATION PROGRAMS ARE USED IN THE BLUE RIBBON SCHOOLS?

Table 7 lists all of the different drug education programs found in the Blue Ribbon Schools. In subsequent sections of this chapter, the drug curricula most commonly found in the Blue Ribbon schools are described and assessed with regard to effectiveness and appropriateness as components of character education programs.

DARE

The mostly popular drug curriculum program, used in 30% of the schools, is DARE (Drug Awareness Resistance Education), created in 1983 by the Los Angeles Police Department. Steve Duke, the principal

Table 7 Drug education programs used in the
Blue Ribbon Schools to develop character.

Category	Count	Percent of Responses
Babes	7	2
DARE	99	30
Here's Looking at You	40	12
Just Say No	36	11
McGruff	79	24
Me-ology	7	2
Pride	13	4
Project Charlie	10	3
Quest	40	12
School Developed Program	46	14

Cases, 330; missing cases, 20

at the Quailwood Elementary School in Bakersfield, California, states that "the DARE program has been highly successful." He explains:

Sixth graders receive lessons related to the dangers of drugs, alcohol, and tobacco. The weekly forty-minute lessons emphasize positive approaches for avoiding these substances. The district has provided funding for having one police officer on campus one day a week for fifteen weeks to be a model for students. The DARE officer plays sports, eats with the students and informally talks to the students throughout the day in addition to conducting the classroom presentations and discussions. Three sessions are also taught by the officer in each K–5 classroom. The positive response to this program by students, parents, and staff has been outstanding.

The DARE curriculum focuses on teaching pupils the skills needed to recognize and resist social pressures to use drugs; it teaches decision-making skills, builds self-esteem, and helps students to choose healthy alternatives to drugs (Ennett et al., 1994). The program is now used in all states. The County Line Elementary School in Georgia echoes what many schools reported:

One of the most exciting additions to our school has been the DARE Program. DARE is a unique drug prevention education program designed to equip elementary school children with skills for resisting peer pressure to experiment with drugs and alcohol. This program is offered as a cooperative effort. Every class, K–5, is included in the DARE program. During one phase of the program, high school students, who have vowed never to take drugs, visit with the fifth graders and talk personally about peer pressure and ways to say "no." A DARE graduation ceremony is held at the end of the study. Parents, community members, local Board of Education members, and county officials are invited. Students are recognized for their work in the DARE Program with a DARE T-shirt and certificate. Many parents have commented that this program has opened the door to conversations with their children about the dangers of drug abuse.

Given its widespread use, the effectiveness of DARE has been evaluated by several researchers. Early DARE evaluations (1987–89) were generally favorable; the participants showed decreased drug use and increased self-esteem and sense of responsibility to self and to police (DeJong, 1987), relative to control groups. However, more recent meta-analysis of a group of evaluations (late 1989 to present), comparing the DARE curriculum to other drug education (if any) offered in control schools, show that the DARE program does not significantly reduce the actual use of drugs (Walsh, 1993). (A review of all existing DARE evaluations to date can be found on-line: http://hyper-real.com/drugs/politics/dare/dare.evaluations). These evaluation results contrast dramatically with the program's popularity and prevalence and lead to an important implication: perhaps DARE is taking the place of other, potentially more beneficial drug education curricula that students could be experiencing (Ennett et al., 1994).

Who teaches DARE and how it is taught may provide possible explanations for the program's limited effectiveness. Lori Wiley (in press) has reviewed the DARE lesson plans and finds them to be more of a self-esteem program and a way for the police to interact in a friendly way with students than a real character education program. Perhaps greater emphasis in the DARE core curriculum on social competencies and less emphasis on affective factors might result in greater program effectiveness (Ennett, et al., 1994). Reader are encouraged to examine the DARE K–8 curriculum themselves by contacting the Los Angeles Police Department, Juvenile Division, 150 N. Los Angeles Street, Los Angeles, CA 90028; phone: 213-485-4856.

Here's Looking at You

One of the most widely used alcohol education and abuse prevention programs in the nation is Here's Looking at You. This "state-of-the-art" K–12 curriculum uses a variety of participatory activities to enhance self-esteem, improve decision making, develop students' coping skills and provide information on alcohol and other drugs. The curriculum is divided into grade level packages: K–3, 4–6, 7–9, 10–12. A revised version of the program is called Here's Looking at You 2000. These two programs were found in 12% of the Blue Ribbon Schools. The Dorothea Simmons School, a K–5 school of 367 homogeneous students in suburban Ambler, Pennsylvania, piloted the revised program. Rita Klein, the principal, acted as the district trainer:

> Students in third, fourth and fifth grades received eight weeks of lessons taught by the health and classroom teachers and the guidance counselor. This program included drug and alcohol information, self-esteem, decision making and development of refusal skills at each level. High school students visited the school and talked with fourth- and fifth-grade students about the natural highs available in a teen's life.

> The effectiveness of the "Here's Looking at You 2000" curriculum was evident in reviewing the pre- and post-tests given. . . . These tests showed a marked improvement in students' knowledge of drug- and alcohol-related information. The effectiveness of the refusal skills segment of the program was seen in the videotape the fourth-grade students prepared. Parents were invited to see the tape . . . and they expressed positive feelings about the program and recommended its continuation. They mentioned the increased communication in the home about this subject.

A comprehensive short-term and long-term evaluation of the program found that, just as Klein reported for Dorothea Simmons students, there was a significant short-term knowledge gain about alcohol and alcoholism on the part of the recipients of the program, based on the pre- and post-test scores. However, when this group was evaluated in a long-term, longitudinal study, their attitudes toward alcohol use and their actual alcohol-drinking behavior was indistinguishable from those students who had not been exposed to the program (Kim, 1987).

Another comprehensive evaluation study found that the program had only "minimal impact on the psychosocial variables assumed to be involved in drinking behavior and had essentially no measurable carry-over effect on problem drinking behavior" (Hopkins et al., 1988). Other critics of this program have stated that it is an affective education curriculum for grades 3–6 that uses values clarification techniques to teach about drug abuse and decision making, and therefore it should not be used in the schools (Kilpatrick 1992).

The curriculum is also rather expensive, so readers will have to decide if it is worth the cost, given these results. In order to obtain a curriculum review package contact Here's Looking at You, 2000, Comprehensive Health Education Foundation (CHEF), 20832 Pacific Highway South, Seattle, WA 98198; phone: 206-824-2907.

Just Say No

The federally sponsored program Just Say No is found in 11% of the Blue Ribbon Schools. The sixth of the National Education Goals 2000 states: "By the year 2000, every school in America will be free of drugs and violence and will offer a discipline environment conducive to learning" (U.S. Department of Education, 1991). Currently, all school districts receiving federal funds must establish standards of conduct for all students regarding drug use, possession, and sale, as well as provide a K–12 developmentally appropriate drug prevention education program. Research conducted by the Office of Substance Abuse Prevention (OSAP) has shown that ages 10–16 are the ages when alcohol- and drug-use attitudes and beliefs are being formed and when alcohol and other drug use is initiated. Therefore prevention efforts are strongly encouraged during the elementary and preteen years (U.S. Department of Education, 1993).

County Line Elementary School in Georgia celebrates "Red Ribbon Week" by having students make T-Shirts with original designs and the "Say No To Drugs" slogan. All students, faculty and staff receive stickers and the school doors and signs are decorated with red ribbon bows and red balloons to signify that the school is drug free. Students conclude the observance of Red Ribbon Week by marching through the building and declaring war on drugs and by dressing in camouflage on the last day of the campaign.

The Blue Ribbon Schools are following the national guidelines for implementing substance abuse programs. Nevertheless, the research shows that although these programs are able to show positive gains in knowledge, they are unsuccessful in changing attitudes and the drug-using behaviors of students (Bangert-Drowns, 1988). A large comprehensive study of 5000 students, 240 schools, commissioned as part of the California Department of Education study of the DARE and Red Ribbon Week programs, found that as students age, they become progressively more convinced that drug prevention programs are ineffective. As these programs rely on lectures and assemblies to promote the evils of drugs, they lack credibility with students and fail to reach them (Texeira, 1995). A growing body of research is finding that the most effective drug education programs help children deal with peer pressure to use drugs by engaging them in group discussions and role-playing, rather than by having an adult stand in front of the class lecturing (Bangert-Drowns, 1988). Peer- or student-led programs have achieved greater reduction in drug use than teacher-led programs partly due to greater fidelity in curriculum implementation by peer leaders and arguably because of higher credibility with high-risk students (Botvin et al., 1990).

The federal document *What Works: Schools without Drugs* (U.S. Department of Education, 1989) blames the widespread drug use in part on the influence of television and movies that make drugs and drinking seem attractive. A good classroom curriculum is a start, but it cannot do the job alone. In order for a positive reduction in drug abuse to occur, a comprehensive approach must be implemented: families, schools, and communities must work together. Parents need to be educated, society needs to promote and reward the right kind of behavior, and the media needs to change their message and stop the glorification of the drug world.

McGruff the Crime Dog

McGruff the Elementary School Puppet Program is used in 24% of the Blue Ribbon Schools. This substance abuse program is targeted for grades 1 and 2 and seeks to promote student confidence and self-esteem around the entire topic of drug awareness and abuse. At the Hill Elementary School in Austin, Texas, McGruff the "Take the Bite Out of Crime Dog" is used in primary classrooms to teach students in a non-threatening manner about the dangers of drug and alcohol abuse. Hill is a large urban school with a diverse student population of over 700 students who speak seven languages besides English. Hill students come from a socioeconomic mix ranging from lower- to upper-middle-income families. McGruff the Crime Dog, through his actions, is able to speak an international language to all of the students.

Project Charlie

Project Charlie is a drug abuse prevention program for elementary school children based on building self-esteem, teaching social competencies and discouraging the use of drugs as a way to avoid problems. Project Charlie is found in about 3% of the Blue Ribbon Schools. According to the curriculum authors, the program emphasizes feeling good about yourself without sacrificing anyone else's well-being.

However, Project Charlie uses values clarification techniques instead of directive instruction and has come under criticism by some parents. According to the *Watchman Expositor*, the Arlington *Citizen-Journal* reported on July 29, 1990, that "Project Charlie approaches drug abuse prevention from a perspective other than telling kids what they shouldn't do." The curriculum explains to the teachers that they should not instruct the students by "advising, providing answers or solutions." How, then, are the teachers of Project Charlie to help students make difficult decisions? In the lesson plan entitled "Decision-Making," the curriculum instructs the teachers with this advice: "As children ask questions, tell them to use their own judgment as you do not know any more than they do" (*Watchman Expositor*, 1996). One should note that character educators often make use of indirect methods (such as questioning and discussion) as well as direct methods (such as explaining why something is right or wrong) but in all cases for the purpose of guiding children toward morally correct conclusions that adults have judged to be in children's best interests.

Readers who would like to review this curriculum themselves should contact Project Charlie, 5701 Normandale Road, Edina, MN 55424; phone: 612-925-9706.

Quest

The Quest program is a commercially prepared curriculum in self-esteem and decision making that emphasizes how to deal with drugs and respond to social pressures. Quest International, a nonprofit educational organization, was established in 1975 to "help create a world that cares more deeply about its young people." Quest develops and makes available comprehensive, broad-based programs and services that enable young people to gain the self-confidence, good judgment and social skills they need to cope with the challenges they face in today's world. The Quest curriculum was found in 10% of the total sample of Blue Ribbon Schools: The Skills for Adolescence curriculum for grades 6–8, first written in 1985, was found in 5% of the Blue

Ribbon Schools in the award years 1985–86, 1987–88, and 1989–90. The Skills for Growing curriculum, written in 1990 for grades K–5, was found in 20% of the schools in the 1991–92 and 1993–94 award years. Some of the Blue Ribbon Schools cite the use of the Quest program as their character education program, as their drug education program, and/or as their guidance program. The Quest program curriculum guide states that it is meant to be a "life skills" program that helps to develop positive social skills, decision-making skills, character, and citizenship in children.

At the Westwood Elementary School, a school with a growing population of linguistically diverse students in suburban Santa Clara, California, all of the students participate in the Quest: Skills for Growing Program:

> The program is included as part of the curriculum at each grade level and teaches skills in self-discipline, responsibility, good judgment and getting along with others. A unique quality of the program is that 100% of the Westwood staff has participated in the training. The staff integrates this program into daily classroom activities such as daily classroom meetings, conflict resolution activities, and leadership role playing.
>
> An important aspect of Skills for Growing is the link between home and school. It helps parents resolve family conflicts with love and limits. This schoolwide program also allows us to use a common language for respect, tolerance, and acceptance. Some student's opinions were: "I liked cooperating on the friendship chain." "It helps me deal with situations in everyday life." "It helps me communicate in a way that does not make both of us angry."

Many of the students at Westwood are refugees from Ethiopia, South America, Vietnam, and Eastern Europe, with a considerable number of Korean, Spanish, and Chinese students. Quest letters to the family allow students to share with their parents what they are learning in school.

Critics of Quest, such as Kilpatrick (1992), state that it is a humanistic education curriculum that uses values clarification techniques to enhance students' self-esteem. He states that it is an affective curriculum that is nondirective and allows students to choose for themselves whether or not to take drugs. Kilpatrick says that the real problem is that Quest is not clearly a drug education program because it has units on thinking, feelings and emotions, decision making, communication, and action, while only one unit on drug education.

Humanistic or affective education is concerned with the formation and development of emotions, feelings, values, attitudes, and morals (Beane, 1986). It is important for students to develop this moral feeling aspect if they are to avoid drugs; however, for Kilpatrick, the preferred curriculum would be more directive—"Don't take drugs"—and less values clarification. Kilpatrick cites an evaluation of Quest made by Professor Stephen Jurs at the University of Toledo in 1985 in which he found that program participation was followed by an increase in drug experimentation relative to a comparison group that did not experience Quest.

Quest has responded to Kilpatrick's allegations with a thirteen-page document correcting the misconceptions he raises. In particular, the document notes that "Quest's programs are based on the principle of skills acquisition, and teach traditional civic values, including self-discipline, good judgment, responsibility, honesty and positive commitments to family, school, peers and the community." By promoting these values, Quest's programs are clearly *not* non-directive. The program defenders cite Dr. Jurs as saying that Kilpatrick has erroneously summarized his research findings. Dr. Jurs clarified that there was evidence of increased drug use by about 2% of the students who had taken the Skills for Living compared to an increase of about 5% among students not taking Skills for Living. This, he noted, was a positive finding: Quest students showed less drug use than nonQuest students.

Carol Apacki, Quest Program Development Writer explained in a phone conversation that Quest has mirrored what has been the "best thinking" on educational methodology over the years that it has been in the schools. In the 1970s values clarification methods were used, in 1980 a child-centered/learning styles approach was used, and now in 1990 a more directive approach is used to inculcate certain values such as citizenship, responsibility, honesty, good judgment, and self-discipline. She stated that Quest has responded to criticisms of its program with revisions that rely less on the previous "affective education techniques" and more on the current "directive approach." In its current programs it balances decision-making exercises with a "no use" stance toward drugs, and it supplements self-esteem activities with a list of school service projects. The new edition of Skills for Adolescence even includes criteria for making decisions:

(*1*) Will it lead to trouble?

(*2*) Is it against the law, rules, or teaching of my religion?

(*3*) Is it harmful to me or to others?

(*4*) Would it disappoint my family or other important adults?

(*5*) Is it wrong to do? (Would I be sorry afterwards?)

(*6*) Would I be hurt or upset if someone did this to me?

Many Blue Ribbon Schools state that they foster character development through the use of the Quest curriculum. The new curriculum is more directive and does include some character education components but is mostly a "life skills" program that emphasizes the development of social and emotional competencies. The old Quest curriculum, even though it was written by the "current educational experts" of that time, could actually be considered one of the causes for the sorry state of values education in American schools today. Readers can review the Quest curriculum themselves to decide if it would be an appropriate component of their school's character education program by contacting Quest International, 537 Jones Road, P.O. Box 566, Granville, OH 43023-0566; phone: 800-446-2700.

Other Programs

The *Discovery* textbook series has been adopted by several of the Blue Ribbon Schools, including St. Damian's in Oak Forest, Illinois. The textbook series goes from grades K–8 and provides a comprehensive program of personal development, decision making, and drug and substance abuse prevention.

Another substance abuse program implemented in these exemplary schools is Babes, which was found in 5% of the schools. Babes is an alcohol awareness program for the primary grades. It has lessons that focus on self-esteem and drug awareness and emphasizes the development of a positive self-concept with the ability to say no.

Teachers in the Como Park Elementary School in New York are trained in the Growing Healthy curriculum, a nationally recognized program for substance abuse prevention, which is described below under health programs. In addition, Como Park students are trained in the Prevention is Primary (PIP) program, which has been used in their district for many years and includes drug- and alcohol-prevention instruction.

Me-ology is yet another drug prevention education program found in the Blue Ribbon Schools. Me-ology, a program developed in the early 1980s, has also been criticized for using values clarification techniques (Kilpatrick, 1992).

Students Teaching Students

There is a movement, especially in the area of substance abuse curricula, to have students who have quit using drugs talk to other young people. Some programs include Kids Teach Kids, which is a mentorship for drugs and alcohol prevention, and Peer Outreach, which helps students develop a positive self-image, explains peer pressure, and provides factual information on drugs and alcohol. Let's Talk Turkey and Stars are two programs in which students talk about the risks of smoking. Research reviews of substance abuse programs have found significantly more attitude change and less drug use on the part of peer-taught students as compared to adult-taught students (Bangert-Drowns, 1988).

The China Grove Elementary School in North Carolina uses different programs at different grade levels:

- 3rd grade—Here's Looking at You, 2000
- 4th grade—I'm Special
- 5th grade—Be Smart, Don't Start
- 6th grade—DARE

China Grove is a K–6 school with a heterogeneous population of almost 800 students, 11% of whom are African-American and over one-fourth of whom are from lower-income families.

RESEARCH RESULTS

William Kilpatrick (1992) criticizes many of these drug prevention programs—Quest, Positive Action, Project Charlie, Here's Looking at You, Me-ology, and Values and Choices—because they were developed in the 1970s and early 1980s and are modeled on Carl Rogers's therapeutic education scheme and values clarification techniques that put a heavy emphasis on feelings. Research studies have shown that drug education programs alone have minimal effect. Although there is an increase in knowledge by students who are in the programs, it is very hard to change students' attitudes and behavior by a curricular program alone. On a long-term basis, the actual drug use of students is the same as students who have not been exposed to the program (Bangert-Drowns, 1988). In some cases, with nondirective drug education programs, there has been an actual increase in drug use; students have chosen to use the less serious drugs, but more students show greater drug use (Hopkins et al., 1988; Kim, 1987). Consensus is developing that a curricular program alone will not change students' attitudes and actions. What is needed is a comprehensive, multimodal approach.

WHAT DOES WORK?

The U.S Department of Education (1988) has published a guide to selecting drug prevention curricula. It states that consumers should watch out for outdated theories and avoid curricula that emphasize open-ended decision making, values clarification, and therapeutic educational strategies. The department's research has shown that the drug use prevention field has evolved from a reliance on simplistic approaches to one of combining multiple strategies to address multiple risk factors for substance use. Programs that target a single risk factor, such as low self-esteem or poor school achievement, are unlikely to have a significant impact (U.S. Department of Education, 1993). The *Third Triennial Report to Congress: Drug Abuse and Drug Abuse Research* from the Department of Health and Human Services (1990) also cite research that shows that although site-specific interventions have had limited impact on reducing drug use, there is evidence that a comprehensive approach is effective.

Perhaps the Murdock School, a very large school of over 1000 students in the suburb of La Mesa, California, is one of the best examples of this multipronged effort.

In the educational community and the community at large, Murdock School is known for high standards of behavior and an educational environment that is conducive to learning. Through a comprehensive and cooperative approach at Murdock, students and parents are presented with the knowledge and skills to help prevent substance abuse now and in their future. All aspects of the school community coordinate their resources to promote healthy alternatives to illegal drug use.

Ongoing skills in responsible decision making, refusal skills and positive self-concept building are encouraged through a teacher-presented curriculum. The school counselor collaborates on total school and community activities which include community speakers, letter writing to local government officials, poster contests, and classroom lessons. Murdock's staff and parents conduct an intensive parent education program. Through this joint effort between the district, school, and community, Murdock School is promoting a drug-free lifestyle.

As Murdock's broad-based program indicates, drug prevention is not simply a matter of developing good curricula; it needs to be a communitywide effort involving teachers, parents, students, and community members working together to fight drug and alcohol use and abuse by any member of the community. Clear messages need to be given about the moral implications of abusing alcohol and/or using drugs. Older students should be involved in encouraging younger students to resist drugs. These messages need to be clear in the school policies, in community social events, and in the media.

Kilpatrick (1992) found that the most successful schools do not limit themselves to providing drug education courses. A more important factor is the school's atmosphere of expectations. A strong school policy against substance abuse—clearly articulated, consistently enforced, and broadly communicated—is the foundation upon which any program should be built. Kilpatrick states:

> Their first priority is to create a drug-free environment and a sense of pride in achieving and maintaining a drug-free school. Such schools take academics seriously and assign significant amounts of homework. In addition they emphasize extracurricular activities. They attempt to create a school atmosphere rather than a group therapy atmosphere. They focus on science, history, art, and the marching band rather than on self-esteem. They enlist the help of families, business, police, and community groups. (pp. 50–51)

Visits to the Blue Ribbons Schools revealed that the most successful drug prevention programs are those that are integrated as an essential part, although not the only part, of an all-school effort to promote good character in the students. Whether the school uses one of the character education curricula outlined in Chapter 3 or integrates character education throughout the curriculum as done in the Princeton School District in Ohio and the Plano School District in Texas, students are able to see that people of character, for many reasons, do not use drugs because they have no need for drugs. They get their "high on life" from doing good deeds, from helping others, and from being positive leaders among their peers. They have learned to use the character values to help them to make good choices. Using their moral knowledge and moral feelings, they have chosen to perform good moral actions. As Daniel Goleman (1995) writes in *Emotional Intelligence*,

> Information is not enough. The most effective programs supplement the basic information given with the development of essential emotional and social skills. These programs taught children to find ways to solve interpersonal conflicts more positively, to have more self-confidence, not to blame themselves if something happened and to feel they had a network of support in teachers and parents to whom they could turn. (p. 257)

SEX EDUCATION

There is no specific question in the Blue Ribbon Schools application regarding sex education programs in the schools. Therefore, there was little information given regarding this area of the curriculum. Some schools did report on their health education program in the same category as that regarding the keeping of their school drug, alcohol, and tobacco free; others reported that it was part of the programs they used to promote good character.

Only seventeen states and the District of Columbia include sex education as a mandated part of the school curriculum, specifying that the program should promote abstinence until marriage; however, they usually specify that such a curriculum should begin at grade six (McClellan, 1987). The Urban Institute and the National Association of State Boards of Education, in a 1982 survey of 180 school districts in cities with populations over 100,000, found that three-fourths of the districts provided some instruction in sex education in high school or junior high school and two-thirds provided it in elementary school (Kenney, 1987). Most of the schools in this Blue Ribbon sample were K–5 organization, which would account for the general lack of program information in this area.

Need for Character Based Sex Education

The Medical Institute for Sexual Health (1996) has developed "National Guidelines for Sexuality and Character Education" that state that character-based sex education should be directive, using thoughtful curricula, accurately interpreted medical data, and ethical reasoning to guide students toward right decisions about sex—that is, sexual abstinence until they are ready to establish a mutually faithful monogamous relationship within marriage. Abstinence education presents young people with the moral dimensions of sexual conduct. It helps them apply core ethical values such as respect, responsibility, and self-control to the sexual domain.

Research has repeatedly shown little correlation between participation in a unit on sex education and level of sexual activity (this is similar to the findings on drug education). Simply incorporating a unit on sex education into other course work may increase students' knowledge, but it rarely changes their behavior (Buie, 1987). In fact, some have argued that it is the introduction of "too much explicit information at too early of an age" that has led to the dramatic increase in sexual activity among the young.

A five-year project sponsored by the W.T. Grant Foundation distilled and studied the active ingredients of successful programs. The key list of emotional skills to be covered included self-awareness; identifying, expressing, and managing feelings; impulse control and delaying gratifications; and handling stress and anxiety. A key ability in impulse control is knowing the difference between feeling and actions and learning to make better emotional decisions by first controlling the impulse to act, then identifying alternative actions and their consequences before acting (Goleman, 1995).

The "Principles of Character-Based Sex Education" adopted by the Character Education Partnership, state that character-based sex education must be holistic, addressing the physical, social, and emotional needs of young people as they move from childhood through adolescence. Character education must help young people develop the virtues that underlie the ability to make and live out good decisions about sex.

Lickona emphasizes that the best hope for developing sexual self-control is directive sex education—teaching students why sexual abstinence is the only medically safe and morally responsible choice for unmarried teenagers (Lickona, 1994).

In 1981, the federal government approved the Adolescent Family Life Act, called Title XX, that approved public funds for abstinence-only sex education programs. The goal of abstinence-only programs is to convince teens that the only morally acceptable sexual behavior takes place within marriage.

Character-based sex education should help young people understand that while condoms may reduce some of the physical risks of premature sexual activity, serious risks remain. These risks include pregnancy, disease, and the negative psychological consequence of temporary sexual relationships. Character-based sex education should help students develop the values and moral reasoning in support of abstinence. In teaching abstinence, the school should stress that abstinence can be regained. If the school discusses condoms/contraception, it should do so in a way that does not undermine its advocacy of abstinence and related character goals.

The *National Guidelines for Sexuality and Character Education* (Medical Institute for Sexual Health, 1996), concur that abstinence sexuality education is directive sex education, it emphasizes making the right decisions. Through ethical reasoning, medical evidence, videos, role-plays, and real-life stories, abstinence education unambiguously promotes the reasons for waiting to have sex. It assumes that young persons respond positively when instruction is well reasoned and supported, and when it comes from an adult whom they respect and trust.

Sex Respect is a nationally known program used in several Blue Ribbon Schools. Developed by Colleen Kelley Mast, Sex Respect provides teens with information, identifies the emotional, psychological, and physical consequences of teenage sexual activity, and helps students to develop positive and healthy attitudes. The program's effectiveness has been documented in a series of evaluation reports for the federal office of Adolescent Pregnancy Programs (Lickona, 1994). For more information on this curriculum, contact Sex Respect, Inc., c/o Colleen Kelly Mast, Bradley, IL 60915.

Values and Choices is another curriculum mentioned by the Blue Ribbon Schools. The curriculum focuses on seven values essential for maintaining positive human relationships: equality, self-control, promise keeping, responsibility, respect, honesty, and social justice. The curriculum includes abstinence messages throughout the fifteen lessons. It also includes a lesson on birth control as the second-best alternative to abstinence, and therefore cannot be considered a true character-based program.

AIDS Curriculum

AIDS instruction began in most school districts about ten years ago. Responsibility for the curriculum was given to the school nurse, guidance counselor, or science or health teachers, who were to teach it as one unit in their classes. Some of the Blue Ribbon Schools explained to the author that condoms were demonstrated as part of the original AIDS health classes curricula, but parents protested and demanded "abstinence only" instruction. These schools immediately modified the lessons plans in the curricula to meet the desires of the parents, and they had no further problems in this area.

Our nation's leaders are urging educators to undertake an intensive educational effort that has a chance of influencing the sex-related and drug-related behaviors that place young people at risk of becoming infected with HIV. Effective AIDS education should encourage students to be abstinent and not offer "protected sex" as a "responsible" second option. The clear expectation of abstinence is the only message consistent with character education, since it alone truly respects self and others. Any sex education worthy of the name must help students develop self-control and the ability to apply core ethical values such as respect and responsibility to the sexual domain (Lickona, 1993).

"HIV, You Can Live Without It" is a curriculum for grades 5–12 that emphasizes that abstinence from premarital sexual activity is the best and only sure prevention of AIDS and other sexually transmitted diseases. It provides coverage of the topic of AIDS age-appropriately in the sensitive upper elementary grades within a directive, abstinence-based, family-centered conceptual framework. For more information contact Teen Aid, E. 723 Jackson, Spokane, WA 99207; phone: 509-482-2868.

HEALTH CURRICULUM

Growing Healthy is a comprehensive, sequential K–7 health curriculum. It is designed to equip students with the knowledge and skills to make choices that are conducive to good health and to help children to establish good health habits. Miriam Remar, principal at Howard Reiche Community School in Portland, Maine, explains that the school dedicates a minimum of one class period per week per grade level, ranging from twenty to sixty minutes, to the curriculum. It includes information on health, substance abuse, the anatomy and biology of the body, and sexuality education. The curriculum uses a hands-on approach to guiding students through the decision-making process, so students can relate the information and concepts to their daily lives. Teacher in-service training for implementation of Growing Healthy takes four days. Teachers usually integrate the curriculum into the science or physical education courses. Evaluations of this curriculum have shown a positive correlation between the degree of in-servicing received by the teacher and the success of implementation (Smith et al., 1993).

Family Life Education was also mentioned by a few of the Blue Ribbon Schools. The Hillside School in Montclair, New Jersey, is a magnet middle school with a very diverse student body. The school uses this curriculum to help its middle-grade students learn to deal positively with the emotional, social, and physical changes experienced at puberty. The curriculum also deals with drugs, alcohol, and character development. Responsible decision making is the major focus of the curriculum; however, it does not emphasize abstinence as the best choice and therefore cannot be considered a character-based curriculum. A goal of the curriculum is to foster increased communication between parents and children about sexuality. The Hillside School has guest speakers to address the students on issues such as dating, fighting, and drugs.

Character Building Health Education

According to Kathleen Sullivan of the Project Reality organization, health curricula are more effective than sex education curricula because they help students to understand not only the physical aspects of sex but also the emotional aspects, which are very much related to character education. No contraceptive will ever be able to prevent the emotional trauma involved in having intimate relations with someone who is not ready or able to make a true commitment.

A true "composite" approach to sex education would include character education as an integral part of the program. It helps build self-esteem by teaching students that there is a profound purpose for their lives, showing them how to develop caring relationships of all kinds, and encouraging them to think beyond the present and to set long-term goals. Students thus are given the skills they need in order to make moral decisions about the appropriate use and care for their body.

CHILD ABUSE AWARENESS

We Help Ourselves (WHO) is a program used in the Plano School District in Texas to encourage students to voice their concerns and opinions about child abuse. Arlene Carnes, the counselor at the Saigling School in this district explained the program during a visit to the school. The Junior League in Plano started the program. It is a curriculum that includes videos for different grade levels. Carnes comments:

> It talks about strangers, stranger dangers, verbal abuse, physical abuse, and sexual abuse. Then it also talks about inappropriate touching. There are little puppets that go with the primary grades and then the older students do role plays as news commentators. One issue which we just discussed included a role play of a girl who comes home from school and gets a phone call. Saying it is a radio station, they ask her to answer who is the first president. She gives the answer—they say she has won and ask her for her address. They ask, "Do your parents work outside the home?" "Well yes," she replies, "But why do you need to know that?" They hang up. She realizes that she has given out too much information. Then the students brainstorm and discuss what she should have done, what she should do now, and then they make some decisions.

Come in from the Storm is another curriculum used in the Plano schools that deals with abuse—sexual, verbal, and physical. Parents are very involved in most of the Blue Ribbon Schools, approving these different curricula and giving their input on how they would like a program to be delivered. Parents have requested that boys and girls be separated for these classes, and the counselors and teachers have honored the parents' request.

RESEARCH RESULTS ON
HEALTH/SEX EDUCATION CURRICULA

Research studies have shown that students who have taken comprehensive sex education programs (those that also teach about contraceptives) were significantly more likely to have sexual intercourse than teens in sex education courses that did not discuss contraceptives (Dawson, 1986). In addition, health programs that are simply knowledge dispensers lead to high incidents of different types of abuse. Like the findings on substance abuse programs, knowledge alone is not enough to change behavior. Effective sex and health programs need to be multifaceted and an essential element of a comprehensive character education program (Lickona, 1993). These programs should teach moral values, develop healthy self-esteem, and foster attitudes that lead students to choose chastity as a virtue of a person of character. Schools should recruit parents, faith communities, and other community groups as partners in character-based sex education. All of the Blue Ribbon Schools visited by the author had succeeded in this area.

SUMMARY

As this chapter shows, the majority of the Blue Ribbon Schools indicated that their drug education program is the main way in which they foster the development of character in their students. However, research has shown that substance abuse and drug education programs alone have not been effective in changing students' behavior and have in fact increased students' use of these chemicals. Many of the programs that different Blue Ribbon Schools use are based on values clarification techniques and are the exact opposite of character-building curricula. A drug prevention program alone cannot be a school's entire character education program, for research has shown that drug education will only succeed when it is part of a comprehensive character education program that involves the entire community.

Very few of the Blue Ribbon Schools reported on their health education and or sex education programs, as there was no specific question in the application form regarding this area. However, some did mention these programs as part of the way in which they foster character or as part of their health and substance abuse prevention curricula. Research has shown that the effectiveness of sex education programs is similar to that reported for drug education programs: they are only effective when they are based on fostering the development of character through the living of core moral values.

REFERENCES

Bangert-Drowns, Robert. 1988. "The Effects of School-Based Substance Abuse Education — A Meta-Analysis," *Journal of Drug Education*, 18(3):243–264.

Beane, J. 1986. "The Continuing Controversy Over Affective Education," *Educational Leadership*, 43(4):26–31.

Botvin, G.J., E. Bake, L. Dysenbury, S. Tortu, and E. Botvin. 1990. "Preventing Adolescent Drug Abuse through a Multimodal Cognitive Behavioral Approach: Results of a 3-Year Study," *Journal of Consulting and Clinical Psychology*, 58(4):437–447.

Buie, J. 1987. "Teen Pregnancy: It's Time for the Schools to Tackle the Problem," *Phi Delta Kappan*, 68(10:737–739.

Character Education Partnership. 1996. *Character-Based Sex Education in Public Schools: A Position Statement*. Arlington, VA: Character Education Partnership.

Dawson, D. 1986. "The Effects of Sex Education on Adolescent Behavior," *Family Planning Perspectives*, 18(4):162–170.

DeJong, W. 1987. "A Short Term Evaluation of Project DARE (Drug Abuse Resistance Education): Preliminary Indications of Effectiveness," *Journal of Drug Education*, 17:279–294.

Ennett, S., N. Tobler, C. Ringwalt and R. Fewelling. 1994. "How Effective Is Drug Abuse Resistance Education? A Meta-Analysis of Project DARE Outcome Evaluations," *American Journal of Public Health*, 84(9):1394–1401.

Goleman, D. 1995. *Emotional Intelligence: Why It Can Matter More than IQ*. New York: Bantam Books.

Hawley, R. 1987. "School Children and Drugs: The Fancy That Has Not Passed," *Phi Delta Kappan*, 68(9):K1–K8.

Hopkins, R.A., A.L. Mauss, K. Kearney and A. Weisheit. 1988. "Comprehensive Evaluation of a Model Alcohol Education Curriculum," *Journal of Studies on Alcohol*, 49(1):38–50.

Kenney, Asta. 1987. "Teen Pregnancy: An Issue for Schools," *Phi Delta Kappan* 68(10) Special Report: 728–736.

Kilpatrick, W. 1992. *Why Johnny Can't Tell Right from Wrong*. New York: Simon and Schuster.

Kim, S. 1987. "A Short- and Long-Term Evaluation of Here's Looking at You Alcohol Education Program," *International Journal of Health Services*, 17(1):235–242.

Lickona, T. 1991. *Educating for Character: How Our Schools Can Teach Respect and Responsibility*. New York: Bantam Books.

Lickona, T. 1993. "Where Sex Education Went Wrong," *Educational Leadership*, 51(3):84–89.

Lickona, T. 1994. "Directive Sex Education Is Our Best Hope," *Educational Leadership*, 52(2):76–78.

London, J. 1987. "Character Education and Clinical Intervention: A Paradigm Shift for U.S. Schools," *Phi Delta Kappan*, 68(9):667–673.

Males, M. 1993. "Schools, Society and 'Teen' Pregnancy," *Phi Delta Kappan*, 74(7):566–568.

McClellan, M. C. 1987 "Teenage Pregnancy," *Phi Delta Kappan*, 68(10):789–792.

Medical Institute for Sexual Health. 1996. *National Guidelines for Sexuality and Character Education.* Austin, TX: MISH, p. 11.

Nucci, L. 1991. "Doing Justice to Morality in Contemporary Values Education," in *Moral, Character, and Civic Education in the Elementary School.* J. Benninga, ed. New York: Teachers College Press, pp. 21–37.

"A Different Look at DARE." [On-line] Available URL: http://www.drcnet.org/DARE/

Smith, D., L. McCormick, A. Steckler and K. McLeroy. 1993. "Teachers' Use of Health Curricula: Implementation of Growing Healthy, Project SMART and the Teenage Health Teaching Modules," *Journal of School Health,* 63(8):349–354.

Sylvester, R. 1994. "How Emotions Affect Learning," *Educational Leadership* (52) 2: 60–65.

Texeira, E. 1995. "Study Assails School-Based Drug Programs," *Los Angeles Times,* Oct. 21, 1995 [On-line] Available URL: http://turnpike.net/~jnr/dareinef.htm

U.S. Department of Education. 1988. *Drug Prevention Curricula: A Guide to Selection and Implementation.* Washington, D.C.

U.S. Department of Education. 1989. *What Works: Schools Without Drugs.* Washington, D.C., p. v, 37.

U.S. Department of Education. 1991. *America 2000—An Education Strategy: Sourcebook.* Washington, D.C., p. 4.

U.S. Department of Education. 1993. *Reaching the Goals. Goal 6: Safe, Disciplined and Drug Free Schools.* Washington, D.C.: Office of Educational Research and Improvement, pp. 20–26.

U.S. Department of Health and Human Services. 1990. *Third Triennial Report to Congress: Drug Abuse and Drug Abuse Research.* Washington, D.C.: Department of Health and Human Services, pp. 1–12.

Walsh, T. 1993. "Drug Abuse Education Information and Research: Review of Existing DARE Evaluations." [On-line] Available URL: http://hyperreal.com/drug/politics/dare/dare.evaluations

Watchman Expositor. 1996. "New Age Drug Education Programs." [On-line] Available URL: http://rampages.onramp.net/~watchman/drugs.htm

Wiley, L. In press. *Character Education.* New Hampshire: Character Development Foundation.

Wynne, E. 1989. "Transmitting Traditional Values in Contemporary Society," in *Moral Development and Character Education: A Dialogue,* L. Nucci, ed. Berkeley: McCutchan, 1989, pp. 19–36.

Chapter 5

MOTIVATING STUDENTS

In praising or loving a child, we love and praise not that which is, but that which we hope for. —Goethe

Teaching that impacts is not head to head, but heart to heart.
—Howard Hendricks

In teaching, and almost any other profession, they won't care how much you know until they know how much you care. —Anonymous

WILL KNOWING THE GOOD LEAD TO DOING THE GOOD?

This book began with Meno's question to Socrates, "Can virtue be taught?" and it has tried to show how the Blue Ribbon Schools indeed help to develop students' virtue, values, and character. However, the less-than-encouraging research reported in the previous chapter regarding the effectiveness of the drug education programs suggests that mere knowledge of something being the good or the better thing to do does not necessarily lead to a student choosing to do this action. This bears on an ancient question asked by many philosophers (e.g., Plato, Aristotle, Augustine): "Will knowing the good necessarily lead us to doing the good?"

In Chapter 1, Lickona's model of good character was described as a combination of moral knowing, moral feeling, and moral action (Lickona, 1991). It is a valid construct that can be used to categorize all of the different Blue Ribbon Schools' programs for character

85

development. Programs that teach core virtues and decision-making skills emphasize moral knowing; those related to discipline and citizenship emphasize moral doing. In this chapter we look at how motivation, guidance, and self-esteem programs promote the moral feeling that serves as a bridge between moral knowing and moral action.

DEVELOPING THE AFFECTIVE SIDE OF CHARACTER

This chapter looks at the programs in the Blue Ribbon Schools that attempt to develop the affective or feeling side of students, focusing on inspiring students to *want* to live the good character values. It reports on the various motivational programs found in the Blue Ribbon Schools, reviews their curricular components, and cites research that evaluates their effectiveness. The chapter tries to answer the following questions:

- Can and should schools try to develop the affective and emotional side of students?
- What are some effective ideas that schools can use to motivate students towards living a life of good character?
- Which guidance programs are more effective in promoting character development?
- Do self-esteem programs promote genuine character development in students?
- Why are so many Blue Ribbon Schools using ineffective programs based on techniques that range from values clarification to new age philosophy?

There are two sources for the information reported in this chapter. First of all, there are the programs mentioned in response to the main question, "How do school programs, practices, policies, and staff foster the development of sound character, democratic values, ethical judgment, good behavior, and the ability to work in a self-disciplined and purposeful manner?" In addition, there are answers given to another question in the section on "Student Environment" that was often referred to in answering the question above: "What specific programs, procedures, or instructional strategies do you employ to develop students' interest in learning and motivate them to study?" The answers given to these questions, as seen in Table 2, fell into three categories: motivation programs, guidance programs, and self-esteem programs. These categories provide the organizing paradigm for this chapter.

Emotional Intelligence

It is important for students to develop the emotional side of themselves in order that they may not only know the good but also love the good. Every teacher should read Daniel Goleman's book *Emotional Intelligence* (1995) in order to understand the important role emotions play in the successful education of students. Goleman shows in this text the importance of developing the emotional aspect of human potential, for there is growing evidence that fundamental ethical stances in life stem from underlying emotional capabilities. Emotional intelligence is a set of traits and qualities that make us more fully human, and they matter immensely for our personal destiny: "Emotional intelligence = abilities such as being able to motivate oneself and persist in the face of frustration; to control impulse and delay gratification, to regulate one's moods and keep distress from swamping the ability to think, to empathize, and to hope" (Goleman, 1995, p. 34).

MOTIVATION PROGRAMS

Student motivation is a very important factor in character education. Motivation is related to students' inner desires and is thus closely associated with their values (Frymier, 1974). Values represent what people believe in: what they are committed to and what they cherish. Values give direction to behavior. A school tells students what it values by what it rewards and by what activities it deems are important enough to sponsor and include during school time. Typically, motivation is a durable phenomenon, although it is not fixed. Students who are not motivated to learn in schools can be helped by nurturing a positive self-concept. Giving students positive feedback helps them to take responsibility for their own learning. Students come to realize that their success can be attributed to their own personal effort and abilities.

At the time of nomination, all the Blue Ribbon Schools appeared to be effective in motivating students. However, some of the schools cited their move from unmotivated and undisciplined school bodies to highly motivated school bodies as one of the reasons they should be nationally recognized. These schools suggested that the implementation of some of the following ideas throughout the school resulted in more motivated student bodies. These student motivation ideas fall into four different categories: awards, ceremonies, high academic expectations, and school mottos (see Table 8). Ideas are included here if they satisfy either of two criteria: they were mentioned so often by schools that they might be considered as an integral part of elementary school student motivation, or they seemed so interesting that other schools might want to consider them.

Awards

In *Reclaiming Our Schools: A Handbook on Teaching Character, Academics, and Discipline*, Edward Wynne and Kevin Ryan (1993) state that awards and ceremonies are important ways of emphasizing and transmitting character values. A school—and, in fact, a culture—shows what type of character it values by the awards, recognitions, and ceremonies (or celebrations) it sponsors. If all of the awards go to athletes (including the monetary "award"), the school or society says it values athletics. The Blue Ribbon Schools do give awards for athletics, but they also recognize and celebrate good character, hard work, effort, and good citizenship. There is no better way to build up children's "self-esteem" than for them to win an award well-earned. One-third of the Blue Ribbon Schools stated that granting awards was one of the ways they promoted character development in students.

TABLE 8 *Motivational methods used in the Blue Ribbon Schools.*

Category	Count	Percent of Responses
Activities	12	6.0
Assemblies	5	2.5
Awards	49	24.0
Catch students being good	20	9.8
High expectations	43	21.0
Mascot, motto	10	4.9
Positive reinforcement	38	18.6

Awards have been found to be effective motivators for students, especially when they help students to link their success in achieving the reward to their own efforts (Alderman, 1990). It can be noted that some of these awards given at the Blue Ribbon Schools directly express aspects of character development in the very name of the award.

- Athlete of Month (must show good sportsmanship)
- American Legion Award for Leadership
- Good Citizen Award
- Knights of the Month
- Most Improved Student of the Month (sign on school van)
- Presidential Academic Fitness Award
- Student of the Month Award
- Super Kids Awards
- Terrific Kids Program

Other schools use acronyms to tell what their award stands for:

- DUDE: doers of unusual deeds of excellence
- TOPGUNS: totally organized pupils who are gentle, understanding, neat, and sensible
- VIP: very important person

David Derby, the principal at the Mountain View School in California when the school won the Blue Ribbon Award, explains in the school application why awards are important:

> Awards can be said to serve four functions. First, they are a vehicle to motivate students to become active participants in the activities of their school. Second, they are a *blueprint* for parents and teachers to use in planning, encouraging, and setting goals with children. Third, they are a means of affirming that the nurturing of responsible, well-rounded individuals is important. Fourth, they are a significant form of recognition for students who have met the criteria for the award.

Some schools have set up awards based on their school mascot. The Tarkington School located in Wheeling, a middle-class suburb northwest of Chicago, Illinois, has "The Tarkington Tiger." Tarkington is a K–6 school with 674 students in a diverse student body that is 5% Hispanic, 5% Asian, and 3% African-American. Eight percent of the students come from lower-income families and 5% come from families in which English is not the primary language spoken at home. A visit to the school revealed that Arvum Poster, the principal, was the key factor in creating and maintaining the school "ethos" or "climate"—the spirit of enthusiasm among members of the group for one another, their group, and its purposes (Kilpatrick, 1992). Mr. Poster came from another school in the same district, which had won the Blue Ribbon Award in 1990–91. When he came to Tarkington, he purposefully sought to create a nurturing, happy, and excellent environment where children were encouraged to develop the many facets of their unique personalities and talents—with an eye to the school model, the Tarkington Tiger. The "Tarkington Tiger Traits" are a list of academic and behavioral expectations of students that are posted throughout the school building. Students are encouraged to participate in activities that require self-discipline, good behavior, and sound character—what their school award is all about. Students who are nominated by their peers or teachers for having done something nice are awarded "Paw Pats on the Back."

Kilpatrick (1992) would likely compliment Mr. Poster on what he has done at Tarkington:

> The primary way to bring ethics and character back into schools is to create a positive moral environment in the school. The ethos of the school, not its course offerings is the decisive factor in forming character. The first thing we have to do is to change the moral climate of the schools themselves. (p. 226)

Tarkington School has a happy climate. Climate refers to the group's shared attitudes, beliefs, and values of a community of people or of a group (Wynne & Ryan, 1993). A Tarkington Tiger greets you on the carpet as you enter the school; another hangs in the lunch room and smiles at you from the walls. Students love giving one another tiger-paw waves using the three middle fingers of their hands.

There is also a consistent trend emerging in some of the Blue Ribbon Schools, in both inner-city as well as in white, middle-class districts, to discourage competition among students for awards and recognition. In these schools, awards and recognitions are available for *all* students who meet the criteria; they are not competitively "won." Instead, students are encouraged to participate in all curricular and extracurricular events and to measure themselves against the standards and criteria that must be met to receive the award, not against peers.

Alfie Kohn (1993), in his book *Punished by Rewards*, criticizes our American system for what he considers the excessive use of awards. He, however, would prefer this non-competitive system, as he feels that the most destructive way to administer rewards is to limit the number that are available; if awards are to be given, they should be distributed equitably to all who manifest the desired behaviors at the appropriate level and quality of performance. For instance, the Schuster Elementary School, in El Paso, Texas, reports that "students are encouraged to compete against norms, instead of each other. Noncompetitive games are even found in physical education classes." Schuster is a pre-K to sixth-grade urban school with a very diverse student population of 363. More than half of the students are Hispanic, and 64% of the students are from lower-income families.

Ceremonies

The ceremony that goes along with receiving the award is perhaps just as exciting as actually receiving the award. Ceremonies are important because they teach the participants that there are certain values that we all collectively and publicly acknowledge are important (Wynne & Ryan, 1993). The main ceremonies utilized in the Blue Ribbon Schools are the assembly and the morning announcements. There are assemblies to announce and explain the weekly/monthly/ yearly character traits and assemblies to award those who have developed and manifested the traits. Assemblies provide students with the opportunity to practice "good audience behavior." During assemblies, students who have excelled in reading, math, and spelling, as well as attendance and citizenship, are given their awards. Sometimes these are simple certificates, and sometimes they are coupons to use at local merchants and fast food restaurants. This helps students to see that community businesses too are interested in promoting good character and good citizenship in young people.

Schools use the morning announcement time to explain the weekly character trait and to identify those who have been "caught doing something good." They also award students with visual displays such as banners, an Honor Roll, a Hall of Fame bulletin board, or a bulletin board highlighting excellent student work. Some schools use the school marquee and newsletter to announce the names of students who have excelled in some way.

In addition, some schools have special clubs for students who agree to pursue the character goals of the club. Fairfield North Elementary School is a K–5 school of almost 900 white, mostly middle-class students from the suburb of Hamilton, Ohio:

> Fairfield North has a "Principles Club" which is an all-inclusive, school-wide effort to reinforce self-concept and basic principles of cooperation, perseverance, and responsibility. Themes such as "Responsibility" are worked on for one month. Simple goals like "cleaning up your work area" or "handing in homework on time" are stressed. Children who are observed by any teachers as meeting one of these goals are given a badge to wear. At the end of the month, the principal hand-delivers small favors to all students who have demonstrated the principle of the month. Since our major emphasis is on reinforcing positive behaviors, each student who has received even one month's reward will receive special recognition in the spring.

Engaging Instruction

The Blue Ribbon Schools make schoolwide efforts to motivate students, but as every good teacher knows, motivated students primarily result from excellent and stimulating instruction in the classroom.

Christi Wiens is the current principal at Mountain View Elementary School in Fresno, California. She explained to the author that the cornerstone of the instructional process at their school is the faculty's belief that "how they teach children is as important as what they teach them." Mountain View is a newly formed suburban K–6 school that continues to experience enrollment increases each year. The student body consists of a growing number of linguistically diverse students encompassing thirteen different languages.

> We know that we cannot force students to be motivated, but we can create an environment that enhances motivation. In fact our Faculty and Staff Handbook summarizes our philosophy well: Children learn best when they: (1) feel someone cares about them; (2) are curious about what they are learning; (3) are actively involved in the learning process; (4) receive appropriate feedback for tasks completed; (5) see a chance for success; (6) are interested and challenged in what they are learning; and (7) feel they are doing something worthwhile.

The Blue Ribbon teachers know how to teach to all students in a challenging, motivating, and rewarding way. A major principle of current motivation theory is that tasks associated with a moderate probability of success (50%) provide maximum satisfaction. Moderate probability of success is also an essential ingredient of intrinsic motivation (Clifford, 1990). Intrinsic motivation is motivation due to reinforcers that are inherent in the activity being performed (Gage & Berliner, 1991). Knowing that one can succeed in a learning task if one applies oneself is essential for a student.

The Argonaut Elementary School in Saratoga, California, serves a diverse, affluent population from the Silicon Valley. The ethnic makeup of the student body of 517 is about half Caucasian and half Asian. Parents have high expectations of their children and for the school. The principal, Sheri Hitchings, explained:

> Research has proven that intrinsic motivation is a powerful long-term effective means to success; therefore, our staff strives to create a stimulating learning environment based on mutual respect and trust where students may experiment and take risks. Asking students what they want to learn is one of the highly motivating teaching techniques used by our teachers. Teachers strive to make learning relevant and to develop intrinsic motivation as well as extrinsic rewards.

At the St. Joseph's Montessori School in Columbus, Ohio, a teacher explained that

> The Montessori materials are developed to be challenging and exciting. The hands-on manipulative materials often attract the child to the work and to learning much more than before. These materials have proven to promote learning and make natural extensions in learning. Responsibility for work lies with the student. Much of the learning is on topics children are drawn to; sparking their imagination has caused great active participation in and enthusiasm for attaining knowledge. We are proud of the excitement and interest in our students.

St. Joseph's is a private, pre-K through eighth-grade school with a diverse student population of 236.

Kohn (1993) would agree with the way these Blue Ribbon Schools engage students in learning, as he advocates the promotion of learning conditions that facilitate intrinsic, rather than reward-based, motivation.

> The job of educators is not to make students motivated, but to set up the conditions that make learning possible. The challenge is to offer a stimulating environment that can be perceived by students as presenting valid and valued options that can lead to successful learning and

performance. It is necessary to establish the conditions that facilitate motivation, to create the right curriculum and the right school climate. (p. 194)

Many of the Blue Ribbon Schools would agree with Kohn as they emphasize the importance of the teacher's role in tapping the students' intrinsic motivation by engaging them with meaningful instructional tasks. Kohn (1993) summarizes intrinsic motivation as the desire to engage in an activity for its own sake — that is, just because of the satisfaction it provides.

The teachers at the Bellerive School in Creve Coeur, Missouri, are firm believers that true learning comes from a desire within the student to learn. The subject matter need not necessarily always be fun, but it must be meaningful. Teachers know that they must convey expectations to students sensitively and realistically, because each student learns differently; therefore their curriculum is structured to bring out the best in students. The school's application explains:

> Science and social studies units culminate with celebrations in each grade level's yearly or monthly themes. One first-grade monthly theme is "Bernstein Bears at Bellerive" and they have a Bear Day. Second grade has "From Squiggly Sprouts to Towering Tigers." . . . Fifth grade uses a different piece of literature each year for their theme. This year it is "Follow the Yellow Brick Road" based on the Wizard of Oz. They used "Oz" to help students be the best they can be by encouraging them to have courage to learn and try their best; the heart to understand their peers and the world; and the brains to be successful in the information age, i.e, the 21st century.

> Bellerive teachers have a positive attitude toward students and they believe that all students can learn. They encourage students in their academic work and provide appropriate incentives and rewards. Sometimes rewards are in the form of assemblies, bound books of students' work, a bulletin board of photographs, or pizza parties. These and other strategies assist our students to become independent and prepare them for a lifetime of self-education.

Paul Chance (1992) disagrees with Kohn's dismissal of the value of other forms of motivation. He cites research showing that, although intrinsic rewards are important for maximally efficient learning, students need to have all three forms of positive reinforcement: encouragement (praising, complimenting, and applauding students), extrinsic rewards (special privileges, certificates, and prizes), and intrinsic rewards (pleasure in learning, satisfaction from a job well done). Many of the

Blue Ribbon Schools would agree with this position as they indicate that "catching students doing something right" as well as awarding good behavior and citizenship are key elements of their schoolwide effort to promote character development in students.

Mottos

Schools have found, as have successful organizations, that mottos, slogans, and symbols strengthen school spirit and unite and motivate school members to strive toward a common goal. There is positive effort on the part of the teachers and administrators in these outstanding schools to create an image, a common goal around which the whole school unites. Blue Ribbon School leaders explain their school goals: "We create climate: we do not just maintain it." And again: "Good climate is promoted, not taken for granted." Several schools specifically mentioned in their applications that positive climate is one of the reasons why they should be nominated for Blue Ribbon recognition.

The Jefferson Center for Character Education STAR program (Success Through Accepting Responsibility), explained in Chapter 3, is a also a schoolwide systematic program for improving school climate. It is used in the Parkway School in a suburb in New Jersey. Parkway has a diverse student body of 350, 12% of whom are Asian. STAR teaches these children personal and social responsibilities through the use of the monthly themes that become like the school motto for the period.

From New York to California, schools use mottos just as they use awards—to express their values and unite the whole school around certain character traits that all strive to obtain:

- Be All You Can Be
- BE PLAN—Be Fun, Be Neat, Be Kind, Be Polite, Be Prompt, Be Careful, Be Honest, Be Alert
- Everyone Helps One
- MAGIC—Make a Greater Individual Commitment To Learning
- Olympic Creed—Always Strive to Do One's Best
- Onward to Excellence
- Project PRIDE=Personal Responsibility In Developing Excellence
- Reach for the Stars—Fulfill Your Dreams

- Rising to the Needs of Others
- Say Yes to Friends
- Sharing Is Caring
- What I'm Going to Be Is Up to Me.
- Where Eagles Learn to Fly
- You Can If You Think You Can.
- You Must Give Your Best.

These nationally recognized schools recognize and reward student achievement through schoolwide systems of awards and activities that promote school spirit.

Alfie Kohn (1993) points out that this system of awards and ceremonies can only be considered character-forming if the students continue to manifest these behaviors even when there are no more awards to be earned: "Children who come to believe that their prosocial behavior reflects values or dispositions in themselves have internal structure that can generate behavior across settings and without external pressures" (p. 270). Mottos, awards, and ceremonies have to help students feel a sense of control over their own lives by giving them the guiding concepts that will help them to make judgments about what constitutes good moral behavior: "Research has shown that motivation for academic learning comes from the reinforcements of one's social environment for specific learned skills . . . and that self-concept changes are likely to be an outcome of increased achievement with accompanying social approval" (Biehler & Snowman, 1990, p. 530).

The above-cited methods show how these Blue Ribbon Schools were able to motivate their students to achieve by: (1) emphasizing a schoolwide atmosphere of high ideals and values; (2) rewarding students who succeeded in developing the specified character qualities outlined by the school awards, ceremonies, and mottos; and (3) recognizing the value of engaging instruction, which taps a student's intrinsic motivation.

GUIDANCE PROGRAMS

Guidance Programs That Develop Character

The many different guidance programs mentioned by the Blue Ribbon Schools as ways in which they promote character are found in

Table 9. Guidance programs can be considered traditional "character development" when they follow a curriculum or program aimed at developing moral values or virtues. Judgment can best be made about the philosophy of a guidance program by looking at the curriculum to see if its components focus on content or process.

MegaSkills is perhaps a good example of a "character development" guidance program. It is a community-building program used by the Perley School in South Bend, Indiana. There are ten "MegaSkills" that the program seeks to develop: confidence, motivation, effort, responsibility, initiative, perseverance, caring, teamwork, common sense, and problem solving. MegaSkills is a classroom curriculum and a schoolwide program with parental involvement and training. It seeks to help students to develop strong study skills and good work habits, stimulate their creative thinking, involve families in educational activities at home, and build student self-discipline in coping with pressures, making individual choices, and developing a strong value system. Memphis State University researchers evaluating MegaSkills as implemented in the Tennessee schools found that those who participated in the program doubled the time they spent on homework and decreased the time spent watching

TABLE 9 Guidance programs and self-esteem
programs found in the Blue Ribbon Schools.

Category	Count	Percent of Responses
Advisor system	4	2%
Children Are People	6	3%
CLASS	13	5%
DUSO	8	4%
Kids on the Block	6	3%
Magic Circles	8	4%
Positive Action	8	4%
PRIDE	23	10%
Project Self-Esteem	4	2%
Rainbows for All	7	3%
School program	34	15%
Self-Respect & Responsibility	24	10%
Super Me, Up with Kids	4	2%
Workshop Way	5	2%

Valid cases, 254; missing cases, 104.

television. In addition, the parents spent 2 to 2¼ hours more per week with their children. [These research results are reported in the MegaSkills information package and by Dorothy Rich (1991) in an *Educational Leadership* article entitled "Parents Can Teach MegaSkills to Their Children."] For more information on this curriculum, contact The Home and School Institute, MegaSkills Education Center, 1500 Massachusetts Ave., NW, Washington, DC 20005; phone: 202-466-3633.

Children Are People Program

The Children Are People (CAP) program was found in several of the Blue Ribbon Schools. It is a basic part of the primary social studies and K–5 health curriculum at the Independence Primary, the Forest Elementary, and St. Thomas More schools in Ohio. These three schools each represent a different socioeconomic mix of students, but the CAP program is successful at each. Independence is a K–4 school of 315 students from white- and blue-collar, middle-class families located in Independence, Ohio, a suburb fifteen minutes from Cleveland; Forest is a K–6 school of 359 middle-class white students in North Olmstead, Ohio; and St. Thomas More is a Catholic K–8 school in Cleveland with a diverse student population from lower-income settings that include single-parent homes and racially mixed families.

The objectives of the CAP program are to foster self-awareness, positive self-concept, decision making, values, ethics, and self-discipline and prepare students for responsible independence in the future. Students learn how to develop friendships that are rewarding and encourage individual growth. Character, good behavior, and sound judgment are developed by teaching strategies that help children cope with rejection, frustration, disappointment, and failure. The CAP program deals with students' emotions and helps to incorporate the discussion of emotions into the classroom in a comfortable way.

Robert Sylvester (1994) reports that emotions are an area that even today we do not understand fully. Yet we realize they are very important for the overall health of our students and in order to have a stimulating and emotionally positive classroom. The CAP program seeks to teach these emotional competencies to children. These competencies include self-control, zeal, and persistence and the ability to motivate oneself. As Goleman (1995) explains: "Whether there is a class explicitly devoted to emotional literacy may matter far less than how these lessons are taught. There is perhaps no subject where the quality of the teacher matters so much since how a teacher handles her class is in itself a model — a de facto lesson in emotional competency — or lack thereof" (p. 279).

Dilemma Discussions

Guidance program curricula are usually based on versions of Kohlberg's cognitive developmental theory of character development (as cited in Power et al., 1989). Kohlberg maintained that moral reasoning is the most important factor in understanding and predicting moral behavior. His psychological theory and his educational interventions studied the relation between moral reasoning and moral behavior. Character development programs subscribing to Kohlberg's theory present students with moral dilemmas for discussion. The purpose is not to solve the dilemmas, because they usually can have two or three defensible solutions, but to aid students in developing more complex reasoning patterns. Critics maintain that Kohlberg's theory is more concerned with *how* we think about moral issues, that is, the structure of thinking — rather than *what* we think or what we do (Ryan, 1981).

One example of this type of program found in the Manoa Elementary School, a pre-K to sixth-grade school in Honolulu, Hawaii, is the Foundation Program on Career Education and Guidance. It provides opportunities for students to examine their behavior, values, and judgments through class discussions, role playing, and other activities. The goal of the program is to develop a positive self-concept and an enthusiasm for learning along with a sense of responsibility to self and others. The program helps students practice cooperation skills and develop responsibility in problem-solving situations that they encounter as safety patrols and as library, cafeteria, and office monitors.

Another dilemma discussion program is the Developmental Guidance Program, found in several Blue Ribbon Schools, including the Los Encinos School in Corpus Christi, Texas. Los Encinos is a large, very diverse K–6 urban school that is 86% Hispanic students and 60% students from lower-income families. The goal of the Developmental Guidance Program is to help students become purposeful, responsible, and honest. The counselor provides organized thematic units in all of the classrooms in forty-minute sessions every other week. The units include such topics as self-awareness, respect, decision making, interpersonal relationships, responsibility, and drug education. These topics are all approached through moral dilemmas relevant to students' ages and interests. The counselor helps students to recognize the importance of their own worth and take personal responsibility for their choices and their behavior. Emphasis is placed on making decisions, being an individual, and respecting the feelings of others. The school considers this developmental guidance to be an essential component of their character development program.

A Three-Pronged Approach

Joseph M. Roma, the principal at the Parkway School in New Jersey, explains that the school uses a three-pronged approach to teach values that involves character qualities, discussions of moral dilemmas found in good literature, and role models:

> 1. Standards of excellence, honesty and cooperation are set for the social and moral behavior of students and communicated on a daily basis within the framework of the classroom environment.
> 2. Teachers, through the study of literature and moral dilemma discussions, heighten the students' awareness of moral issues and possible solutions to problems. As problems are discussed, children realize that people change their views when they gain a new perspective on a situation and may change the basis for their own moral judgments.
> 3. Students are exposed to the lives of outstanding personalities to foster emulation of strong character traits. Classroom situations are created for learning character traits through dramatic productions, role playing and creative writing.

Leadership Programs

Guidance programs to promote leadership are found in 5% of the Blue Ribbon Schools. The CLASS program (Community Leadership Activities for StudentS) is one popular leadership program; another is the STOP program (Students Thinking of Others and Peers) found in the Plano School District and other schools. The STOP program allows students to develop leadership qualities by encouraging them to think of others and to think about the consequences of their own actions. This extracurricular program permits all interested children to receive training in developing skills for responsible decision making

and resisting peer pressure. One strategy teaches students the importance of being responsible leaders by developing their sensitivity to
the new and lonely student. The counselor appoints STOP students to
be "pals" or buddy partners with new students or students needing special friends. These students take them to class and lunch, call them to
offer help with any assignments, buddy with them at recess, and just
let them know that they have a "pal" to help them with problems and
events. This program is also aimed at helping children build self-
esteem and keep themselves drug-free. Students in this peer support
program learn and model ethical decision making in skits at student
assemblies. STOP members also fill Christmas baskets, package gro-
ceries, and give toys and the like to less fortunate families.

At the Westwood Elementary School in Santa Clara, California, students are expected to be leaders, tutors, peer coaches, and problem
solvers. The student body is ethnically, economically, linguistically,
and religiously diverse, and students are taught to accept others and
help others. Character education is a thread that runs throughout their
curriculum, integrated within each subject matter, and taught at appropriate "teachable moments." Class meetings are held regularly by
teachers to discuss school, class, and personal issues. Students are
thereby given the opportunity to apply their character lessons by solving school problems and by getting involved in service to others as tutors, coaches, or conflict mediators.

The PLUS program (Peers Leading to Ultimate Success) is found at
the Mount View Elementary School in Virginia. Mount View is a large
K–6 school with a homogeneous population of white, largely middle-
class students. The goal of the school is to "develop ethical standards
of behavior in order for students to participate in society as responsible family members and citizens." Students are taught by trained high
school students who introduce them to the wider world that the students will enter after elementary school. The lesson plans include an
introduction to making course choices in high school, extracurricular
options open to students, tips on how to make good decisions, and an
explanation of the different ways in which older students communicate, cooperate, resolve feelings, and form friendships. All of these
goals are approached in interesting and creative ways. This program
helps develop peer leadership and provide young students with appropriate older role models.

Positive Action

Another guidance program that promotes character is the Positive Action program. Positive Action is used in several Blue Ribbon Schools to "teach students a love of learning, how to feel good about themselves and how to become productive citizens" (Allred, 1994). The Positive Action curriculum includes a scope and sequence chart that shows how completely the program teaches character traits. Some of the traits listed on this chart include cheerfulness, citizenship, cooperation, courage, diligence, generosity, honesty, kindness, patience, punctuality, respect, responsibility, temperance, and tolerance.

The parents of students at Cherokee Elementary School in Arizona initiated the Positive Action program so that each child would develop a positive self-image. The parents teach the curriculum as a total self-improvement plan that encompasses physical, mental, and emotional growth with a holistic program for self-improvement based on family values. Cherokee is a K–5 school of over 1000 students, so it is important for each student to feel that he or she is personally important and not just a number in the school.

Linda Kamiyama, principal at the Waiahole Elementary School in Hawaii, explains that Positive Action encompasses guidance, character development, and drug education: "We combine this program with our self-esteem-building and character development activities so that students have numerous opportunities to develop into responsible, resourceful, and self-assured individuals." Waiahole is a "bona fide community school" of 175 students, 88% of whom are Asian, and 70% of whom are from lower-income families.

Positive Action develops pro-social skills using a "structured learning" approach similar to the teaching of academic competencies. Components include modeling, role-playing, performance feedback reinforcement, and transfer and maintenance strategies. At Oklahoma's Monte Cassino School, which has used Positive Action, individual achievement is recognized with ICU ("I see you") notes written by students and teachers. ICU notes give positive acknowledgement to students when they exhibit pro-social behaviors such as sharing and caring for others.

The Mary E. Roberts School, a K–4 school of 350 homogeneous students from the suburb of Moorestown, New Jersey, conducted a schoolwide evaluation following the implementation of Positive Action. The results showed the program was effective. Ralph Scazafabo, the principal, was pleased with the program results: "This project has demonstrated how a program designed to change students' attitudes toward adults, peers, and self can have a dramatic effect on total school-wide climate."

Guidance Programs Supporting Family Issues

Other guidance programs help children to deal with difficult family situations. For example, Fairfield North Elementary School in Hamilton, Ohio, uses the TRIBES program. TRIBES is a preventive mental health program for students who are "at risk." Fairfield is a very large school of Caucasian students. Nevertheless, the student population is diverse, as 14% come from lower-income families and 25% of them qualify for special education services. Classroom teachers have been trained to break students into "tribes" or groups that work together as the Native-American tribes functioned. The "tribe" is a group of five to seven students who meet together regularly during the school year to discuss personal concerns and feelings, plan and problem-solve one another's personal problems together, and at times work on appropriate classroom projects together. The teacher serves as the facilitator, as the students in these supportive peer groups work to improve their self-images and academic achievements. The TRIBES manual contains complete "lesson plans for meetings" in which social development classes and cooperative learning experiences provide a rich background for children who lack a cohesive family unit in their homes. The "tribe" at school becomes their own cohesive peer unit.

Rainbows for All God's Children is found in 4% of the schools. This program, used by its full name in most schools, but referred to just as "Rainbows" in some public schools, is a peer group for those who have experienced loss in their lives. The curriculum includes discussions about anxieties, fears, feelings, frustrations, and beliefs that children often experience as a result of death, divorce, and family separation. This program is explained well in the St. Damian School handbook:

> We are aware that a child does not come to school and leave his/her feelings outside the school door. When children experience the loss of a parent through death or divorce, they experience many feelings that are new to them.

The Rainbows for all God's Children Program is designed to implant in these children a belief in their own goodness and the value of their own families. Rainbows is a support group program for children living in a single-parent family or a blended family. Small groups are arranged by age and meet with a trained faculty facilitator.

Currently at St. Damian, a large Catholic K–8 school located in suburban Oak Forest south of Chicago, there are six teacher-facilitators who work with groups of five or more children. Students meet with a facilitator once a week for twelve weeks when a parent dies or a divorce takes place in a family. The facilitator helps the students work through their grief, build a strong sense of self-esteem, and begin to accept what has taken place in the family. A culminating celebration is held at the end of the twelve weeks for these students and their parents. The celebration helps them to understand that a change in life can be an occasion for a new beginning. Students in the program feel comfortable in seeking out their facilitators whenever they have a problem or just need to talk.

Understanding Students with Special Needs

Kids on the Block is used in almost 10% of the Blue Ribbon Schools with primary-grade students. Developed by Barbara Aiello in Washington, D.C., Kids on the Block uses commercially produced, life-sized puppets who represent children who are nonhandicapped, mentally handicapped, deaf, blind, and learning disabled. Junior League volunteers are the puppeteers and conduct the hour-long performances using a script that focuses on each of the areas of disability. The puppeteers are well informed about each handicapping condition as a result of workshops given by professionals in each disability area, which they have attended in order to become puppeteers. They are able to respond to children's questions, usually using the puppets throughout the presentation. Research into the program has shown that it is effective in increasing young children's knowledge and understanding of handicapped persons (Snart & Maguire, 1987).

SELF-ESTEEM PROGRAMS

Almost 20% of the Blue Ribbon Schools equate character development with their self-esteem programs (see Table 2). In such programs, it is important that the students be given the correct things to esteem: values such as responsibility, industriousness, honesty and kindness— not values such as good looks, popularity, or possessions. Students will feel good about themselves because they know they have done well (worked hard) and have tried to do the right thing. Research has not shown the reverse to be true, that is, that students will do well in school because they feel good about themselves (Kohn, 1994).

Self-Esteem as Reverence/Respect for Oneself

High self-esteem by itself does not ensure good character. However, unless students respect and appreciate their own worth and dignity, they have little to offer to others (Van Ness, 1995). Typically, self-esteem is defined as the personal judgment of worthiness expressed in the attitudes the individual holds towards himself or herself (Kohn, 1994). Self-esteem comes from a Greek word meaning "reverence for self." At a philosophical level, self-esteem is a central feature in human dignity and thus an unalienable human entitlement (Beane, 1991). Nationwide, teachers tell us that the number one problem in the schools today is a lack of respect: a lack of respect of children toward themselves, other students, their teachers, and their parents. Self-esteem allows them to value and respect themselves and thereby to value and respect others. Attributing intrinsic value to children because of their unique qualities and gifts is self-esteem education that is appropriate both in and outside the curriculum (Baniewicz, 1995).

Affective Education

Self-esteem programs are one kind of affective education, that is, concerned with the formation, content, and role of emotions, feelings, values, attitudes, predispositions, and morals (Beane, 1985). Most educators would agree with Bloom (1977) and others that education involves an artful blend of instruction in the cognitive, affective, and psychomotor domains. Many of the programs cited in this book dealing with the areas of citizenship, substance abuse, peace education, and explicit character education include aspects of affective education—educating moral feeling or the "heart side" of character. Controversy arises when affective education is emphasized as more important than the cognitive, and when the content of the affective curriculum is based on a subjective, self-discovery philosophy (held by humanists) rather than on an objective, truth-discovery philosophy (held by "realists"). Controversy also arises when people have different understandings of what self-esteem is. Too many people see self-esteem as "permission to do what I want to do as long as it makes me feel good." By contrast, ethical self-esteem—the kind that is properly part of good character—is permission to do what one wants as long as it results in good moral behavior.

Self-Esteem Based on Truth Discovery

The realists propose that self-esteem comes through focusing on truth-discovery. Their theory is that changes in achievement cause changes in self-concept, that is, self-esteem develops as a by-product of other reality-based factors. The pedagogical focus, then, centers on activities of problem solving, seeking relevant meaning from facts, developing skills, and discovering academic and moral truths. Truth, here, means conformity to fact, fidelity to the standard (Paul, 1990). Real self-esteem develops when a student works hard, learns something worthwhile or accomplishes a challenging task. Edward Wynne states that students then develop the virtue of "diligence" (Wynne & Ryan, 1993). If they are graded strictly but justly and are rewarded and praised when they have earned it, they will come to develop a sense of self-respect. Educators who want to help children "feel good about themselves" will do better by treating them with respect, not merely showering them with praise. Research has demonstrated the validity of the realist model for developing self-esteem, showing a correlation between students' academic success or failure and the resultant high- or low self-esteem (Calsyn & Kenny, 1977). The Blue Ribbon Schools in this study promoted "achievement self-esteem" by implementing the latest pedagogical methodologies in order to ensure academic success for all students and thereby promote their feelings of self-worth and accomplishment. (These teaching techniques are described in more detail in the next chapter.)

Humanist Affective Education

The humanists (Carl Rogers, Abraham Maslow, Arthur Combs) set up a system of affective education based on the human experience philosophy of John Dewey. Dewey proposed that values develop through the cyclical interaction of the individual with his or her environment. Values are open to question and change. This "developmental" approach to affective education proposes that the school's role is to help the child formulate values or beliefs through experiences (Beane 1985). The content of the humanist's curriculum is based on the premise that self-esteem comes through focusing on self-discovery. The theory is that changes in self-esteem cause changes in achievement. The pedagogical focus in these programs centers on activities seeking self-discovery. The teacher becomes the facilitator of student self-discovery. Contemporary self-esteem programs are criticized because of their lack of consistency, absence of clear direction and purpose, and lack of thoroughness in program planning (Beane, 1985; Leo, 1990).

There are no data to show that these self-esteem programs can make a difference in raising students' self-esteem or basic view of themselves (Kohn, 1994). No researchers have been able to show that high self-esteem inclines people toward pro-social behavior or steers them away from antisocial behavior. Some studies have shown a positive correlation between self-esteem and school participation, school completion, self-direction, and various types of achievement and chances for success in life (Beane, 1991; Canfield, 1990), but such correlations could mean that self-esteem was the result of these outcomes rather than their causes.

One can even challenge the desirability of focusing on self-esteem in the classroom, because this kind of affective education program may lead to a preoccupation with self instead of with community. As stated by Kohn (1994), "Affective education should be embraced but in the context of building community rather then attending to each individual separately. . . . Whether our objective is to help children become good learners (that is creative, self-directed, lifelong learners) or good people (that is secure, responsible, caring)—or both, we can and need to do better than merely concentrating our efforts on self-esteem" (p. 174).

There are several commercial self-esteem programs that are currently in use in many of the Blue Ribbon Schools. Most of them are used as one component of their schoolwide program for fostering the character development of their students. Some of these programs, however, should not be used if a school is really serious about character development, because they give students mixed messages, that is, telling students that the most important criteria to use in judging actions is whether or not the actions make them feel good about themselves. Therefore, after each program mentioned in the next section, the author will give criteria for judging the program's effectiveness in fostering character in students.

DUSO

The DUSO (Developing Understanding of Self and Other) guidance materials were mentioned in fewer than 5% of the Blue Ribbon School applications. The DUSO curriculum is designed to help primary students build self-esteem, social awareness, respect for others, and decision-making skills. DUSO 1 is targeted for children in kindergarten and first grade; DUSO 2 for children in the third and fourth grades. The curricular materials feature an awareness kit that includes puppets (DUSO the Dolphin), a teacher's guide book, storybooks, cassette, and lesson cards. Students are presented with unended short stories and discuss appropriate endings with the teacher. Topics of these short stories include a child who wants to be first in line, a child who has an opportunity to share, and making friends. The process or story completion focuses on helping children to understand behavior, listen reflectively, express their feelings, and deal with conflict. The guidance counselors interviewed in the Blue Ribbon Schools were very positive about the DUSO curriculum. One stated that she thought it was the "most well known program being used by guidance counselors in elementary schools across the nation." Many of the activities in both DUSO 1 and DUSO 2 contain stories, songs, writing and art projects that are valuable assets in the classroom (National Association of Christian Educators/Citizens for Excellence in Education, 1996a).

However, DUSO also has a unit that uses imagery lessons in which children are told by their teachers to relax, close their eyes, and then imagine that they are traveling to strange planets and meeting friendly creatures. For this reason, some parents have complained about the DUSO curriculum, stating that its guided fantasy activities asking students to "visualize" are mind-altering psychological techniques that are like hypnotism. For example, a parent in San Diego, California, objected to DUSO because it "encourages a child to explore his inner self, to relax by meditation, and to acquire fantasy companions to help guide him through life's stresses." The main criticism of the program is directed at its philosophic basis. DUSO was written by Don Dinkmeyer, Ph.D., in 1971 and uses values clarification techniques. There are no absolute values in DUSO, no definitive right and wrong. Most of the research conducted on the DUSO program is over twenty years old and consists of doctoral dissertation studies. The findings are mixed: several studies found no significant difference in self-concept in DUSO students and those who were in a classroom without DUSO (Galina, 1973; Quain, 1977); other studies found a positive effect (Eldridge et al., 1973). In 1982, the DUSO curriculum was revised (with fewer values clarification activities) and subsequent studies (Stacey & Rost, 1985) showed that the revised program can be more effective at raising self-concept, academic skills, and other variables than the original DUSO "if given a chance to work." For more information on DUSO and these research studies, contact the American Guidance Service (AGS), 4201 Woodlawn Road, Box 99, Circle Pine, MN 55014; phone: 800-328-2560.

Magic Circles

The Stewart Elementary School in the Princeton School District in Cincinnati, Ohio, uses Magic Circle discussions to foster democratic values and ethical judgments in students. The Magic Circles program was found in 3% of the Blue Ribbon Schools. It is an affective education curriculum and methodology for improving self-concept, teaching self-discipline, and values. It seeks to promote self-esteem through the self-discovery model. It was developed by Bessell, Ball, and Palomares as a means for promoting social adjustment and mental health (Bessell, 1972) by providing students with the opportunity to practice humanistic social skills such as empathy, congruence, and positive regard (Braun, 1989). The curriculum and accompanying small-group discussion are designed to provide practice in displaying empathy for others (perspective-taking), understanding of self, accepting responsibility, and dealing with conflict and are to result in increased self-esteem.

Magic Circles has come under fire by Phyllis Schlafly as sensitivity training that pressures students to express their feelings and seeks to solicit intimate familial information and undermine religious values (Schlafly, 1984). The curriculum authors reply that, when properly led, the process is a safe and rewarding experience; but some teachers have tried the process without adequate training. It is not meant to be sensitivity training, and the teacher is not meant to be a therapist. When sensitive issues are brought up, the teacher needs to bring this information to the appropriate professionals on the school staff (counselor, nurse, social worker) and allow them to follow through with action.

The Ivymount School in Rockville, Maryland, uses the Magic Circles discussion methodology but focuses on more concrete content such as discussing responsibility, respect for others, appropriate behavior, and other issues that contribute to students' ability to function in a society where those qualities are valued. Ivymount, which serves the entire Washington, D.C. metropolitan area, is a private school for children who have disabilities that require special education services not found in the public schools. One class developed a "Civil Rights" document for students, staff, and parents. Ivymount seeks to maximize every child's potential and prepare students for a less restrictive setting and eventually toward living as independently as possible.

The "circle discussions" used at Ivymount are actually more similar to the "circle meetings" Glasser (1990) proposes in *The Quality School* than to the Magic Circle meetings, because they focus on discussing issues from the perspective of the character qualities valued by the group. Glasser recommends that classrooms be permanently set up in a circle configuration, instead of the standard rows with the teacher's desk at the head. In this way, at a moment's notice, students and teacher can begin to discuss any problems that need to be solved. The main purpose of Glasser's class meetings is to teach control theory to students, that is, to teach them that they choose to do everything that they do in order to satisfy one of their five basic needs. Control theory helps students to develop their characters as it teaches them that the better they are able to control their lives and make good, responsible choices, the happier they will be.

Power of Positive Students

According to the counselor at Huffman School in Plano, Texas, this school has a "wonderful" program for teaching self-esteem—Power of Positive Students (POPS). This program was developed by Dr. Billy Mitchell to infuse positive attitudes into all aspects of the school. The program seeks to help all students and staff to develop positive self-images: "We have on the morning announcements every morning a

POP statement, that is, a positive thing we must do right after we do the pledge. For example, one day the goal might be to try to compliment someone in the class for something they do that is good." Every day the staff focuses on the positive, teaching children to think positively and to plan for positive results. Special reinforcement bulletin boards have been designed around the school, and newsletters are periodically sent home to parents, mentioning all of the positive things happening.

Project Self-Esteem

Other schools use Project Self-Esteem, a program that says in its curriculum flyer that it emphasizes sound character, decision-making skills and developing positive self-concept. Project Self-Esteem is an elementary level program to enhance self-esteem, improve memory and communication skills, stress individuality, increase sensitivity to others, and improve self-responsibility.

The National Association of Christian Educators/Citizens for Excellence in Education (1996b), have found that the curriculum is based upon a form of moral relativism (situation ethics) that uses self-interest as the primary motivator for character development. They give an example from the unit in the curriculum on stealing. The objectives for the unit are stated as the child "will be able to state the reasons why people steal" and "understand that stealing hurts oneself and the victim"; however no explicit judgment is made in the lesson concerning the wrongness of stealing (and teachers are instructed to refrain from making judgments about the rightness or wrongness of the act). Self-interest, not society, is the norm of behavior.

The National Association of Christian Educators/Citizens for Excellence in Education (1996c) explains that there are some good lesson plans and activities in these curricula programs, that is, DUSO and Project Self-Esteem, but the lessons are not directive enough to be effective in promoting character. If teachers have a strong background in character education, they could use these creative curricular ideas to stress the development of decision-making skills in students based on reference to specific character qualities such as responsibility, honesty, and justice. Using the situations mentioned in the curriculum, they can be more directive and ask students, for instance, "What would a *responsible* person do in this situation?"

Workshop Way

Workshop Way, a kindergarten through high school program developed by Grace Pilon, is found in several schools including St. Thomas of Canterbury School in New York. St. Thomas is a Catholic K–8 school of 214 white middle-class students. Sister Helen Boyd, the principal at St. Thomas, explains the Five Step Lesson Program of Workshop Way: (1) Communication with a smile, (2) "Power Step"—reinforcing one skill for a few weeks, (3) technical vocabulary drills (flashcards), (4) new lesson each day, and (5) helping students to "live" their knowledge. She explained that the goal of Workshop Way is to help children believe more strongly in themselves as learners and in their ability to learn. Workshop Way is designed to inculcate a love for learning by creating an environment in which each child is accepted, wherever he or she is in the learning process at this particular moment of time. Children learn through Workshop Way that mistakes are a means by which we learn, and that taking risks and making decisions are all part of a very intelligent process.

Workshop Way is "a way for a teacher to organize time, content, and materials so human growth is not left to chance. It's a way teachers can give all students the conditions that release their remarkable human potentials." The most important goal of Workshop Way is to "respect the child's dignity at all costs" (Pilon, 1988).

Critics of Workshop Way cite the fact that it gives priority to nurturing dignity and intelligent living habits and not to academics. It emphasizes changing a child's attitude in order to develop feelings of self-worth but does not associate positive self-concept with knowledge, skills, or right answers. Pilon would direct these critics to look at an evaluation study conducted by Douglas Rose of Tulane University that found that students in Workshop Way classrooms outperformed their peers on SAT scores (Harmin, 1990).

SUMMARY

This chapter shows why it is important for schools to develop the emotional side of students' characters. School mottos, awards, and ceremonies can be effective ways for schools to motivate students to develop and display good character. There are some guidance programs that are effective in promoting character development because they teach character qualities as part of their curriculum. A self-esteem program can promote genuine character development if it teaches that authentic self-esteem is based on the knowledge that one has chosen to do the better thing. However, there are many programs in use in the Blue Ribbon Schools today that do not meet these criteria and therefore cannot be considered to be part of character education. Perhaps this review of these programs will lead schools to evaluate the effectiveness of the programs they are using.

REFERENCES

Alderman, M. K. 1990. "Motivation for At-Risk Students," *Educational Leadership*, 48(1):27–30.

Allred, C. G. 1994. *Positive Action 1994–95 Catalog*. Twin Cities, ID: Positive Action Company.

Baniewicz, J. 1995. "A Parent's Case for Character Education." An Open Letter to the Fairport, N.Y. Education Community, May 21, 1995.

Beane, J. 1991. "Sorting Out the Self-Esteem Controversy," *Educational Leadership*, 49(1):25–30.

Beane, J. 1985. "The Continuing Controversy Over Affective Education," *Educational Leadership*, 43(4):26–31.

Bessell, H. 1972. *The Magic Circle: Methods in Human Development Theory Manual*. Human Development Training Institute: San Diego, CA.

Biehler, R.F. & J. Snowman. 1990. *Psychology Applied to Teaching*, 6th ed. Boston: Houghton Mifflin.

Bloom, B. S. 1977. "Affective Outcomes of School Learning," *Phi Delta Kappan*, 59(3):193–98.

Braun, J. 1989. "The Empathy Lab: A Strategy for Promoting Perspective Taking and Self-Esteem." A paper presented to the Association for Humanistic Education, Denver, CO. April 28, 1989.

Calsyn, R. J. and D. A. Kenny. 1977. "Self-Concept of Ability and Perceived Evaluation of Others: Cause or Effect of Academic Achievement?" *Journal of Educational Psychology*, 69(2):136–45.

Canfield, J. 1990. "Improving Students' Self-Esteem," *Educational Leadership*, 48(1):48–50.

Chance, P. 1992. "The Rewards of Learning," *Phi Delta Kappan*, 74(3):200–207.

Clifford, M. 1990. "Students Need Challenge: Not Easy Success," *Educational Leadership* 48 (1):22–25.

Eldridge, M., Barcikowsk, R. & Witmer, J. 1973. "Effects of DUSO on the Self-Concepts of Second-Grade Students," *Elementary School Guidance and Counseling*, 7 (4): 256–260.

Frymier, J. 1974. *Motivation and Learning in School*. Bloomington, Indiana: Phi Delta Kappa Educational Foundation.

Gage, N.L. and D. Berliner. 1991. *Educational Psychology*, 5th ed. Geneva, IL: Houghton Mifflin Co., pp. 351–358.

Galina, B. 1973. Testing the Stated Objectives of Developing Understanding of Self and Others Curriculum (Doctoral dissertation, Georgia State University, Atlanta 1972). *Dissertation Abstracts International*, 33: 4056A.

Glasser, W. 1990. *The Quality School*. Perennial Library. New York: Harper & Row Publisher.

Goleman, D. 1995. *Emotional Intelligence: Why It Can Matter More Than IQ*. New York: Bantam Books.

Harmin, M. 1990. "The Workshop Way to Student Success," *Educational Leadership*, 48 (1): 43–47.

Kilpatrick, W. 1992. *Why Johnny Can't Tell Right from Wrong*. New York: Simon and Schuster.

Kohn, A. 1994. "The Truth about Self-Esteem," *Phi Delta Kappan*, 76(4):272–282.

Kohn, A. 1993. *Punished by Rewards*. Boston, MA: Houghton-Mifflin.

Leo, J. 1990. "The Trouble with Self-Esteem," *U.S. News & World Report*, April 2:16.

Lickona, T. 1991. *Educating for Character: How Our Schools Can Teach Respect and Responsibility*. New York: Bantam Books.

National Association of Christian Educators/Citizens for Excellence in Education. 1996a. *Duso & Pumsy. Special Report #19*. Costa Mesa, CA: NACE/CEE, p. 1.

National Association of Christian Educators/Citizens for Excellence in Education. 1996b. *Affective Education Special Report #18*. Costa Mesa, CA: NACE/CEE, p. 2.

National Association of Christian Educators/Citizens for Excellence in Education. 1996c. *Creating Healthy Self-Esteem in Children*. Costa Mesa, CA: NACE/CEE, p. 4.

Paul, R.W. 1990. *Critical Thinking*. Rohnert Park, CA: Sonoma State University, Center for Critical Thinking and Moral Critique, p. 570.

Pilon, G. 1988. *Workshop Way*. New Orleans: The Workshop Way, Inc.

Power, C., A. Higgins and L. Kohlberg. 1989. "The Habit of the Common Life: Building Character Through Democratic Community Schools," in *Moral Development and Character Education*. L. Nucci, ed. CA: McCutchan Publishing Corporation, pp. 125–143.

Quain, P., Jr. 1977. Affective Education, Teacher Training for Affective Education: Change in Self-Concept and Affectivity in Kindergarten Children (Doctoral dissertation, St. Louis University, 1976.) *Dissertation Abstracts International*, 37, 7604A.

Rich, D. 1991. "Parents Can Teach MegaSkills to their Children." *Educational Leadership*, 49(1):42.

Ryan, K. 1981. *Questions and Answers on Moral Education*. PDK Fastback 153, Bloomington Indiana: Phi Delta Kappa, p. 20.

Schlafly, P. 1984. *Child Abuse in the Classroom*. Westchester, IL: Crossroads Publisher.

Snart, F. and T. Maguire. 1987. "Effectiveness of the Kids on the Block Puppets: An Examination," *B.C. Journal of Special Education*. 11(1):9–16.

Stacey, S. & J.O. Rost. 1985. "Evaluating the Effectiveness of the DUSO-1 (Revised) Program. *Elementary School Guidance and Counseling*, 20: 84–90.

Sylvester, R. 1994. "How Emotions Affect Learning," *Educational Leadership* 52(2):60–65.

Van Ness, R. 1995. *Raising Self-Esteem of Learners*. Phi Delta Kappan Notebook #389: Bloomington, Indiana, p. 5.

Wynne, E. and K. Ryan. 1993. *Reclaiming Our Schools: A Handbook on Teaching Character, Academics, and Discipline*. New York: Macmillan Publishing Company.

Chapter 6

TEACHING TECHNIQUES THAT PROMOTE CHARACTER

Work while it is called today, for you know not how much you will be hindered tomorrow. One today is worth two tomorrows; never leave that till tomorrow that you can do today.—Benjamin Franklin

Whatever I have tried to do in life, I have tried with all my heart to do well.—Charles Dickens

Teach your students to use what talents they have; the woods would be silent if no bird sang except those that sing best.—Anonymous

Meno tells Socrates that if virtue is knowledge, there can be no doubt that virtue is taught. Socrates replies that if it is taught, there must be teachers of virtue. Socrates was not able to identify any teachers of virtue in Athens before the end of the dialogue, but Aristotle in his writings described such teachers of virtue. He said that teachers help students to become good when they teach in such a way that they help students to cultivate good habits, or virtues. For "with regard to virtue, it is not enough to know, but we must also try to have and use it, and in this way become good" (1179a).

The Blue Ribbon Schools have found teachers of virtue. They promote character in students by challenging them to develop good study habits in order to be the best students that they can be. The teachers have high academic standards for all their students, but they also have high standards for themselves, seeking to do their best as teachers. Blue Ribbon teachers implement the latest pedagogical methodologies which enable students to have academic success while helping them develop their character through the effort to do their work as a student well. In order to be nominated as a Blue Ribbon School, applicants had to show that they were doing an exceptional job with all of their students in developing a solid foundation of basic skills and knowledge of subject matter in addition to promoting the development of their character. The bulk of the application form (see Appendix A) concerns the former. It asks for evidence that the students are developing a solid foundation of skills in reading, writing, and mathematics; the schools must include separate documentation on each of these areas. For a complete review of these academic areas, the reader should refer to other books that have been written about the Blue Ribbon Schools: *The Nation's Best Schools: Blueprints for Excellence, Volume 1: Elementary and Middle Schools* (Ogden & Germinario, 1994), *Best Ideas from America's Blue Ribbon Schools, Vol. 1 and Vol. 2* (National Association of Elementary School Principals, 1994, 1995).

This chapter reports on those teaching techniques, methods, or programs that the schools specifically mentioned in the section on "promoting the development of sound character, a sense of self-worth, democratic values, ethical judgment and self-discipline in students." This chapter looks at the "teaching techniques that promote character" as found in the Blue Ribbon Schools. It shows how these schools develop the academic ability of students, and, in so doing, help them actually to live good character traits. It reports on a few of the instructional programs mentioned by the Blue Ribbon Schools as important for the development of character; it makes connections between these pedagogical methodologies and the development of character, and cites research that documents the effectiveness of these techniques in promoting learning. The chapter tries to answer the following questions:

- Why is it important for a school to stress academics in order to promote character development in students?
- Why must the value of work be understood if a student is to become a person of character?
- Why is cooperative learning such an important technique for developing character in students?
- How do learning styles and multiple intelligence instruction, and portfolios and alternative assessments contribute to the character development of students?

• Why is it important to develop thinking skills in students through whole language, thematic instruction, or other methods in order to develop their characters?

THE ROLE OF ACADEMICS IN PROMOTING CHARACTER DEVELOPMENT

The actual role of students places them in this key environment for developing their characters. Their job is to be the best students that they can be (Lickona, 1991). If we understand good character as the intersection of moral knowing, moral feeling, and moral action, we can see that studying and learning give students key opportunities to show their character through their actions.

Although learning can be very exciting and fulfilling, it is hard work. As Wynne and Ryan (1993) note, profound learning is difficult and uncomfortable. Profound learning is learning about important things, and this knowledge brings about important changes in students' conduct or way of looking at things. Profound learning includes learning about the basic events and features of Western culture and developing an understanding of other cultures. It helps students to develop both a cultural and a moral literacy, that is, a knowledge of culture's moral wisdom and those enduring habits or traits needed for good character.

Learning and studying these demanding subjects not only is the heart of students' liberal education but also helps develop their characters. For example, children develop self-discipline and responsibility if they devote the necessary time to studying and doing their homework instead of watching television. They develop the courage to attack difficult assignments and the perseverance to keep at the assignments until they have completed them. They acquire diligence if they do this day after day (Kilpatrick, 1992). Studying and learning also help to develop intellectual virtues in students such as a love of learning, valuing the opportunity to learn, respect for the truth, objectivity, prudence to think critically, understanding, humility to accept limitations, and a concern for excellence.

THE VALUE OF WORK AND OF A STUDENT'S WORK

Given a challenging curriculum, excellent instruction, and high expectations, students come to recognize that they need to work in school if they are to learn. They see that they need to do their school work the best that they can: neatly, with care for details, by expending appropriate effort and time. Finally, students learn to check and evaluate their work before they turn it in or call it finished, to be sure that it is done well and meets standards of excellence. Lickona (1991) states that it is important for students to learn the value of work done well, as this is a fundamental source of their dignity and sense of worth as human beings. One could summarize all of the problems in our society today as resulting from a lack of care in work. Many people work for money alone and fail to see that work is the way in which they can fulfill themselves and develop their characters, affect the lives of others, and contribute to the betterment of society.

In the words of Josemaria Escriva de Balaguer (1973):

> A complete range of virtues is called into play when we set about our work with the purpose of doing it well: fortitude, to persevere in our work despite the difficulties that might arise and to ensure that we never let ourselves be overwhelmed by anxiety; temperance, in order to spend ourselves unsparingly and to overcome our love of comfort and our selfishness; justice, so as to fulfill our duties toward God, society, our family and our fellow workers; prudence to know in each case what course to take, and then to set about it without hesitation. (p. 62)

According to Donna Barton, principal of the St. Joseph Montessori School in Columbus, Ohio, work is often discussed in terms of being the student's "job" for that is the Montessori philosophy. School is their workplace. Pride in work, completion, and content knowledge are expected. The curriculum used stresses knowledge in the content areas and is enhanced with daily discussions and tasks necessary to survive in the world of work.

ACADEMIC WORK IN THE BLUE RIBBON SCHOOLS

Schools need to help students to take their work seriously, perform it to the best of their ability, and thereby develop the qualities of character inherent in the capacity to work well. The Blue Ribbon Schools do this by setting high expectations for all students and finding ways to challenge gifted, average, and at-risk students. They realize that in order for students to be productive citizens and workers in the next century, they will need a strong foundation in literature, history, geography, science, economics, the arts, and other subjects. Therefore high-quality instruction appropriate to each child's age, grade and learning styles needs to be provided. Alternative modes of assessment help children to show what they have learned and thereby develop a positive self-image regarding their work as students.

Table 10 lists the instructional innovations mentioned by the Blue Ribbon Schools as key in their effort to develop the character of their students through schoolwork well done.

LEARNING THAT PROMOTES "ACHIEVEMENT SELF-ESTEEM"

Historically, one can see the different instructional emphases in different Blue Ribbon Award groups. Cooperative learning was in vogue in 1985–86. Then consideration of learning styles theory led to brain-related instruction and modality instruction in 1988–89. Whole language and thematic instruction dominated the early 1990s. The latest years of award winning schools tell about the value of teaching to the seven intelligences and using multiple forms of assessment. Why do the Blue Ribbon Schools cite these instructional methodologies as important contributors to the development of character? They are methodologies that help students to succeed at the work of learning. Academic success promotes a student's feeling of self-worth and accomplishment, the "achievement self-esteem" mentioned in the previous chapter.

The Red Bank Elementary School in California is "dedicated to preparing students for the 21st century by providing an academically rigorous and emotionally supportive program that promotes positive self-esteem, values, and personal growth for the leaders of tomorrow."

TABLE 10 Instructional methodologies cited by Blue Ribbon Schools.

Category	Count	Percent
Cooperative learning	39	15%
Learning styles	11	8%
Portfolio assessment	10	7%
Whole language	14	9%

Red Bank is a very large K–6 school with a population of 883 students, 21% of whom are ethnically and racially diverse. Students come from families that are middle- to upper-middle-class, well-educated semi-professionals who have a high regard for schools and education. In order to provide this environment, teachers target learning modalities, using both whole-class and small-group instruction. They use portfolios, journals, and new assessment techniques, hands-on science and field trips, and a relevant "real-life curriculum" that is developmentally appropriate while seeking to exercise higher-order thinking processes. They seek to integrate technology into the curriculum as a tool for the students to access in the learning process.

COOPERATIVE LEARNING

In cooperative learning, students work together to achieve shared learning goals and complete specific tasks and assignments. Students seek outcomes that are beneficial to all those in the cooperative learning group. A criteria-referenced evaluation system is used. Cooperative learning is different from traditional small-group work in the sense that there is individual accountability along with group or team rewards. Students need to develop interpersonal and small-group skills because there is positive interdependence as members of the group. "We sink or swim together" is a common cooperative learning motto (Johnson and Johnson, 1986a, 1986b).

There are many different cooperative learning methods in use that are applicable to a wide range of grade levels, subjects, and classrooms: Learning Together, Group Investigation, Jigsaw, Student Teams—Achievement Divisions and Teams-Games-Tournaments. For a complete description of these methods the reader is referred to *Learning Together and Alone* by David and Roger Johnson (1986b) and *Cooperative Learning* by Robert Slavin (1990). However, there are two cooperative learning methods that are particularly helpful in promoting high academic performance and the value of a student's work well done, as they are keyed into learning specific subject matter: Team Assisted Individualization (TAI) and Cooperative Integrated Reading and Composition (Slavin, 1990).

TAI provides for conceptually rich instruction in mathematics and can accommodate a wide range of student skills in one classroom. Unlike the more generic cooperative learning methods mentioned above, TAI includes its own set of instructional materials and implementation guide. Students work on different mathematics units in teams, check one another's work, help one another, and then take formative tests. The emphasis is on mastering the mathematical concepts of the unit before going on to other concepts. Research on the effectiveness of TAI has shown that the combined use of homogeneous teaching groups and heterogeneous work groups is both practical and effective (Slavin, 1991).

Cooperative Integrated Reading and Composition (CIRC) is a comprehensive program for teaching reading, writing, and language arts in the upper elementary grades. It emphasizes the metacognition activities in reading, and writing for revision. The major component of CIRC is heterogeneous reading groups that divide into pairs or triads (teams). After direct instruction from the teacher, the teams use their basal readers and do "partner reading," story-related writing, vocabulary and spelling, and story retelling. Students check one another's work, complete comprehension tests on the story, and engage in writing activities. Research on the effectiveness of CIRC has shown that solid gains in reading comprehension and vocabulary are achieved in comparison to students who did not participate. The most important result is that the process of working together helped students to improve academic skills and develop their characters. Curriculum materials for TAI and CIRC are available from The John Hopkins Team Learning Project, John Hopkins University, 3505 N. Charles St., Baltimore, MD 21218; phone: 301-338-8249.

One of the goals of the Spring Glen Elementary School in the state of Washington is to "encourage students to engage in cooperative strategies and team building techniques." Its staff believes that cooperative learning helps students practice proactive social skills by working together. Leadership, social skills, and democratic values are fostered in cooperative group-learning activities. Spring Glen tries to build a positive nurturing environment where each individual is valued and enriched, by providing students with

(*1*) An integrated curriculum that uses conceptual themes for the entire school, thus creating greater opportunity for meaning-driven learning to occur at all levels

(2) Learning modalities/styles instruction that teaches to the auditory, visual, tactual, or kinesthetic strengths of the students, thus increasing learning success

(3) Cooperative learning groups that emphasize team-building and communications skills for students to peer-tutor, problem-solve and make decisions

Research has consistently found that students in cooperative learning classes have significantly greater achievement than do students in control group classes not using cooperative learning (Slavin, 1991). Several researchers working on cooperative learning techniques have found that in addition, these methods increase students' self-esteem due to the sense of accomplishment engendered. Most importantly, cooperative learning leads to other benefits that are more directly related to character development. A 1990 study by Solomon and others found that students who had been taught cooperatively ranked significantly higher than control students when measured for supportive, friendly, and pro-social behavior, and they were better at resolving conflicts and supporting democratic values (cited in Slavin, 1991). Johnson and Johnson (1986a) acknowledge that to achieve mutual goals, students must develop skills at working together that include (1) getting to know and trust one another, (2) learning to communicate accurately, (3) accepting and supporting one another, and (4) resolving conflicts constructively. Lickona (1991) states that character development benefits of using the cooperative learning instructional process include growth in interpersonal moral skills such as increased perspective-taking, appreciation of those who are different, and valuing cooperation. Philip Fitch Vincent (1994), author of *A Primer: Developing Character in Students*, agrees that cooperative learning is a valuable tool in the development of character. He has found that this process helps students to develop good character traits such as being responsible for their work, being respectful of the abilities of others, and caring for others and for the finished product.

LEARNING STYLES

"Learning style" is conceptualized as a biologically and developmentally determined set of personal characteristics that influence the way students perceive, process, and learn. The Blue Ribbon Schools are well versed in the different theories of "characterizing" learning styles instructional strategies. Some use right- and left-brain instruction; some mention 4MAT or Gardner's work on "Multiple Intelligences"; others use a combination of teaching for learning styles and learning modalities. Research has found that student achievement is significantly higher whenever students are taught through approaches that allow them to learn through their preferred styles. In addition, the research shows that when students are permitted to learn difficult academic information or skills through their identified preferences, they tend to achieve statistically higher test and attitude scores than when instruction is dissonant with their preferences (Dunn et al., 1989). This success at the "work of learning" helps students to realize the high expectations for learning that the Blue Ribbon Schools hold for all students. "High expectations for student achievement" have been found to be "what works" in schools; that is, it is one of the characteristics of effective schools and a mark of a high standard of excellence in the school (U.S. Department of Education, 1987).

In order to actualize their philosophy that "All Children Can Learn," the staff at the Quail Creek Elementary School in Oklahoma use instructional strategies geared towards learning styles and "hands-on" techniques:

> Children at Quail Creek are allowed to experience the educational process in the style most conducive to their individual modes of learning. Teachers develop strategies around visual, tactile, auditory, and manipulative modalities, within the learning process. Children have the opportunity to excel in their learning mode. This is important as all children have different abilities and talents. Our desire is to see that all children are comfortable in the learning process.

Quail Creek is a K–5 school in Oklahoma City with a heterogeneous student body of 350, 10% of whom are African-American, and 5% Asian; with almost 10% from lower-income families.

Dr. Cherry Jones, the principal at Flanders Elementary School in Connecticut, explains that her teachers are aware of the many different types of intelligences as reported by Gardner (1983) in *Frames of Mind: The Theory of Multiple Intelligences,* and the different learning styles summarized by McCarthy (1983):

> We approach our students as individuals who *all* have special gifts and talents. Each teacher plans lessons that address the various types of learning

styles of individual students and stimulates them through both individual and group activities. All children have gifts and talents and we attempt to let every child shine.

According to Lickona (1991), Gardner's theory of multiple intelligences helps students to develop their unique talents. By helping students identify their strengths, that is, their intelligences, teachers can guide them toward fields of work in which they will be competent and satisfied because their talents will fit these jobs well. As Gardner (1995) points out, "there are hundreds and hundreds of ways to succeed and many different abilities that get you there."

Nadine Mouse, principal at St. Thomas More School in Houston, Texas, explains how learning styles instruction also helps students to develop their characters:

> Taking responsibility for one's own learning is an important goal at our school. To help students achieve this, we all completed learning style inventories during orientation at the beginning of the school year. The following week, an afternoon was devoted to acquainting each student with his or her special style—visual, auditory, or bodily-kinesthetic. Students formed groups with others of their preferred style. Teachers then shared research data and personal learning experience concerning the most effective ways of receiving, processing, and giving back information for each style.

Knowledge of learning styles helps students appreciate their own uniqueness and to understand the different needs of others. It gives them knowledge of their intellectual strengths and awareness of areas in which they will be more challenged. It helps them to make informed choices that will help them to study and learn better. Learning styles helps students to learn about their personality and character. All of us are unique, with certain strengths and certain areas of concern. People of character seek to capitalize on their positive qualities while learning to change or compensate for their weaknesses.

INTEGRATED LANGUAGE ARTS OR "WHOLE LANGUAGE" INSTRUCTION

Years of research in linguistics, psycho-linguistics, sociology, anthropology, philosophy, child development, curriculum, composition and literary theory, semiotics, and other fields have contributed to the development of the concept of whole language. Whole language seeks to connect skills, concepts, and content through integrated, theme-based, learning activities (Robbins, 1990). Instead of using short selections of stories in a basal text, this methodology has students reading whole books starting in kindergarten. The story in each book leads to major theme-related projects. A comprehensive and extensive array of classical literature forms the backbone of an integrated language arts program. Although one of the criticisms of whole language instruction was its failure to teach phonics, most of the Blue Ribbon Schools have integrated phonics and spelling instruction within this reading program (Ogden and Germinario, 1994).

The use of a whole language program at Burrus Elementary School in Marietta, Georgia has greatly helped to motivate students who now see a clearer purpose for reading and writing, according to Jerry Locke, the principal. Burruss is a school of 570 culturally diverse students; 24% African-American, 20% from low-income families, and 11% who qualify for special education services.

> Other instructional strategies that motivate students are extensive use of cooperative learning . . . integrated content areas, hands-on math activities and a continually changing assortment of interesting learning activities. The school motto, "Burruss Beavers are Real Achievers," reflects a commitment to motivation and learning.

Research evaluating the effectiveness of whole language instructional techniques has found that "student achievement is strongly affected when reading and writing are taught as integral and connected processes" (Robbins, 1990).

Why do the Blue Ribbon Schools consider whole language instruction relevant to the development of the character of their students? First, whole language instruction helps students to see the unity of knowledge; instead of seeing academics as discrete subjects that have no connection to one another, students read, write and speak about topics that naturally flow from the content of the book they have read. Second, a good whole language program has students reading classical literature. According to Vincent (1994), "Great readings illuminate human struggles, successes, strengths, weaknesses, virtues, and vices. A study of great ideas allows us to gain greater understanding of ourselves" (p. 111). Third, whole language engages students in reading for the sake and excitement of reading. There is no better way to discover the joy in working hard to learn, than to discover the joy inherent in learning to read.

THEMATIC INSTRUCTION

When teachers are able to apply whole language principles that link reading and writing activities to other subject matters, students are able to make interdisciplinary connections. At the Whittier Elementary School in Lawton, Oklahoma, teachers use Expressions, a cross-discipline curriculum that utilizes the interrelationships of the physical, mental, and creative processes:

> The purpose of Expressions is to organize the students' experience in art, music, language, drama and movement into a curriculum rich with multi-sensory experiences. It also provides for the students' growth in attitude, conduct and self-esteem. A strand of values runs through Expressions: truth, beauty, justice, love and faith. These values give their students an understanding of humanity.

Whittier is a K–6 school of 287 racially/ethnically diverse students living in a small town, 20% of whom come from low-income families.

Interdisciplinary, or thematic instruction, while maintaining the centrality of content-based knowledge, integrates social studies, science, mathematics, and literature to foster the pursuit of knowledge and understanding of a particular theme or the resolution of a specific problem (Hiebert & Fisher, 1990). At Centennial Elementary School in Tucson, Arizona, higher-level thinking skills, curricular, and technological areas are integrated into thematic units. These units often have differentiated assignments and a variety of activities so that students of different academic levels are challenged and enriched:

> An example is the fourth-grade unit on Native Americans. Students use reading, writing, and spelling to prepare a research report and oral presentation on authentic Indian weapons, tools, games, homes, artwork, and handcrafts. They learn the science of firing pots, the importance of math as the kachina maker teaches them about proportions. Through art, students use authentic colors and materials to make corn jewelry, sand paintings, and story turtles. Higher-level thinking becomes a natural part of the unit as students compare and contrast different cultures and draw conclusions about environmental adaptations tribes have had to make.

When students are presented with a real problem that needs to be studied and solved, they have the satisfaction of working on an authentic task that has tangible consequences for them. Participation in these authentic activities allows them to develop a real sense of purpose and motivation as they seek to arrive at "action-oriented" solutions to real social problems. One of the most popular themes mentioned in the Blue Ribbon Schools was the study of the environment, which often led students to set up recycling programs in their schools and even in their communities.

Thematic instruction helps students to develop their thinking skills and strategies. Students develop higher-order thinking skills as they compare and contrast two characters in a story and analyze and evaluate characters' choices and authors' purposes. Developing thinking skills is key to developing character, as students need to be able to reason, make decisions, and take the perspective of others in order to develop moral knowing, an essential element of good character (Lickona, 1991).

At Saigling School in Plano, Texas, the emphasis on critical, evaluative, and creative thinking seen in the rigorous, content-rich academic program extends into the citizenship program. Students express their social responsibility by regular community service projects that address areas of concern that the students with their teachers have identified. Philip Vincent (1994) states that one of the major functions of education is to develop in students the ability to think clearly and consistently. Only by becoming adept at thinking can we know the good and therefore pursue it.

Thematic instruction shares many of the character-building advantages of whole language instruction mentioned above. In addition, it gives students opportunities to investigate further the areas of interest to them that are related to the unit. Letting students' interest be the subject of their investigation maximizes their involvement in learning and often liberates astonishing energies for work. This gives students the opportunities to make commitments to develop real expertise in given subjects or skills. When students achieve this expertise, competence becomes part of their self-images, and they are more motivated to do quality work in other areas as well (Lickona, 1991).

PORTFOLIOS AND AUTHENTIC ASSESSMENT

Dr. Joya Chatterjee, principal at Westwood Elementary School in Santa Clara, California, explained that the school has moved from a traditional grade-based report card to a portfolio-based authentic evaluation system in order to realize a profound change in the instructional process. Many Blue Ribbon Schools have turned to portfolio assessment as a strategy for creating a classroom assessment system that includes multiple measures taken over time. "Portfolios have the advantage of containing several samples of student work assembled in a purposeful manner. Well-conceived portfolios include pieces representing both work in progress and "showpiece" samples, student reflections about their work, and evaluation criteria" (Herman et al., 1992, p. 120).

The Summerville Elementary School in Summerville, South Carolina, uses portfolios to measure the effectiveness of their instructional strategies. They have students include works in the portfolios that show what they have learned. These may include teacher-made assessments, class projects or activities completed, writing samples, and completed exercises in any other subjects. The teachers' efforts to foster critical and creative thinking enable these students to become active learners rather than passive receivers, with the ability to do productive thinking, forecasting, decision making, and planning.

Portfolios allow students to evaluate their own work according to the high standards expressed in a rubric. Students are able to strive on their own to meet these high standards, making them their own. Through authentic assessments, students are allowed to show that they have learned the given content to such a high level that they can actually perform the new skills in a real-life situation. Authentic assessments help students to develop their character because they help them to see that they are not just learning for the sake of test scores and grades; they are learning so that they can help make a difference in the world by using their knowledge to solve real-life problems.

SUMMARY

As this chapter demonstrates, the Blue Ribbon teachers use the latest pedagogical methodologies to enable their students to be successful academically. The students' success helps them develop their characters through the efforts they expend in doing their work as students well. Specifically, cooperative learning methodologies help students develop character qualities of responsibility, understanding of others, and team spirit. Learning styles instruction allows students to learn about themselves and take responsibility for their own learning. Whole language and thematic instruction help students develop thinking skills that are key to developing moral reasoning. Portfolios and alternative assessments enable students to show that they have worked hard at their job as students and have learned the required knowledge and skills. The Blue Ribbon Schools successfully engage their students in learning and thereby develop their intrinsic motivation. Students develop healthy self-esteem built on the realization of jobs well done.

The role of education is to help develop students into good people. Since students do not become good just because one tells them to be good, we have to look at how what they study and how they study it helps them develop good character traits (Vincent, 1994). The Blue Ribbon Schools help students develop their character by giving them the opportunity to do their work as students well by encouraging them through different instructional methodologies to work hard at their job of learning.

REFERENCES

Armstrong, T. 1994. *Multiple Intelligences in the Classroom.* Alexandria, VA: ASCD.

Dunn, R., J. Beaudry and A. Kavis. 1989. "Survey of Research on Learning Styles," *Educational Leadership*, 46(6):50–58.

Escriva de Balaguer, J. 1973. "Working for God," in *Friends of God.* New York: Scepter, p. 62.

Gardner, H. 1983. *Frames of Mind: The Theory of Multiple Intelligences.* New York: Basic Books.

Gardner, H. 1995. "Reflections on Multiple Intelligences: Myths and Messages," *Phi Delta Kappan*, 77(3):200–209.

Herman, J., P. Aschbacher, L. Winters. 1992. *A Practical Guide to Alternative Assessment.* Alexandria, VA: Association for Supervision and Curriculum Development.

Hiebert, E. and C. Fisher. 1990. "Whole Language: Three Themes for the Future," *Educational Leadership*, 47(6):62–63.

Johnson, D. and Johnson, R. 1986a. *Circles of Learning: Cooperation in the Classroom*, revised edition. Edina, MN: Interaction Book Co.

Johnson, D. and Johnson, R. 1986b. *Learning Together and Alone*, 2nd ed. Englewood Cliffs, NJ: Prentice-Hall.

Kilpatrick, W. 1992. *Why Johnny Can't Tell Right from Wrong.* New York: Simon and Schuster.

Lickona, T. 1991. *Educating for Character: How Our Schools Can Teach Respect and Responsibility.* New York: Bantam Books.

McCarthy, B. 1983. *4-MAT in Action*. Oak Brook, IL: EXCEL, Inc.

McKeon, R. 1941. *The Basic Works of Aristotle*. New York: Random House.

National Association of Elementary School Principals. 1994. *Best Ideas from America's Blue Ribbon Schools*. Thousand Oaks, CA: Corwin Press.

National Association of Elementary School Principals. 1995. *Best Ideas from America's Blue Ribbon Schools, Vol 2*. Thousand Oaks, CA: Corwin Press.

Ogden, E. and V. Germinario. 1994. *The Nation's Best Schools: Blueprints for Excellence, Vol. 1: Elementary and Middle Schools*. Lancaster, PA.: Technomic Publishing Co., Inc.

Robbins, P. 1990. "Implementing Whole Language," *Educational Leadership*, 47(60):50–51.

Slavin, R. 1990. *Cooperative Learning: Theory, Research, and Practice*. Boston, MA: Allyn & Bacon.

Slavin, R. 1991. "Synthesis of Research on Cooperative Learning," *Educational Leadership*, 48 (5):71–82.

United States Department of Education. 1987. *What Works: Research about Teaching and Learning*, 2nd ed. Pueblo, CO: USDE.

Vincent, P.F. 1994. *A Primer: Developing Character in Students*. Chapel Hill, NC: New View Publications

Wynne, E. and K. Ryan. 1993. *Reclaiming Our Schools: A Handbook on Teaching Character, Academics, and Discipline*. New York: Macmillan Publishing Co.

Chapter 7

HOW DO DISCIPLINE PROGRAMS DEVELOP GOOD CHARACTER?

To be what we are, and to become what we are capable of becoming, is the only end of life.—Robert Louis Stevenson

A good teacher is one who drives the students to think.—Anonymous

It isn't what the student is today that counts. It's what the student will be tomorrow.—Anonymous

DISCIPLINE AS MORAL EDUCATION

Discipline is a fundamental element of moral education, according to Emile Durkheim (1973). This concurs with what the National Education Association's Committee of Fifteen wrote over 100 years ago: "the substantial moral training of the school is performed by discipline rather than by the instruction in ethical theory. The essence of moral behavior is self-control" (cited in Bennett, 1988, p. 56). The criteria set up by the U.S. Department of Education's National Recognition Program states that "for any school to be judged deserving of recognition . . . the school should have an atmosphere that is orderly, purposeful, and conducive to learning and good character. . . . There must be a strong commitment to educational excellence for all students and a record of progress in sustaining the school's best features and solving its problems" (U.S. Department of Education, 1994, p. 2).

Nearly one-fourth of the Blue Ribbon Award–winning schools (see Table 5) defined character development as "having good discipline and good behavior," and almost as many (about one-fifth; see Table 2)

133

stated that they used their discipline programs to promote character development. One could assume that all of the Blue Ribbon Schools maintained effective classroom and schoolwide discipline, even if they were not conscious of this as a form of character education and did not mention it in their answers to this particular question. Schools with good discipline have students whose behavior shows that they are living the third aspect of good character, moral action. They are choosing to perform the appropriate actions in different school situations.

This chapter summarizes the main ways the Blue Ribbon Schools promote character development through their discipline programs. It tries to answer the following questions:

- What are some important qualities of proactive discipline programs that help to foster the development of good character?
- How can a character development program help a school to create a safe and orderly environment?
- What are the most effective discipline programs found in the Blue Ribbon Schools today?
- What are the "character development" advantages of having class meetings?
- Why is it important that school rules be stated positively if they are to be an important means for promoting character development in students?
- Why is it important to teach children how to resolve conflicts and mediate disagreements peacefully in order for them to develop good characters?

DISCIPLINE PROGRAMS
THAT EMPHASIZE CHARACTER TRAITS

Several Blue Ribbon Schools have discipline programs that could be considered character-developing because they emphasize specific good character traits. Richard Curwin (1995) believes that discipline programs should not be based on a system of rewards and punishments, but should be based on values. The best way to set up a values-based discipline program is to develop the value principles prior to rules. The principles are general attitudes, (e.g., be respectful) and provide the reason for following the rules. The Brookridge Elementary School in Shawnee Mission, Kansas, a large K–6 suburban school with a homogeneous student body, has "Five Key Behaviors" that it expects students to demonstrate at all times: "caring, concern, courtesy, responsibility, and respect." The handbook states:

> We believe that the best decisions for managing student behavior are based on a value system that maintains the dignity of each student in all situations. Behaving responsibly is more valued that behaving obediently. It is our goal to help students develop appropriate behaviors through understanding and acceptance in lieu of excessive extrinsic rewards and punishments. We know that good teaching is holistic and discipline is an integral part of the entire teaching experience. Good discipline is related to fair rules, consistency of application, and most importantly, to outstanding teaching.

Similarly, the Perley Elementary School in South Bend, Indiana, has its "Five C's—Caring, Courteous, Cooperative, Considerate, Committed to Learning" that define its expectations for character and behavior in its students. Perley is a K–6 school located in the inner-city section of South Bend. The students are from diverse socioeconomic and racial backgrounds. A visit to the school reveals that the 5 C's hang at the front hallway and in each classroom. The 5 C's are reinforced many times throughout the day and thus encourage students to act appropriately and to use them to resolve problems appropriately.

As mentioned in Chapter 3, the character traits promoted in the Plano, Texas, School district include courtesy, courage, discipline, honesty, human worth and dignity, justice, patriotism, personal obligation for the public good, respect for self and others, respect for authority, tolerance, and responsibility. To reinforce these traits, the staff refers to them during any disciplinary actions. Saigling Elementary has the most diverse population of the Plano schools. It has over 600 students in pre-K to fifth grade. The student body includes over 10% Asian-American students. Arlene Carnes, the counselor, mentioned during the author's visit to the school that when a student is disciplined with an in-school suspension, she discusses the incident with the student, reviewing the school's character traits and deciding which ones were negatively demonstrated by the student's actions. Then, to reinforce the meaning of the citizenship traits, the student reads books that demonstrate traits being used positively and writes a one-page essay discussing the traits. Finally, the principal, student, and parents discuss the essay.

DISCIPLINE THAT DEVELOPS CHARACTER

As mentioned in Chapter 2, some researchers define "character" as "practicing good discipline and being positively helpful to one's peers and to all adults" (Walberg & Wynne, 1989). A discipline program that teaches self-control can truly be a character development program because it spells out specific qualities or virtues to be developed. It seeks to help students internalize the locus of control of behavior. The New Canaan Country School in Connecticut states in its goals its belief that "mannerly behavior contributes significantly to the learning environment as well as to the character development of students." New Canaan is an independent K–9 school founded with the mission of "helping every child in its charge to develop a character built upon sound moral, spiritual, and intellectual values." New Canaan is located in a very affluent, homogeneous community. The staff believes that helping young people learn the skills of self-control and motivation to become productive, contributing, and knowledgeable adult participants in society is one of the most important tasks that good teachers undertake. They would agree with other educators who maintain that these are teachable and learnable skills (Schultz, 1995).

TRUE DISCIPLINE IS SELF-DISCIPLINE

At St. Thomas More School in Ohio, students learn the value of self-discipline when they turn in homework assignments on time; of courtesy when they raise a hand before answering; of punctuality when they come to class on time; of good judgment when they hear teachers emphasize that there is a difference between good and bad, and right and wrong. Ethical judgements are formed when students begin to see and understand the connection between education and "real life." St. Thomas More School is a Catholic K–8 school with students from both suburban and urban middle- and lower-class economic backgrounds, most of whom are the third generation coming from a European ethnic background.

DISCIPLINE AS PART OF THE EDUCATIONAL PROCESS

The teachers at the Monte Garden Elementary School in suburban Bakersfield, California, believe that discipline is an educational process in which students are taught expectations for behavior and re-inforced for achieving those expectations. Monte Garden has a large diverse student population that includes 10% Hispanic students and 10% Asian students. Effective and consistent communication with parents is another key factor in its discipline program. All teachers have a discipline program in place in their classrooms. Some use a unique money system at the intermediate level whereby bank accounts are established for each student in which he or she can earn money for good behavior decisions or have money taken out for poor behavior decisions. The policy is to reward the positive.

ROLE OF THE TEACHER
IN PROMOTING GOOD DISCIPLINE

An interesting trend found in the later years of reports is an emphasis on the role of the teacher in promoting good discipline: "Good classroom control is largely dependent upon a well-planned, interesting program and mutual respect between pupil and teacher. A pleasant orderly environment is conducive to good discipline." Another example: "Effective classroom management, appropriate planning and interesting material are the primary means for preventing discipline problems." Schultz (1995) asserts that teachers bear moral and ethical responsibilities for promoting responsible social behavior in the classroom. They elicit the best work and behavior from children by modeling this themselves. Teachers are asked to teach to different learning styles and thereby involve all students in learning: "With a focus on multiple intelligences, children at Governor Bent Elementary School [in Albuquerque, New Mexico] learn to recognize and appreciate the strengths of others. Students are applauded by their peers for their differences and those differences serve to strengthen and unite the community of learners within each classroom."

HIGH EXPECTATIONS

Many of the Blue Ribbon Schools explicitly mentioned having high expectations of students' behavior, encouraging them to be self-disciplined and to take personal responsibility for their actions, and fostering in students a respect for others, thereby helping them develop their characters. Some of the schools stated their discipline philosophy in their applications: "True discipline is self-discipline"; "Discipline stresses personal pride in being responsible"; and "High expectations is the key to discipline."

Sister Lora Ann Slavinski, the principal of St. Stanislaus School, a Catholic K-8 school with a diverse Polish and Hispanic student population in Chicago, Illinois, explains: "A consistent discipline program sets a standard which encompasses all aspects of character development. The staff sets the example by appropriate role modeling, respect toward others, compassion, and a professional demeanor with students. Expectations are high. Students are held accountable for their actions. Mistakes are not character flaws but opportunities to grow." A visit to the school revealed that the strong ethnic background of the students is a great influence on their characters. A strong work ethic and an appreciation for the value of education is a part of the Polish culture; and the Hispanic students are taught by their parents to obey and be respectful.

THE PROACTIVE APPROACH TO DISCIPLINE

John Leuke, the principal at Frankfort Junior High School in Illinois, explains that their goal has always been a proactive instead of a reactive approach to discipline. Frankfort is a relatively new school located on a seventeen acre site in a rural setting forty miles southwest of Chicago. The school has a homogeneous student body of 400 from a rapidly developing, upper-middle-class suburban community. The school's Tiger Gold Card Program focuses on responsibility and good citizenship. Students earn a card and its privileges by observing the school rules:

- Respect the rights and property of others.
- Be on time.
- Be prepared.
- No gum or candy.

The gold card can be used in the business community for discounts when purchasing items at cooperating establishments. Mr. Leuke commented that the middle-school students at Frankfort strive very hard to get and to keep their Gold Card. It is as important to them as getting a driver's license is for their older brothers and sisters.

One can ask, what is the character-development rationale for such a system? Rewards like this are successful in increasing the probability that students will act respectfully in school. But these rewards must be judged on whether they lead to lasting change—change that persists even when the extrinsic motivation is no longer there. Will they help students develop the habits and good character of a responsible person? Will the Frankfort Middle School students bother to follow rules in other situations—the mall, the family, and so on—where there is no pay-off? Mr. Leuke thinks that the students will, as the Tiger Gold Card is something important to them. It represents a personal commitment that they have made to be responsible in their behavior. As developing adolescents, it is important for them to make this emotional commitment to following rules.

CREATING SAFE SCHOOLS

Several of the schools reported that one of their claims to meriting the Outstanding School Award is the fact that they have changed in a few years from having poor discipline to very good discipline. They answered in detail the application question: "Summarize your school's overall approach to discipline. Describe any special procedures or programs used to maintain order and discipline throughout your school. What factors contribute most to order in your school?" These award-winning schools created safe schools through very conscious school-wide efforts to integrate character development throughout the curriculum and throughout the school community. Table 11 lists the various discipline programs or approaches mentioned by the Blue Ribbon Schools.

ASSERTIVE DISCIPLINE
AND "MODIFIED" ASSERTIVE DISCIPLINE

The most common commercial program found in 26% of the schools is Assertive Discipline by Canter and Canter (1976). The key to this pro-

*TABLE 11 Discipline programs
used in the Blue Ribbon Schools.*

Category	Count	Percent of Responses
Assertive discipline	92	26%
Modified assertive discipline	9	3%
Behavior modification	3	1%
Catch them being good	19	5%
Class meetings and problem solving	43	13%
Conflict management	22	6%
Cooperative discipline	22	6%
Discipline with love and logic	4	1%
Good citizenship	9	3%
Handbook/class rules	78	22%
Moral discipline	19	5%
Positive discipline	63	18%
Quality schools	15	8%
Red yellow green	3	1%
Respect, responsibility	16	5%
Schoolwide	11	3%
Missing values	4	1%

Cases, 339; missing cases, 11.

gram is that the students are told clearly what behavior is expected of them, how that behavior will be rewarded, and what the consequences will be when behavioral expectations are violated. Behavior modification is the predominant philosophy of education underlying Assertive Discipline. Although Assertive Discipline was found in a total of 26% of the sample of Blue Ribbon School applications examined, it was most common in the 1987–88 year. Assertive Discipline—with its emphases on rewards and punishments—reinforces immature character development (Stages 1 and 2 in Kohlberg's theory—Punishment-obedience and Instrumental-relativistic) and therefore *cannot* be considered a good character education strategy. It is a model that fosters obedience to an authority figure rather than personal responsibility (Render et al., 1989; Curwin & Mendler, 1988; Lickona, 1991).

In more recent years, there has been a definite trend toward using what schools call a "modified" Assertive Discipline program, in response to research showing that Assertive Discipline worked only when the teacher was present. The Susan Lindgren Intermediate Center in St. Louis Park, Minnesota, explains that its student discipline policy has been modified from a more Assertive Discipline "ticketing" approach to one that inserts reason between impulse and action. Students explained the change in these words: "Last year we had yellow and white slips. This year we have lessons." The focus is on helping the students understand about being good. The school's discipline program now utilizes a participatory process that involves all students. Guidelines for responsible behavior are developed cooperatively by, the teacher and the students. The diverse student body in this large, grades 3–6 middle school, located in a suburb of Minneapolis, includes Russian and Asian immigrants as well as white and African-American students. Family income level is also diverse, from upper-middle-class income to over 15% from lower-income families. The staff at the Lindgren School strongly believes that when students have input into classroom and school policy, they become better executors of the policies. This practice is supported by substantial research indicating that people are more inclined to obey rules when they have had a significant part in determining them (Ban, 1994).

BEHAVIOR MODIFICATION TECHNIQUES THAT PROMOTE CHARACTER DEVELOPMENT

Behavior modification per se was mentioned in only a very few of the school reports but behavior modification techniques were listed in many applications: for example, rewarding appropriate behavior by giving first place in line, a star on the classroom or behavior charts, or the issuance of good behavior slips that can be refunded. "Time-out" often takes the form of a "Time to Think Room," or a special place in the room, and is mentioned as an effective method for modifying inappropriate behavior. At St. Mark the Evangelist Catholic School, staff explained, "In the formative years of a child's development, external rewards and punishment may be necessary, but the ultimate goal is that the child internalize modes of acceptable behavior." St. Mark's is a relatively new K–8 Catholic School in Plano, Texas, with a diverse student body of almost 450 that includes Hispanic, Asian, and white students.

Whenever behavior management is used in the Blue Ribbon Schools, staff try to preserve the dignity of the individual student. For example, Shirley E. Anderson, the principal at the Washington School in

Mundelein, Illinois, explains: "Our discipline program is based on the belief that all children can behave appropriately, all children have human dignity and worth, and that behavior is maintained by consequences. Positive consequences are most powerful." Washington is a K–5 school of over 400 students including almost 10% Hispanic students.

CATCH STUDENTS DOING SOMETHING RIGHT

In 10% of the Blue Ribbon Schools, The One Minute Manager philosophy of Spenser Johnson and Ken Blanchard (1982) has been applied, and teachers, staff, and administrators seek to "catch students doing something right." With this proactive system, students are encouraged to act correctly because these positive actions are acknowledged. There is clearly a trend in the last few Blue Ribbon Award years, to emphasize a proactive approach to promoting pro-social behaviors. Another example of this is found at the Eric Norfeldt School in West Hartford, Connecticut, which stresses kindness, consideration, and respect for others. Students have rights and responsibilities. Norfeldt is a school of 400 students. The school has a diverse student population due to its participation in a voluntary desegregation program that buses students from the inner city of Hartford to the school.

THE CLASS MEETING

The class meeting has become very popular in both private and public schools as a means for solving classroom management problems and as a component of their character development and good discipline programs. The St. Rosalie School, located in Harvey, Louisiana, a suburb of New Orleans, uses the classroom meeting in order to solve class or school behavior problems cooperatively. St. Rosalie School is a Catholic K–8 school with over 1000 students, representing diverse racial and ethnic backgrounds including Italian, Cajun, African-American, Oriental, and various European. According to the teachers, the classroom meeting "helps develop students' self-confidence, self-respect, and ultimately self-discipline." It also helps to create a good moral environment, provides an experience in democracy, and involves students in making decisions about the life of the classroom (Lickona, 1991).

One procedure for conducting a problem-solving class meeting, using a circle discussion, is as follows (Pereira, 1988):

(*1*) At the teacher's signal, all chairs are arranged in a circle so each participant has eye contact.

(*2*) The agenda is announced, and students are welcomed to add other items to the agenda.

(*3*) A method is determined for allowing each person who wishes to speak.

(*4*) No interruptions are permitted while students are sharing their ideas and comments.

(*5*) All comments are recorded and discussed; consensus is arrived at regarding the planned course of action.

(*6*) A timeline is agreed upon in order to implement the solution decided: tasks are assigned to volunteers.

(*7*) The date of the next meeting is announced. At that time the outcomes of this new decision will be evaluated.

CONFLICT RESOLUTION AND PEER MEDIATION

The most popular movement today in all schools, including the Blue Ribbon Schools, is teaching students and teachers how to resolve conflicts or disagreements in a peaceful manner. This proactive mode teaches social skills, for example, for negotiation, mediation, anger control, refusal, and problem solving. It teaches students how to listen, instead of punishing them for not listening. Teaching all students negotiation and mediation procedures and skills results in a schoolwide program empowering students to solve their own problems and regulate their own and their classmates' behavior (Johnson et al., 1992).

Richard O'Brien, the principal at the Snug Harbor Community School in Quincy, Massachusetts, explains that his school has adopted a philosophy of nonviolence. It implemented a schoolwide (preschool through fifth grade) violence prevention and conflict resolution program called "Second Step" that has improved the overall school climate, created an environment more conducive to learning, and helped to end acts of violence. The program teaches conflict resolution and provides students with concrete skills to deal with empathy, anger, and peer pressure. Snug Harbor is an ethnically and linguistically diverse school with limited-English students who represent six different language backgrounds. The school also has a successful Conflict Manager program. All fifth-graders are trained in Conflict Management by the end of the year. These Conflict Managers are cited by the students as people to whom they can go if they had academic or personal problems.

Conflict resolution is a method that enables people to interact with each other in positive ways in order to resolve their differences. Peer mediation programs take the next step: They empower students to intervene in the conflicts of others and thereby share responsibility for creating a safe and secure school environment. A peer mediation program's first objective is to ensure that all students have learned the basic skills required to resolve conflicts. Then a staff member, usually a guidance counselor or teacher, supervises fifteen to twenty hours of training the student mediators. Peer mediators may be nominated by teachers or chosen by peers. Stomfay-Stitz (1994) suggests that all students serve as peer mediators on a rotating basis after mastering the basic skills. This gives all students the opportunity to benefit from having this special kind of social responsibility.

Johnson and Johnson (1995) have found that a comprehensive conflict resolution program has three major components: (1) creating a cooperative context, (2) implementing a conflict resolution/peer mediation program, and (3) using academic controversies for instructional purposes.

At the Pioneer Elementary School, with its homogeneous population of 688 students located in the mid-size city of Colorado Springs, "discipline is a growth from dependence to independence. Students resolve their own conflicts using I messages. Conflict management training promotes participatory citizenship and personal responsibility." Research on the effectiveness of conflict resolution programs has been very positive (Johnson & Johnson, 1995). When conflicts are managed successfully, they can increase achievement, develop higher level reasoning, and build problem-solving skills; they also energize individuals to take action, promote caring and committed relations, and help students to understand others.

RESOLVING CONFLICTS PEACEFULLY

One example of a conflict resolution program, found in the Aikahi Elementary School in Hawaii, is Peace on the Playground. Students are trained as mediators or Recess Refs to arbitrate disputes and help other students work out misunderstandings. Aikahi is a K–6 school with a culturally diverse population of almost six hundred students, 25% of whom are Asian and 12% from lower-income families. Another program used in this same Hawaiian school is "Peace Begins with Me," which promotes nonviolent attitudes and behavior. The program teaches that each person is unique and has strengths and limitations, rights and responsibilities. The concept of peace education is multifaceted and cross-disciplinary; it includes peace and social justice, economic well-being, political participation, nonviolence, conflict resolution and concern for the environment (Stomfay-Stitz, 1993). For more information on the curriculum "Teaching Students to Be Peacemakers," contact: David and Roger Johnson, 7208 Cornelia Drive, Edina, MN 55435.

From Moorestown Friends School in New Jersey to Argonaut Elementary School in Saratoga, California, and from Centennial Elementary School in Tucson, Arizona, to the Volker Learning Magnet in Kansas City, Missouri, peer mediation and conflict resolution are being taught to students as this decade's solution to discipline problems. While traditional discipline procedures teach students to depend on authority figures to resolve conflicts, peacemaking programs teach students how to mediate disputes and negotiate solutions themselves (Johnson et al., 1992). In the process, such programs are also developing strengths of character such as good judgment, perspective-taking, self-control, and personal responsibility.

COOPERATIVE DISCIPLINE

A number of schools reported using Cooperative Discipline (Albert, 1990), a classroom management system that promotes self-esteem by reinforcing cooperative behavior on the part of students. Using a comprehensive approach, Cooperative Discipline deals with all three discipline types: corrective, preventive and supportive. It addresses the topics of motivating students, avoiding and defusing confrontations, reinforcing desirable behavior, building student self-esteem, involving parents, and applying discipline cooperatively. A multimedia package for implementing this system can be obtained from the American Guidance Service, P.O. Box 99, Publisher's Building, Circle Pines, MN 55014-1796.

DEVELOPING GOOD DECISION-MAKING SKILLS

There is a clear emphasis in the Blue Ribbon Schools on developing good decision-making skills in students as a way to promote good behavior. At Spring Glen Elementary School in Renton, Washington, the principal explains that the values emphasized at the school are respect, responsibility, and safety. In order to promote these values, the teachers encourage the students to use problem-solving strategies to make responsible choices. This results in a safe and respectful physical and emotional environment. Staff believe that appropriate behavior is self-motivated and is celebrated and recognized through clear, consistent consequences. Spring Glen is a K–6 school of about 400 students, almost 10% of whom are of Asian background.

DISCIPLINE WITH LOVE AND LOGIC

Jim Fay's "Discipline with Love and Logic" (cited in Fay & Funk, 1995) is mentioned in the 1991–92 and 1993–94 award-winning school applications. It is used at the Pioneer Elementary School in Colorado Springs. Pioneer has 688 students, 10% of whom are from lower income families. The students come from diverse racial and ethnic backgrounds: 85% white and the rest almost an equal percentage of Asians, African-Americans, and Hispanics. The Discipline with Love and Logic program is a system for developing natural and logical consequences instead of rewards and punishments. It involves the teacher giving the student encouragement that communicates love, support, and valuing each child as a person. The Three Rules of Love and Logic for the Teacher are:

(*1*) Use enforceable limits.
(*2*) Provide choices within limits.
(*3*) Apply natural and logical consequences with empathy.

The philosophy of Discipline with Love and Logic is that it fosters personal responsibility and respect for self and others. It states that discipline involves building students *up* so they feel more capable and better about themselves, even after a discipline situation. It asks the teacher not to rely on *external* controls to maintain students' behavior, but to get students to develop *internal* controls. Jim Fay's philosophy states that instead of *making* kids behave, the goal is to make them *want* to behave (cited in Fay & Funk, 1995). This emphasis on developing intrinsic motivation clearly accords with character education's goal of helping students develop the desire to be good (moral feeling). The Four Basic Principles of Love and Logic are:

(*1*) Share the control.

(*2*) Share the thinking.

(*3*) Balance consequences with empathy.

(*4*) Maintain self-concept.

For more information on Teaching with Love and Logic, you can call the Love and Logic Institute at 800-338-4065, listen to Love and Logic Audiotapes, or consult the book *Teaching with Love and Logic* by Jim Fay and David Funk (1995).

JUDICIOUS DISCIPLINE

Judicious Discipline (Gathercoal, 1990) explains discipline in terms of constitutional rights and citizenship. In line with this approach, some classes write their own Constitution or Student Bill of Rights, which is based on the premise that each child has a right to learn and each teacher has a right to teach. At the Caroline Bentley School in Illinois, these rights are summarized as "Every student has the right to learn, teachers have the right to teach, and no one has the right to interfere with the rights of others." Respect must be the basis of discipline. Caroline Bentley is a fourth- and fifth-grade intermediate school located in a middle-class conservative community that places a high value on education and has a strong sense of family values.

The Highlands Elementary School in Saugus, California, outlines the Basic Rights of Students in this way:

(*1*) To learn without interference

(*2*) To work together with respect and understanding

(*3*) To have their property safe

(*4*) To be safe from bodily harm

Highlands is a large K–6 school located in a middle-sized urban setting with a diverse student population that is 10% Hispanic and 5% Asian students.

MORAL DISCIPLINE

There has been a definite change in discipline philosophy in the 1990s. Seeking to help students internalize the reasons why they should behave, schools have sought to practice Moral Discipline—that is, to use discipline as a tool for teaching respect and responsibility. This approach holds that the ultimate goal of discipline is self-discipline; the kind of self-control that underlies voluntary compliance with just rules and laws is a mark of mature character and is what every society expects of its citizens (Lickona, 1991). In 20% of the applications, the school is equated with societal institutions, and students are taught behaviors that are required in the larger society. For example, in the Quincy Public Schools, located in a suburb of Boston, Massachusetts, the discipline program is based on the philosophy, explained in the handbook, that all members of the community have rights and responsibilities as defined in the U.S. Constitution. Students are expected to respect the rights, feelings, and property of others.

POSITIVE DISCIPLINE

Nearly one-fourth of the schools, most of them in the last two award years (1991–92 and 1993–94), reported using Positive Discipline instead of Assertive Discipline. Positive Discipline is based on the philosophy of Alfred Adler and Rudolph Dreikurs. It seeks to teach children self-discipline, responsibility, cooperation and problem-solving skills by allowing the teacher and students to cooperate in setting logical and natural consequences and limits. This method considers the students' needs for self-respect and positive reinforcement (Nelson, 1987). As stated by the Cedar Island Elementary School in Maple Grove, Minnesota:

> Our philosophy of discipline is based on the premise that students need to be recognized for doing the right thing and that they need to have clear rules about behavioral expectations and consequences so that they can

choose their course of action. We work toward creating an environment that is respectful, orderly, safe and predictable. We believe that effective discipline has to be self-motivated. Have few rules and emphasize positive action. Good behavior is infectious.

Cedar Island School is a K–6 school with a homogeneous population of 800 students.

The County Line Elementary School in Georgia has found the same to be true. Its discipline program is based on the theory that the reward for good behavior is as important as the consequence for inappropriate behavior. Each teacher writes a classroom discipline plan with positive and negative consequences. The school's philosophy of discipline works toward prevention instead of intervention. Its policies are designed to teach positive behavior. The principal stated, "We pride ourselves on being proactive instead of reactive." Over one-fourth of the County Line students are from families of low income.

QUALITY SCHOOLS

Glasser's ideas, that is, control theory in the classroom, affective discipline, and reality therapy are used in several of the schools (Glasser, 1986, 1990). Historically, one could see the development of the different Glasser ideas as they came out in his different books. In *Control Theory in the Classroom* (1986), Glasser suggests that effective teachers are those who use cooperative learning instead of lecturing and who manage their classrooms in such a way that all of their students do quality work in school. Nancy Martin, principal of the Conder Elementary School in Columbia, South Carolina, explains: "This program emphasizes agreements for individual behavior. It results in a consistent method of dealing with discipline problems throughout the school."

In the 1993–94 Blue Ribbon applications, schools mentioned implementing Glasser's latest ideas as found in his book, *The Quality School* (1990). Specifically, his main ideas are

(*1*) Projecting an image of quality in the work that the students are asked to do by helping them to find quality in the subjects they study and by drastically reducing homework and emphasizing the importance of seatwork

(2) Creating an atmosphere in which the idea of being kind and courteous prevails

(3) Empowering students by allowing them to discuss and establish rules and the punishment if the rules are not followed

(4) Speaking to students in a noncoercive way to persuade them to take responsibility for what they do

(5) Asking students to evaluate every aspect of the school in which they are involved

Many of the Quality School ideas are being implemented in the Blue Ribbon Schools as ways of fostering good discipline and character development. As the principal at St. Isidore School in Danville, California, explains: "Using the Quality Schools idea means that students are encouraged to take responsibility for their behavior. They design the classroom poster which outlines their expectations of what they can do without infringing on the rights of others." St. Isidore is a K-8 Catholic school of 350 homogeneous students of suburban, middle-class, white families.

SCHOOL HANDBOOKS AND DAILY PLANNERS THAT PROMOTE CHARACTER

There is a clear trend found in nearly one-fourth of the schools, especially in the applications from recent years, to have a schoolwide discipline code in a handbook. In the handbook, the motto of the school, the expected behaviors of students, and the rules of the school are clearly spelled out. It is important that school handbooks express their expectations positively, telling students what kind of behavior is expected of them instead of listing every possible type of misbehavior with its consequence. Some of the schools issue bookmarkers or folders listing the school rules or have classroom posters that illustrate the rules.

Daily planners are used at Bryant Ranch School in Yorba Linda, California. Bryant Ranch is a K–6 school with almost 1000 students from diverse ethnic backgrounds. The 16% Asian students speak Mandarin, Korean, Vietnamese, Chinese, and Tagalog. The daily planners are very effective because they post the school rules and class schedule on the inside and help to keep the large diverse student body organized and moving quickly. Students record their homework in the planners, and parents can sign them. The planners can be used to teach character qualities, as they focus on different character values each week with catchy little sayings and pictures. For example, in the week of October 20, 1996, the focus was on motivation. Some of the sayings included: "Motivating yourself to learn is the key to doing well in school—and in life" and "The secret of joy in work is contained in one word, excellence." Daily planners can be purchased from the Premier School Agenda Company, 6161 28th Street, SE, Suite 11, Grand Rapids, MI 49546; phone: 800-447-2034.

SCHOOL RULES THAT PROMOTE CHARACTER

Schools express their focus on character development by the rules they promote. Like other institutions, schools need rules to accomplish their goals. Rules are guides to behavior. They tell the student what is acceptable behavior and what is unacceptable. Rules help children learn the skills and attitudes needed to live in harmony with others (Wynne & Ryan, 1993). When rules are a positive expression of expectations, they are character-building. Rules written negatively list every possible type of misbehavior imaginable but do not successfully communicate to students the correct behavior.

The Blake School is a private school in Hopkins, Minnesota, that includes both a K–8 building of 700 students and a high school of almost 400 students. The school has three rules posted in all classrooms and published in the handbook:

(*1*) The Safety Rule: Do not endanger oneself or others.

(*2*) The Respect Rule: Respect ourselves, classmates teacher, and property.

(*3*) The Welcome Rule: All children must be welcomed into any activity as long as they play according to the rules.

Similarly, the Pine Grove School has four basic school rules:

(*1*) We respect other people and their property.

(*2*) We try to make each other's day as pleasant as possible.

(*3*) In school we talk, not fight.
(*4*) In school we walk, not run.

Pine Grove is a K–6 school with a homogeneous student body of almost 500 students located in the small town of Rowley, Massachusetts. The rules found at the Blake School and the Pine Grove School are formulated to convey clear standards of respect and responsibility.

SCHOOL-WIDE DISCIPLINE PROGRAMS

Red, Yellow, Green is a system used by three of the Blue Ribbon Schools in their cafeterias that communicates to students appropriate levels of conversation. There are three cardboard circles that can be displayed. If green is shown, children are allowed to talk normally. If yellow, they may talk in a whisper. If red is shown, there is to be no talking.

The Pride Program (Positive Reinforcement of Individual Discipline and Enthusiasm) is found in several schools. This system helps students develop a sense of responsibility and respect for others by achieving good conduct and work habits, which are goals every student can attain. Some school programs emphasize "manners," others emphasize "being a lady" or a "gentleman," but the common element is a group of agreed-upon behavior expectations.

Skill Streaming is the character development discipline program found in the Clara Barton Open School in Minneapolis, Minnesota, based on the following behavior principles:

(*1*) Be courteous to others.
(*2*) Use time wisely.
(*3*) Respect property.
(*4*) Respect the rights of others.

Classroom techniques target the development of fair play and concern for others. Clara Barton is a K–8 school with 600 students located in a large city. The student body is diverse; 17% of the students are from an African-American background and 6% are Asian-American. As potentially disruptive situations occur, the teacher helps the students to process the incidents, practicing conflict resolution skills and including students in the discussion. The students use the behavior rules as their guide. The goal of Skill Streaming is to develop an atmosphere of trust that fosters self-discipline and responsibility.

TEACHING RESPECT IN SCHOOLS

Lickona (1991) says that respect and responsibility are the "fourth and fifth R's" that schools not only may but must teach if they are to develop ethically literate persons who can take their place as responsible citizens of society. In these Blue Ribbon Schools, the rights of self and others and responsibilities to others are both emphasized.

The Primary 4 R's of Respect were found in the Livonia Primary School, in New York State:

(*1*) Respect the school and its property.
(*2*) Respect your teacher.
(*3*) Respect fellow students.
(*4*) Respect yourself.

Livonia is a K–4 rural school with some 800 students, over 10% of whom are from lower-income families.

TEACHING RESPONSIBILITY IN SCHOOLS

A recurring theme in these schools is that effective discipline means teaching children how to become responsible. Far too many young people have little idea of what it means to be responsible. The Governor Bent School in Albuquerque, New Mexico, uses the responsibility mode of discipline. They attempt to involve students in decisions regarding behavior and responsibility at school so the students internalize rules and develop as problem-solvers. Governor Bent has a heterogeneous student body of over 700 students. This very diverse population is 40% Hispanic and 40% white. One-third of the students are from lower-income families.

Allen Mendler (1988), the author of *Discipline with Dignity*, has developed the responsibility model of discipline that teaches children how to (1) accumulate knowledge, (2) see the options available, (3) learn to anticipate consequences, and (4) then choose the path that they feel is in the best interest of themselves and others. Responsible students learn that they have choices, and that they need to plan their behavior (Mendler, 1993). When students misbehave, they should be encouraged to ask themselves, what would happen if others acted this way? Why are these rules needed for the effective functioning of our society?

Neubert Elementary School, in the small middle-class town of Algonquin, Illinois, has an interesting "society-based" program:

> Keystone Kids is based on the "Drivers License" concept; a license is issued to each student which is good for the entire year. Failure to accept responsibility for one's behavior results in a written "citation." One copy of the citation is recorded in the office by the "meter maid" while the student copy must be signed by a parent and returned. Three citations results in a detention and a hole punch on the driver's license, which means the student is not entitled to the benefits of a popcorn movie each semester. An honor roll in the hall lists the names of responsible citizens. A videotape presentation acquaints the children with the program at the beginning of the year and a certificate is awarded at the end of the year to the "responsible citizens."

The East Elementary School in Pendleton, Indiana, compares being in school to holding a job and has developed a program called "Learnball" that unites the classroom into a company.

> Learnball is a classroom management program that helps build character. Students may earn points for their "companies" through appropriate behavior, good grades, neatness, etc. The accent is on the positive, not the negative. Winning teams are rewarded by having their company's picture in the winner's place or by receiving special privileges. *The real reward, however, seems to be merely the satisfaction of a job well done!* This system has provided dividends of good behavior, pride in work, and the development of student leadership.

Students at East experience intrinsic motivation from knowing that they have done their very best. East Elementary is a K−8 school of over 800 students from blue- and white-collar white families in the small industrial town of Pendleton.

Durkheim would agree that most of the discipline programs used in these Blue Ribbon Schools are truly promoting character development and morality in the classroom. "Discipline is not a simple device for securing superficial peace in the classroom; it is the morality of the classroom as a small society" (Durkheim, 1973, p. 148).

SUMMARY

As this chapter shows, in order for a school to foster the development of "sound character . . . good behavior and the ability to work in a self-disciplined and purposeful manner," it must have an effective discipline program that promotes self-discipline. Some of the programs that successfully do this emphasize character qualities, class meetings, and conflict resolution and peer mediation training programs. The latter promote character development by teaching students prosocial skills, thus ensuring that the school has an orderly and safe environment.

REFERENCES

Albert, L. 1990. *Cooperative Discipline: Classroom Management That Promotes Self-Esteem: Teacher's Manual*. MN: American Guidance Service.

Ban, J. 1994. "A Lesson Plan Approach for Dealing with School Discipline," *The Clearing House*, 67(5):257–261.

Bennett, W. 1988. *First Lessons: A Report on Elementary Education in America*. Washington D.C.: U.S. Government Printing Office.

Canter, L. and M. Canter. 1976. *Assertive Discipline*. Los Angeles: Lee Canter & Associates.

Curwin, R. 1995. "A Human Approach to Reducing Violence in Schools," *Educational Leadership*, 52(5):72–75.

Curwin, R. and A. Mendler. 1988. "We Repeat, Let the Buyer Beware: A Response to Canter," *Educational Leadership*, 46(2):68–71.

Durkheim, E. 1973. *Moral Education: A Study in the Theory and Application of the Sociology of Education*. New York: The Free Press.

Fay, J. and D. Funk. 1995. *Teaching with Love and Logic*. Golden, CA: The Love and Logic Press.

Gathercoal, F. 1990. *Judicious Discipline*. Ann Harbor, MI: Caddo Gap Press.

Glasser, W. 1986. *Control Theory in the Classroom*. New York: Harper & Row Publishers.

Glasser, W. 1990. *The Quality School*. Perennial Library. New York: Harper & Row Publishers.

Hill, D. 1990. "Order in the Classroom," *Teacher's Magazine*, April 70–77.

Johnson, D. and R. Johnson. 1995. *Teaching Students to Be Peacemakers*. Edina, MN: Interaction Book Co.

Johnson, D., R. Johnson, B. Dudley and R. Burnett. 1992. "Teaching Students to Be Peer Mediators," *Educational Leadership*, 50(1):10–13.

Johnson, S. and Blanchard, K. 1982. *The One Minute Manager*. New York: Morrow.

Lickona, T. 1991. *Educating for Character: How Our Schools Can Teach Respect and Responsibility*. New York: Bantam Books.

McDaniel, T. 1989. "The Discipline Debate: A Road Through the Thicket," *Educational Leadership*, March, 81–82.

Mendler, A. 1992. *What Do I Do When . . .: How to Achieve Discipline with Dignity in the Classroom*. Bloomington, Ind.: National Educational Service.

Mendler, A. 1993. "Discipline with Dignity in the Classroom: Seven Principles," *The Educational Digest*, 58(7):4–10.

Mendler, A. 1988. *Discipline with Dignity*. Alexandria, VA: ASCD.

National Education Association. 1895. The Report of the National Education Association Committee of Fifteen, as cited in W. Bennett. *First Lessons: A Report on Elementary Education in America*. 1996. Washington, D.C.: U.S. Government Printing Office.

Nelsen, J. 1987. *Positive Discipline*. New York: Ballentine Books.

Pereira, C. 1988. "Educating for Citizenship in the Elementary Grades," *Phi Delta Kappan*, 69(5): 429–431.

Render, G., J. Padilla, and M. Krank. 1989. "Assertive Discipline: A Critical Review and Analysis," *Teachers College Record*, 90 (4):607–627.

Schultz, F., ed. 1995. "Managing Life in Classroom" in *Education: Annual Editions 95/96*. Guilford, CT: Duskin, pp. 104–105.

Stomfay-Stitz, A. 1993. *Peace Education in America 1828–1990*. Metuchen, NH: Scarecrow Press.

Stomfay-Stitz, A. 1994. "Conflict Resolution and Peer Mediation Pathways to Safer Schools," *Childhood Education*, 70(5): 279–282.

United States Department of Education. 1994. *Application for Elementary School Recognition Program*. Washington, D.C.: U.S. Department of Education.

Valett, R. 1991. "Teaching Peace and Conflict Resolution," in *Moral, Character, and Civic Education in the Elementary School*, J. Benninga, ed. New York: Teachers College Press, pp. 243–258.

Walberg, H. and E. Wynne. 1989. "Character Education: Toward a Preliminary Consensus," in *Moral Development and Character Education: A Dialogue*. L. Nucci, ed. Berkeley, CA: McCutchan Publishing Corporation, pp. 37–50.

Wynne, E. and K. Ryan. 1993. *Reclaiming Our Schools*. New York: Macmillan Publishing Company.

Chapter 8

HOW DOES GOOD CITIZENSHIP CONTRIBUTE TO GOOD CHARACTER?

You will remember that all the End of study is to make you a good Man and a useful Citizen.
—John Adams in a letter to his son, John Quincy Adams

Great schools are the result of great cooperation. Let's remember that it takes both the white and the black keys of the piano to play "The Star-Spangled Banner."—Anonymous

The only ones among you who will be really happy are those who have sought and found how to serve.—Albert Schweitzer

EDUCATION FOR CITIZENSHIP AS THE GOAL OF UNIVERSAL EDUCATION

"Citizenship" is a quality that most Americans would agree should be promoted in the schools. "Values education," as we have seen, provokes controversy and the question "Whose values are you going to teach?" An acceptable response is, "Values of citizenship, American democratic values, and the values upon which our country was founded."

Jefferson, Madison, and Adams each said that a well-constructed constitution was not enough to maintain our democracy; a free society ultimately depended on its citizens and on their knowledge, skills, moral, and civic virtues. The "habits of the mind" and "habits of the heart" that Alexis de Tocqueville saw in the American democratic ethos need to be taught by word, study, and example (Quigley, 1996).

157

Noted historian R. Freeman Butts (1991) says that education for citizenship was the primary reason for establishing universal education in the American Republic. The purpose of universal school, Butts explains, is to develop among all students, whether in private or public schools, the virtues, sentiments, knowledge, and skills of citizenship. In short, the health and survival of our democracy rests on the character of its citizenry.

This chapter shows us how the Blue Ribbon Schools use their citizenship programs to assist in the development of the character of their students. Citizenship programs are usually found within the social studies curricula but are also found integrated throughout the school in various other programs. This chapter presents answers to the following questions:

- What are the key characteristics that make a citizenship program character education and not just civic education?
- What are the democratic values that we want to foster in America's schools?
- Why is it important to involve students in decision making in order to develop character and citizenship?
- What are some ways that students can develop good character by caring within the classroom?
- How does community service help students develop character?
- How do the Blue Ribbon Schools prepare students to live effectively in our culturally, ethnically, and economically diverse society and on the globe?

CIVIC EDUCATION VERSUS CHARACTER EDUCATION

One needs to note what a school means by citizenship in order to judge whether or not its citizenship program can be considered character education. If the school considers citizenship only to be learning about voting and laws, observing national holidays, and knowing leaders and historical figures, it is limiting citizenship to civic education, not character education (Letwin, 1991). Character education is much broader than this.

Character education means coming to understand, care about, and practice virtue. It includes learning the moral principles of a democratic society, namely, the perpetual struggle to live rationally within the boundaries of democratic tradition. This moral code is based on cultural history and is accepted as the ethic of society. It should give students the ability to separate good from evil, fairness from unfairness, justice from injustice, and truth from falsehood (Reische, 1987).

DEMOCRATIC TRAITS OF CHARACTER

The Communitarian Network's 1996 task force paper, *The Role of Civic Education*, explains that civic education is not synonymous with character education; however, the two are related, and their aims overlap in important respects. An effective civic education program should provide students with opportunities for the development of desirable traits of public and private character. According to the task force paper, the public traits of character needed for the healthy functioning of our constitutional democracy are "civility, respect for law, civic-mindedness, critical-mindedness, persistence, and a willingness to negotiate and compromise" (p. 5). The private traits of character needed include "self-discipline, moral responsibility, honesty, respect for individual worth, and empathy for others" (p. 5).

Citizenship education is character education if it focuses on helping students develop the moral knowing aspect of their characters while learning about their civic responsibilities. It uses citizenship awards to promote moral feeling in students. Finally, it gives the students opportunities to show good actions to others in the classroom, school, family, and neighborhood, so they manifest the third component of good character, moral action. When citizenship education involves cooperative learning, it provides still another way for students to practice good moral actions and develop morally by having the opportunity to work with others, make fair decisions, and develop pro-social skills such as perspective-taking (Lickona, 1991). Citizenship education can be one of the best forums for developing character in students because it allows the development of all three aspects of character:

> Citizenship practice in the earliest grades is most appropriate in the setting of the classroom and the school itself. Students begin to understand

through participation such as role-playing, games and active discussion how and why rules are made, why people have laws, how people nego-tiate agreements. Through games, simulations, plays and other activi-ties students can experience directly how disputes arise, how they can be resolved without conflict, why people need to agree upon rules or laws. (Reische, 1987, p. 59).

SCHOOL MISSION TO PROMOTE CITIZENSHIP

It is not surprising, then, that developing citizenship was men-tioned as the mission and goal of one-third of the Blue Ribbon Schools (see Table 6). For example, the mission of the Lewis Powell Gifted and Talented Magnet Elementary School in Raleigh, North Carolina, is "to enable students to develop the skills necessary to become capable productive citizens." Lowell is a large pre-K to fifth-grade school with a very integrated student body of 500 stu-dents, 43% of whom are black. Similarly, the mission of the Saigling School in Plano, Texas, is "to develop students who are re-sponsible citizens, who make good decisions, and who try to do their best." To accomplish this mission, they have defined three goals, one of which is that 100% of their students will exhibit good citizenship and character.

The objective of the Normandy Elementary School in Centerville, Ohio, is similar to Saigling's goal: Normandy staff want to produce self-disciplined, morally sound, and socially aware citizens for the next century. Normandy is located in a suburb outside of Dayton and has a small homogeneous student body.

Mill Lake is a primary K–3 school of 380 homogeneous students located in the small town of Spotswood, New Jersey. One of the school's goals is to develop good character, good citizenship, and posi-tive relationships with others. Nancy Richmond, the principal, ex-plains the school goal:

> A commitment has been made to establish a foundation upon which future building blocks of good citizenship, community service and personal re-sponsibility can be laid. These basic concepts are addressed through age-appropriate activities and learning experiences which include social stud-ies lessons, assemblies, awards, bulletin boards, community service, and guidance lessons.

PROMOTING CITIZENSHIP
IN THE SOCIAL STUDIES CLASS

The normal academic setting for instruction in both civic education and character-building citizenship is the social studies class according to the teachers at the Russell Elementary School:

> Good citizenship is the major focus of the social studies curriculum at Russell Elementary School in Missouri. The cooperative learning that takes place in these classes allows the students to assume various roles in a group to prepare them for roles in the community. Class meetings and Student Council speeches and elections allow students to experience democratic processes. Discussion of current events and multicultural units within the social studies curriculum contribute to developing the students' sense of citizenship in a global society.

At the Southwest Elementary School in Howell, Michigan, the social studies program provides opportunities for students and staff to be involved in promoting good citizenship and community service. Southwest is a pre-K to fourth-grade small-town school with a homogeneous student population of over 500 mostly middle-class, white students but also including over 10% lower-income families. Student activities include visiting nursing homes, participating in Scouts, recycling, and being a part of a good citizen recognition program.

CIVITAS

It is only in the last Blue Ribbon Award year (1993–94) that schools mention using the CIVITAS curriculum in their social studies classes. CIVITAS is the result of a collaborative project of the Center for Civic Education and the Council for the Advancement of Citizenship, with support from the Pew Charitable Trusts. The aim of CIVITAS is to provide an intellectual and scholarly curriculum for K–12 civic education in the schools. This consists of a common core of knowledge, skills, and values desirable for all students in the nation to achieve (Quigley & Bahmueller, 1991).

It is interesting to see how much the Blue Ribbon Schools value their citizenship program as an important component of their character education program. Joyce Westgate, the principal at Benjamin Franklin Elementary School in Binghamton, New York, describes their diverse student body as including students from middle-class to lower-middle-class families. Students learn the habits of good citizenship in three ways:

> First is through example. Students witness the cooperation, hard work and friendliness of the staff, administration, and faculty. Secondly, the Character Education Committee regularly plans events around positive character traits. One month highlights "Responsibility" with a new rap song taught in music classes and sung during assembly; another "Honesty " with public acknowledgement of honest actions; and yet another "Helpfulness" with classroom displays of photographs that show children gaining understanding by helping others. The third focus on citizenship is direct instruction through a series of activities emphasizing peaceful conflict resolution, problem solving, cooperation, self-esteem and responsibility. (National Association of Elementary School Principals, 1995, pp. 28–29)

Judith Schulz, principal of the Independence Primary School in the Cuyahoga Valley of Ohio, explained that their schoolwide citizenship programs are very effective in fostering good character and leadership in students. They strive to develop values, such as responsibility for self, trust, and caring for others, and thereby help to ensure that students are prepared to be responsible members of American society.

The Bellerive School in Missouri teaches the civic values of equality, freedom, justice, respect for authority, and respect for property in many of its programs and especially through its Bellerive Cadet Helper Program. As explained in Chapter 3 on character education programs, the Bellerive Cadet Helper program is one in which students volunteer to participate as a service to the school, but one to which they also have to be chosen, based on their possession of good character and leadership qualities. Students are able to choose the teacher, job, and time they are available, but it is basically an opportunity for them to show they are good citizens of the school by helping out in another grade.

East Elementary School in rural Pendleton, Indiana, considers "love of country" to be one of the several cornerstones that support purposeful citizenship. Students raise and lower the American flag each day. The flag is also placed in every classroom and the Pledge of Allegiance is respectfully recited each morning. The annual all-school singing assembly emphasizes America's heritage. Individual classrooms study the important responsibilities of American leaders.

CURRENT EVENTS

At St. Rosalie School in Harvey, Louisiana, current events are addressed daily at all levels. From these topics come the opportunities for discussions of behavior and consequences: Why do we have certain opinions? Are they based on facts? How are we, school, and country working in support of democratic ideals? From these discussions and role modeling, students gain insights into problem solving.

At the Elvin School in Alabama, current events are used to help students live values. For instance, students wrote protest letters concerning ethical issues in South Africa and wrote their Congressmen regarding political issues. The large, very diverse student body of 647 consists of 18% African-American students and 40% students from lower-income families.

Ernest Boyer (1990) believes that civic education means helping students confront social and ethical concerns, even if it involves controversial issues. Students can apply what they have learned to make judgments, form convictions, and act boldly on values held. Schools that advocate citizenship programs for their role in character development provide students with opportunities in which they can find solutions to problems and can then act on these solutions. These programs help them to become active, questioning young adults who are prepared to take on the vital role of citizens in a democracy (Sadowsky, 1991). Moreover, they build personal character by challenging students to translate moral judgment and feeling into moral action as citizens of their classrooms, schools, and communities.

DEVELOPING DECISION-MAKING SKILLS

Recommendation 8 of the National Task Force on Citizenship Education states: "Because values and ethical issues are central to civic education, schools should be encouraged to use moral education concepts, as well as . . . community-based experiences reflecting the values of the community" (Reische, 1987). Some schools have based their citizenship programs on an application of Kohlberg's theories of moral development (outlined in Chapter 2). Kohlbergian methods initially focused on encouraging interactive moral dilemma discussions among students at different levels of moral reasoning. Later, the focus changed to establishing within existing schools, models of participatory democracy called "just community schools" (Reische, 1987). The Blue Ribbon Schools use the moral discussion method extensively; however, instead of discussing hypothetical moral dilemmas, they tend to examine real school issues. Thus, students truly participate democratically in making suggestions for the effective running of their school.

A good citizen must be a thinking citizen (Rowe, 1990). Social studies is one of the school subjects that provides a natural context for teaching thinking skills. The "town meeting" is a method mentioned in several of the Blue Ribbon Schools. It is a problem-solving framework that allows students to use thinking skills, techniques, and processes learned in the social studies content area to solve real school problems. Some schools use the "town meeting" to invite the community to discuss ethical issues. (Many of the character education organizations are now ending their annual meetings with a "town meeting" that allows participants of the conference to make suggestions to the organizational leaders and problem-solve with the other members of the professional group.)

CITIZENSHIP PROGRAMS FOUND IN THE BLUE RIBBON SCHOOLS

More than half of the Blue Ribbon Schools mentioned their citizenship program in response to the question, "How do school programs, practices, policies and staff foster the development of sound character, democratic values, ethical judgment, good behavior, and the ability to work in a self-disciplined and purposeful manner?" and Table 12 summarizes the programs that they mentioned they use.

CARING AS A MORAL VALUE

Lickona says that respect and responsibility are the "fourth and fifth R's" that schools not only *may* but *must* teach if they are to develop ethically literate persons who can take their place as responsible citizens of society. He states that the effectiveness of a character development program is shown in students' actions. Lickona's comprehensive approach to character education emphasizes the importance of caring

TABLE 12 *Citizenship programs*
mentioned by Blue Ribbon Schools.

Category	Count	Percent of Responses
Buddy Program	12	4
Citizen of Week Award	64	23
Community service	66	23
Develop cooperative skills	10	4
Global concerns	6	3
Patrol/Scouts	6	2
Student council	37	13
Tutoring program	19	7

Valid cases, 284; missing cases 68

within the classroom and caring beyond the classroom. The Blue Ribbon Schools also strive to develop these two aspects of caring within their citizenship programs. This focus on caring is especially important in order to begin bridging the differences in the multiracial and multicultural community; it is a virtue that has truly global repercussions.

According to George Noblit and his research colleagues (1995), "Morally and culturally, caring is a belief about how we should view and interact with others," (p. 680). Alasdair MacIntyre (1981), in *After Virtue* states that caring is a moral concept when it is something that is reaffirmed continually in everyday life. Alfie Kohn (1991) concurs, stating that caring is a natural quality in humans and that the school provides a logical setting in which to guide children toward caring about and helping other people. The outcome of good citizenship education is students who know how to care for all of the other people in their world—family, school, community, city, and nation.

CARING WITHIN THE CLASSROOM

George Wood (1990) has spent three years in classrooms observing teachers who see their task first and foremost as nurturing the skills, attitudes and values necessary for democratic life—that is, teaching caring. He believes that, with proper attention to all the individuals within the school, educators can create an experience for students that demonstrates what it means to be compassionate, involved citizens. For it is only within a community that young people learn how important are such principles as working for the common good, empathy, equality, and self-respect.

One of the most common ways for students to show their good citizenship within the classroom is to participate in a buddy program, patrols, or a tutoring program.

"Buddy" Programs

Students show that they care for others by sharing their time with them. Educators can begin to promote the value of caring explicitly by exploring ways in which they can create a more caring culture in the classrooms and schools. Culture is based, in part, on such gestures of caring and other everyday ways of doing things (Noblit et al., 1995). One example is a school's buddy program. Westwood School in Santa Clara, California, describes how its students care for one another through the buddy program:

> Our fourth- and fifth-grade classes are role models for the school. Their leadership program includes working with younger students in developing math and reading skills. Each student selects a buddy, and together they select books to read, stories to write, science or social studies projects to do, and games to play. Consequently, it is a two-way street where both students benefit. A fifth-grade ESL student tutoring a first-grader reinforces his own English skill while the first-grader learns math problem-solving skills.

At Lowell Elementary School in Boise, Idaho, the fifth- and sixth-grade classes use "study buddies" in which children are paired with a partner in class to provide instructional and work habits support. In other grades, peer helpers work with students who are having difficulties academically or motivationally. Lowell is a K–6 urban school of 400 students of growing diversity. The formerly all-white school body now has 8% of its students from other ethnic heritages. Lowell families have the greatest socioeconomic span of the Boise schools; 72% are low-income families, but the others represent middle-income, professional, and even executive-level occupations.

In addition to the "study buddies," Lowell has a cross-grade buddy system in which all fifth- and sixth-grade classes are paired up with a primary class. Besides listening to children read, the upper-grade students teach "mini-lessons" to their buddies. The older students have special projects that combine social studies and science with research skills. They learn the material, then modify it to include hands-on, concrete examples to teach the concepts to the younger children. These "mini-lessons" have included subjects on manners, snakes, and plant growth. Buddies also share field trips and art projects and celebrate holidays together. This year the second-graders read to the kindergarten students. One of the students told about the program: "We have a buddy program, and it helps us to know someone little is looking up to us. My buddy cried this morning because she didn't know why I couldn't come." (She was touring this visitor around the building!)

Good Citizenship Award

Increasingly, schools are teaching citizenship and character in the same way that they are teaching reading and math. They are working with their communities to define those core values such as honesty, hard work, and respect for others and for oneself that make it possible for our democracy to continue (National Association of Elementary School Principals, 1995). Although some schools do give grades to their students on their report cards for citizenship, 23% of the Blue Ribbon Schools have found that a more effective way to promote good citizenship is to recognize those who demonstrate good citizenship in their actions.

Fort Washington Elementary School in Fresno, California, is a large heterogeneous K–8 school of 600 students: 6% Hispanic, 4% Asian and 2% African-American. It became a Blue Ribbon School because of its Exemplary Patriot Award Program:

> The award is based on (1) Academics, (2) Co-curricular Activities, (3) Athletics, (4) School Service and Leadership, and (5) Effort and Citizenship. The Patriot Program reflects a holistic view of the person and presents the students with the motivating challenge of striving to achieve the goals set out by the school in order to become responsible and well-rounded individuals. The school has prepared "A Guide for Earning the Exemplary Patriot Award" which defines in clear terms the character expectations and qualities needed in order to win the Award. Specifically students are asked to be honest, responsible, respectful, dedicated, perseverant, self-respecting, and concerned for others.

The effectiveness of the Exemplary Patriot Award Program was evaluated after five years of implementation. The program was found to be effective in developing a positive, purposeful school climate. Several key outcome variables were observed by evaluators. Specifically, scores on achievement tests improved and the number of students on the honor roll grew; daily attendance to school improved and incidence of school vandalism became non-existent; and the number of students who participated in school extracurricular activities increased greatly (Sparks, 1991).

A visit to the school by the author also verified the effectiveness of this Program. In fact, the Exemplary Patriot Award Program was seen as so effective that, when the principal, Dr. Richard Sparks, moved into the district offices, other schools in the district were also encouraged to implement their own version of the Award Program. Mountain View School, also in Fresno, implemented the Exemplary Bear Award, and other schools have also begun award programs.

Oakbrook School in suburban Ladson, South Carolina, is a very large diverse pre-K to fifth-grade school that has also developed a good citizenship award program:

> Through a grant, the guidance program at Oakbrook has been coordinated with the citizenship program. A good citizen, selected weekly from each homeroom, is recognized in the newsletter, the in-house TV broadcast and receives a ribbon and a pizza coupon. Each month there is a special focus on topics such as responsibility, respect for authority, decision making, good manners, and conflict resolution skills. The "Red Carpet" is given by the principal to the class with exceptional citizenship.

Most of Oakbrook's students come from middle-income families; however, 25% are from a lower socioeconomic background. Sixteen percent of the student body is comprised of minority students.

Kohn (1993) questions the use of good citizenship awards although he admits that they are common across the country: "Sometimes rewards are used in the hope of promoting undeniably worthy qualities such as generosity and concern for others. The evidence however shows that anyone who is rewarded for acts of generosity will be less likely to think of himself as a caring or altruistic person; he will attribute his behavior to the reward instead," (p. 173). The Blue Ribbon Schools in general would not agree with Kohn in this area. Although they would concur with him that "good values have to be grown from the inside out and that no behavioral manipulation ever helped a child develop a commitment to becoming a caring and responsible person," (p. 161) they would tell him that good citizenship awards are important because they teach specific character values to students, and the awards are open to all students who so manifest these values. By encouraging self-discipline these awards help students to develop control over their own lives and help them to make judgments about what constitutes good behavior.

Civic Achievement Award Program

The Civic Achievement Award Program (CAAP), found in several of the Blue Ribbon middle schools, is a citizenship education initiative established by the U.S. Congress that provides students with the knowledge and skills necessary to become responsible citizens. The program, which is now fully funded by Burger King Corporation, targets fifth-through ninth-graders, because these are crucial years for inculcating the basic concepts and values that support American pluralistic democracy. For information, contact the Civic Achievement Award Program, 1235 Jefferson Davis Highway, Arlington, VA 22202; phone: 800-356-5136 (Dolenga, 1990).

The Moriches Elementary School in New York is committed to "developing individuals who can adapt to our changing world." Moriches is a very large first- to fifth-grade school with almost 1000 culturally and economically diverse students. Thirty-six percent of the students are from low-income families; 10% of the students are Hispanic, 6% are African-American, 1% are Asian, and 2% are linguistically diverse students representing seven different languages. Moriches has a very large student transiency rate of 25%, so it is important that students quickly learn about the citizenship qualities the school seeks to foster in them:

> All students in the school understand the responsibilities of being a good citizen. Through citizenship awards and special awards given at monthly assemblies, students are recognized for their outstanding efforts. A bulletin board in the lobby lists the citizens of the month and special award winners. Democratic values are communicated to our students through mock elections, Student Council elections, and a lottery system for selection in school clubs. Elected student council representatives are given a forum for input on policies and procedure.

Almost all of the Blue Ribbon Schools report that their students are recognized for good citizenship and behavior through schoolwide programs and assemblies. These different awards are described in Chapter 5 on motivation.

Patrols

Participation in patrols helps develop good citizenship in students by providing them with the experience of fulfilling a role within a group and serving as a role model to others. The Safety Patrol at Anna Reynolds School, in Newington, Connecticut, is made up of students in grade five and gives them an opportunity to learn self-discipline and control while helping them to discipline and work with primary students. Safety Patrols help reinforce school safety rules and good behavior before and after school.

Scouts

Scouting per se was mentioned in a very small percentage of the schools' applications as one of the programs that contributes to the promotion of character at the school, because these organizations are not sponsored by the schools. However, visits to the Blue Ribbon Schools confirmed the fact that almost all of the schools do have Scouting activities available for the students and allow the organizations to use their facilities. The Scouting program is one which does, at least in its stated aims, foster good character and good citizenship in students because of the character-related criteria that it sets for each member:

The Boy Scout Law

A scout is:
trustworthy
helpful
friendly
courteous
kind
obedient
cheerful
thrifty
brave
clean
reverent

St. John Bosco is a Catholic, K–8 school of almost 800 homogeneous middle-class students in suburban Parma Heights, Ohio. Sister Gretchen, the principal, feels that the Scouting troop provides an outlet for students to interact with adult leaders on camping trips, at meetings, and at outdoor events and provides these students with many opportunities for service to the community.

Sister Schools

Anna Reynolds School in Connecticut has a unique "Sister School Program" that pairs classes from its school with classes from an urban school. Teachers plan joint educational opportunities that allow students from the two communities to work and learn together. Classes from each school send letters, cards, and artwork to each other and visit each others' schools for picnics and other activities. This creates a climate that affirms diversity through personal contact and prepares students to live productively and harmoniously in a society that is culturally diverse.

Programs like these have been shown by research to enhance caring values, attitudes, and behaviors. They do so by providing students with opportunities to discuss caring, to demonstrate caring to others, and to participate thoughtfully in caring relations (Bosworth, 1995).

Student Council

One of the most common ways for Blue Ribbon Schools to involve students actively in practicing decision-making skills is to promote their participation in Student Council. At the Argonaut Elementary School in Saratoga, California, students are given an opportunity to influence classroom and school policy:

> We instill character and ethics traits through student council meetings that include school officers and two representatives from each class. Student opinions and concerns on timely issues are solicited by the class representatives who then present them during their student council meetings. The council then discusses these issues and makes recommendations to the school faculty, School Site Council or other appropriate groups.

Sheri Hitching, principal of Argonaut School, explains that their citizenship and character-building programs immerse students in decision making. Students have many opportunities to be involved with democratic values and ethics, particularly in learning respect for one another and reflecting on individual responsibility:

> In the 1990's, it is especially important for schools to help children learn what individual moral behavior is and also to see the need to improve the social ethic. Since schools can help shape a society with a stronger moral foundation, any proposed moral education program should be judged by the extent to which it takes both individual and social responsibility for ethical behavior into account. It must be a program which helps children think through issues. (Molnar, 1990, p. 74).

Student Suggestion Box

Students at Crest Hill School, in Casper, Wyoming, know that the principal seriously studies the suggestions they put into the "Student Suggestion Box." They look forward to the biweekly assemblies with the principal when the suggestions are read to the whole school. Students know that their suggestions are taken seriously, studied, reported on, and are a vital part of the school, for they have seen how their suggestions have been implemented, even changing school policies. They have new lunch menu selections now, a Chess Club has been added, safety has been addressed on the parking lot, and there are grade-level dances.

The teachers at Baker's Chapel Elementary School in Greenville, South Carolina, believe that students should have some decision-making power in their own lives in order to teach them about democracy and prepare them for later life. Half of Baker's Chapel students are African-American, and half of the students are from low-income families. Most of these parents have never completed high school. In the past few years, Baker's Chapel has transformed its poor image from that of a dull, mediocre, low-achieving school, to that of an award-winning school where its large population of at-risk students achieve and excel:

> The classroom itself is the best place for students and teachers to get involved in activities that promote good citizenship, community service, and personal responsibility. Here there are thought-provoking discussions of current events which involve valuing, training in animal care, making Christmas cards for crippled children, gathering petitions to send to the principal, and practicing democratic practices in cooperative learning groups.

Tutoring Programs

One of the key goals of the Child Development Program used in the San Ramon, California, schools is to "create a caring community within the classroom" (Kohn, 1990). Several of the San Ramon schools have won the Blue Ribbon Award. One of them is the Country Club Elementary School. It reports on the success of its tutoring program:

> Our kindergarten read-aloud program utilizes upper grade level students who read to the young students. This promotes an interest in the kindergarten students to read, while the older students vie for the privilege of reading. Our older and younger students tell us they like this program.

CARING BEYOND THE CLASSROOM

The Value of Caring for Others

Research has found that an intensive experience in caring for others may have a profound effect on young people:

> There are many possible ways for young people to become involved in the community in a meaningful and contributory role: working with senior citizens, caring for and tutoring younger children, working in service-learning placements in health and community programs and taking part in other types of volunteer activity. Those young people who have opportunities to care for others in such programs have been found to show an increased sense of social responsibility, a higher level of self-esteem, and better school attendance. (Chaskin, 1995)

CARE Programs

Some Blue Ribbon School programs that promote character by giving opportunities for students to care for others are called CARE Programs with differing words for the acronym: Citizenship, Achievement, Responsibility, and Education or Cooperation, Appreciation, Responsibility (Respect), Effort, and Sharing. These programs promote social and emotional well-being, kindness, and helpfulness. The "KIDS" Program at Pioneer Elementary School in Colorado Springs, stands for "Kids Involved in Doing Service." Students take their gifts and talent beyond the school walls into the community. Some of the

KIDS projects include performing for convalescent homes, cleaning up the community, sharing with students at the deaf and blind school, sponsoring food and clothing drives, recycling paper, and preparing Thanksgiving food baskets. Pioneer is a very large school with a diverse student body of 688 that is 7% Hispanic, 5% African-American, and 3% Asian students.

Community Service Projects

Community service projects undertaken by schools help students realize that character education includes service to others. These projects build self-worth and allow students to experience themselves as part of the larger network of people who are helping to create a better world (Berman, 1990). Some Blue Ribbon Schools stated that a measure of the success of their character development programs the service activities in which their students engage and the percentage of the total school body who participate.

Fund-Raisers and Drives for Others

Among the student community service projects are the typical drives, bike-a-thons and jog-a-thons to raise money for medical research on cancer, diabetes, cystic fibrosis, or bone marrow diseases and to support an overseas child through UNICEF. At the Dennis Elementary School in Oklahoma City, students help to meet community needs, for example, buying a new animal for the zoo. Its "Adopt a Family Program" enabled a class to provide food and clothing for a family in need either at a holiday or after a disaster such as a hurricane, earthquake, or drought. Dennis is a very large K–6 school with a homogeneous middle-class student body.

At two schools in Louisiana, the Weaver and Rillieux schools, the students participate in community service such as caroling, making centerpieces for the nursing home, or sponsoring an Easter egg hunt for younger children. Both of these are very large urban schools with very diverse student bodies of 50% African-American and 50% Caucasian and/or Hispanic students. These schools are in tune with the events of the times; they sponsored Earth Day, environmental awareness events, litter-control patrols, recycling drives, Heart Smart, the Smokey the Bear program, Statue of Liberty renovation drives, and nutrition/safety awareness events.

Helping Hands

"Helping Hands" is a community service project found at several schools that fosters the habit of giving of oneself for the benefit of others. Indian Trail School is a primary K–3 school with a diverse student body of 341 from suburban Highland Park, Illinois. It believes that "an essential aspect in the development of character is the idea of service." Its slogan is "Just Say Yes"—to friendship, senior citizens, food drives. This school believes that service in the classroom leads to service in the community. The students love to participate in service opportunities at the school.

At the Weedsport School in New York the philosophy is: "We will place more stress in the area of character development by involving students in community projects than by writing a character development curriculum. Teachers feel that children who are already very positive and caring may benefit more from the school community if they are encouraged to become active with senior citizens and handicapped in the community." Weedsport is a K–6 school located in rural Weedsport, New York. The school lacks ethnic diversity, but has students from diverse socioeconomic backgrounds; 17% are from low-income families and the majority of the others are from lower-middle-class families.

Sister Mary Carol Gentile, the principal at St. Rocco School in Rhode Island, explains how "Community service gives students a chance to demonstrate social and civic responsibility, increase service skills, and act ethically in service settings. Our community service is making a difference through actions of caring, and by extending compassion to many in need."

Kathleen Gannon-Briggs, the principal at St. Isidore School in Danville, California, has made a school-wide commitment to the development of character, values, and ethics:

> Students are encouraged to become responsible caring citizens by getting personally involved with charitable efforts. Activities include monthly visits to a local convalescent home, coordinating "care packages" to sister schools in need (both in our country and one in Central America), outreach efforts in the face of natural disasters and clothing drives for the poor, removal of litter from local neighborhoods near our school and fund-raising for the homeless. We also have "service hour" requirements whereby students in the fifth through eighth grade must volunteer at least twenty hours of human services volunteer work each year.

St. Isidore is a Catholic, K–8 suburban school with a homogeneous student population.

GLOBAL CONCERNS

From the very beginning of the award program, Blue Ribbon Schools showed that they were aware of global concerns. Reading the award applications from several years provides a review of recent global history. In 1984–85, students gave to the Red Cross drives for the starving children in Ethiopia; in 1989–90, they supported the earthquake victims in Mexico; and in 1993–94, the concern was for those in India. In 1991–92 and 1993–94, a specific question was added to the award application: "How is your school preparing students to live effectively in a society that is culturally and ethnically diverse and an economy that is globally competitive?" In the answer to this question, many Blue Ribbon Schools also mentioned how learning to live with those who were culturally and ethnically diverse also helped to promote character.

Students are taught these attributes of caring and responsible behavior in grades K–5 at the Hill Elementary School in Austin, Texas. "Respect for difference is emphasized throughout our curriculum. Students at Hill interact with students from schools with a different ethnic and economic population mix. This helps both groups of children appreciate diversity." In addition, the integrated social studies curriculum helps students to value and cherish diversity in ethnicity, culture, and economics as an important "good citizenship" skill.

Celebrating Cultural and Ethnic Diversity

Country Club School in San Ramon, California, hosts many events and celebrations that emphasize cultural and ethnic diversity. These include United Nations Day, Heritage Days, Mardi Gras, Bastille Day, Chanukah, Christmas, and Cinco de Mayo. Some private schools add to their celebration list their cultural religious holidays, such as St. Joseph's Day, St. Patrick's Day and La Posada. For example:

> While the activities of the school are strictly secular, Laurel Mountain Elementary School in Austin, Texas, recognizes the contribution of the United States' diverse religious heritages to formulating a sound character, ethical

behavior, and self-discipline. Parents assist teachers in helping children learn cultural songs for the music programs. Rabbis and ministers are invited in to discuss specific customs and traditions with students.

Laurel is a large suburban school with a heterogeneous school population with 5% Asian, 6% Hispanic, and 3% African-American students.

Schools are making efforts to allow students to experience diversity in their day-to-day lives by seeking to employ staff and faculty that represent diverse groups. Westwood School in Santa Clara has a principal from a minority background, a music teacher from Russia, an art teacher from France, a science aide from Africa, and custodians from Portugal. In addition, the school tries to host guest speakers from various backgrounds and cultures. The Lowell School in Idaho has had assemblies with Native American dancers, a Japanese folktale performer, an Australian storyteller, Japanese students, and a parent from Norway—all of whom shared their culture with the students.

Multicultural Studies

Respect for differences is emphasized throughout the curriculum at the Blue Ribbon Schools, both in the cultural studies in the classroom and through art, music, sports, and school celebrations. More and more schools are offering instruction in foreign languages at the elementary and middle school level. There is an emphasis on using multicultural literature, such as that found in the Heartwood Curriculum, to teach character values such as respect and understanding of others. The literature-based Heartwood Curriculum allows teachers to integrate social studies, language arts, reading, music, and art. Flags of each country are displayed as part of the curriculum, and students learn to sing songs in different languages. For more information on the Heartwood Curriculum, see Chapter 3.

Moorestown Friends School in New Jersey, with its very diverse student population, tries to teach an appreciation of cultures and share this appreciation on a very personal level. The students are involved in service projects that tie into and support other cultures:

> Many Moorestown students come to school from families that instill sound values regarding the importance of cultures. Moorestown teachers also understand the necessity of teaching students to be responsible global citizens and give them many opportunities to enhance their behavior and attitude toward becoming thoughtful citizens. Students are specifically taught

about cultures and ethics in social studies, music, and library classes. Foreign language classes are also offered.

In the past few award years, schools documented their progress in developing technological skills in students. Computer programs that help to develop students' appreciation for other cultures and societies include PC/MAC Globe and Where in the World Is Carmen Sandiego?

Evaluation of the Effectiveness of Citizenship Programs

The focus on citizenship and character seems to be paying off. Many of the schools featured in this chapter report that they are spending less time on discipline and behavior problems and more time on helping children learn (National Association of Elementary School Principals, 1995). Joyce Westgate, the principal at Ben Franklin School in Binghamton, New York, reports that: "We have experienced fewer behavior problems, a kinder atmosphere, and observable positive actions that support exemplary citizenship as a result of our attention to building better habits of character. The best lessons of citizenship, however, are received through living in a caring, nurturing community where all concerned demonstrate good character every day."

Schools have a special and historic responsibility for the development of competent and responsible citizens and the Blue Ribbon Schools show that they are seeking to meet that responsibility by forming good character in America's future citizens. They do this by developing good citizenship in them.

SUMMARY

This chapter reports on the different ways in which the Blue Ribbon Schools promote the character of their students through their citizenship programs. A character-building citizenship program emphasizes the development of specific "democratic" qualities such as justice, respect, fairness, cooperation, persistence, moral responsibility, empathy, and caring. In order to develop these virtues, schools have given students opportunities in the classroom to practice actions of caring, concern for others, generosity, and kindness. Evaluations of these activities in the Blue Ribbon Schools and in other schools that have also implemented these programs have shown them to be effective in helping students develop their character and thereby act as good citizens.

REFERENCES

Berman, S. 1990. "Education for Social Responsibility," *Educational Leadership*, 48(3):75–80.

Borderbund Software. 1990. *Where in the World Is Carmen Sandiego?*

Bosworth, Kris. 1995. "Caring for Others and Being Cared For," *Phi Delta Kappan*, 76(9): 686–693.

Boyer, E. 1990. "Civic Education for Responsible Citizens," *Educational Leadership*, 48(3):4–6.

Butts, R. F. 1991. "Preface," *Civitas: A Framework for Civic Education*, C. Quigley and C. Bahmueller, eds. Calabasas, CA: National Center for Civic Education, p. xxi.

Chaskin, R. and D. Rauner. 1995. "Youth and Caring: An Introduction," *Phi Delta Kappan*, 76(9):667–674.

Communitarian Network. 1996. *The Role of Civic Education*. Washington, D.C.: Communitarian Network, pp. 1–15.

Dolenga, J. 1990. "The Civic Achievement Award Program," *Educational Leadership*, 48(3):89.

Kohn, A. 1990. "The ABC's of Caring," *Teacher Magazine*, 52–58.

Kohn, A. 1991. "Caring Kids: The Role of Schools," *Phi Delta Kappan*, 72(7): 496–506.

Kohn, A. 1993. *Punished by Rewards*. Boston, MA: Houghton-Mifflin.

Letwin, A. 1991. "Promoting Civic Understanding and Civic Skills through Conceptually Based Curricula," in *Moral, Character, and Civic Education in the Elementary School*. J. Benninga, ed. New York: Teachers College Press, pp. 203–211.

Lickona, T. 1991. *Educating for Character: How Our Schools Can Teach Respect and Responsibility*. New York: Bantam Books.

MacIntyre, Alasdair. 1981. *After Virtue*. Notre Dame: Univ. of Notre Dame Press.

Molnar, A. 1990. "Judging the Ethics of Ethics Education," *Educational Leadership*, 48(3):73–74.

National Association of Elementary School Principals. 1994. *Best Ideas from America's Blue Ribbon Schools*. Thousand Oaks, CA: Corwin Press.

National Association of Elementary School Principals. 1995. *Best Ideas from America's Blue Ribbon Schools, Vol 2*. Thousand Oaks, CA: Corwin Press.

Noblit, G., D. Rogers and B. McCadden. 1995. "In the Meantime the Possibilities of Caring," *Phi Delta Kappan*, 76(9):680–685.

P. C. Globe, Inc. 1990. *PC Globe*.

Pereira, C. 1991. "Educating for Citizenship in the Early Grades," in *Moral, Character, and Civic Education in the Elementary School*. J. Benninga, ed. New York: Teachers College Press, pp. 212–226.

Quigley, C. 1996. cited in *The Role of Civic Education*. Washington, D.C.: The Communitarian Network, p. 3.

Quigley, C. and C. Bahmueller, eds. 1991. *Civitas: A Framework for Civic Education.* Calabasas, CA: National Center for Civic Education.

Reische, D. 1987. *Citizenship Goal of Education.* Arlington, VA: American Association of School Administrators.

Riley, R. 1995. "Foreword" in *Best Ideas from America's Blue Ribbon Schools, Vol. 2* by National Association of Elementary School Principals. CA: Corwin Press, pp. ix–x.

Rowe, J. 1990. "To Develop Thinking Citizens," *Educational Leadership*, 48(3):43–45.

Sadowsky, E. 1991. "Democracy in the Elementary School: Learn by Doing," in *Moral, Character, and Civic Education in the Elementary School.* J. Benninga, ed. New York: Teachers College Press, pp. 84–106.

Schaps, E. and D. Solomon. 1990. "Schools and Classrooms as Caring Communities," *Educational Leadership*, 48(3):38–40.

Sparks, R. 1991. "Character Development at Fort Washington Elementary School," in *Moral, Character, and Civic Education in the Elementary School.* J. Benninga, ed. New York: Teachers College Press, pp. 178–194.

Wood, G. 1990. "Teaching for Democracy," *Educational Leadership*, 4(3):32–37.

Chapter 9

EVALUATING THE EFFECTIVENESS OF CHARACTER EDUCATION IN THE BLUE RIBBON SCHOOLS

What people say you cannot do, you try and find that you can.
— Henry David Thoreau

The possibility that we may fail in the struggle ought not to deter us from the support of a cause we believe to be just. — Abraham Lincoln

A ship is safe at shore, but that is not where a ship is meant to be. We cannot discover new oceans unless we have the courage to lose sight of the shore. — Anonymous

EVALUATING THESE RESEARCH FINDINGS

Aristotle begins the *Nichomachean Ethics* by explaining that "every inquiry, every action and pursuit, is thought to aim at some good; this is the end to which all things tend. Although it is good to attain the end for one person, it is finer still to attain it for a nation. Happiness is the end and goal of all human beings; and for one who lives a life of virtue, the good life, is happy" (1094a1-5).

This book can be seen as a compendium of moral and character education programs found within schools selected as among the best in the United States. It shows how these programs help students attain their ends, to develop their characters, to learn to live lives of virtue. However, as pointed out earlier, the presence of a particular character education program in a Blue Ribbon School does not necessarily mean that the specific program is also one of the best in the country. In each chapter, available research has been cited to help the reader eval-

181

uate the character education program for its effectiveness and desirability as a component of a comprehensive, schoolwide approach to character education.

This chapter addresses the importance of evaluating character education programs in order to assess whether or not they are achieving their end. It reports on the few programs that have been evaluated and gives readers guidelines on how they might go about evaluating the effectiveness of character education programs implemented in their own schools. It seeks to answer the following questions:

- How are schools' applications evaluated in selecting Blue Ribbon winners?
- Must schools have an effective character education program to be named Blue Ribbon Schools?
- How should a researcher or school set up an evaluation study of a character education program?
- What programs have been found to be effective in promoting character development? How do we know that they work?
- What key components can be extracted from the many programs cited in this book that have been found to be effective in promoting character in students?

THE BLUE RIBBON SCHOOL EVALUATION PROCESS

All of the Blue Ribbon Schools, through the selection and review process, were judged to be educating their students effectively, striving to strengthen subject-matter content in English, mathematics, science, history, geography, art, and foreign languages, while using instructional techniques that motivate students to learn and study. These schools have environments that support and recognize excellent teaching, involve the parents and the community in the education of children, and prepare the students to live effectively in a global world. These schools are safe and free from drugs, have a climate conducive to learning, and foster the development of sound character in their students. They had to show that they were meeting these goals in order to be named as worthy of National Recognition as Exemplary Schools. They were evaluated at several different stages of the application process before they received the Blue Ribbon Award.

A school's completion of all of the required parts of the application to the Department of Education's School Recognition Program is the first step in the selection process (see Appendix A). These applications are then sent to the Chief State School Officers who review them and choose the schools from their state to nominate for consideration at the national level. These nominations are then reviewed by a National Review Panel that selects schools to recommend for site visits. Two-day visits are conducted to each school so chosen. (The author has participated as a U.S. Department of Education site visitor to two of the schools that applied for Blue Ribbon Recognition). The responsibility of the site visitor is to verify that what the application reports is indeed happening in the school. The site visit is the qualitative evaluation of the school's application. The site visit reports are then forwarded to the Review Panel, which meets a second time to review all of the schools that have received site visits. The panel then selects the final group of schools for recognition by the Secretary of Education. (As an illustration, in 1985–86, 525 schools were chosen for site visits, and 212 of these schools were chosen as Exemplary Schools.)

The National School Recognition Program uses an "expertise-oriented evaluation approach" that depends primarily upon professional expertise to judge an educational institution, program, product, or activity (Worthen & Sanders, 1987). Using a very specific checklist, in conjunction with observations, document analysis, and interviews, the site visitors gather information on school leadership, teaching environment, curriculum and instruction, student environment, parental and community support, success indicators, and organizational vitality. They then judge the school's application as accurate, understated, or overstated in each of these categories in terms of the criteria for recognition delineated in the program guidelines.

In order to be nominated for Blue Ribbon recognition, the school must show evidence that its policies, programs, and practices foster the development of sound character, a sense of self-worth, democratic values, ethical judgment, and self-discipline. The Blue Ribbon schools do *not* have to have an explicit character education or moral education program in place in order to be chosen. However, they do have to show that the school programs and policies in general, whether or not they are called "character education," foster the development of sound character and good discipline and promote a safe, drug-free environment in which students are motivated to learn and prepare themselves to become participating citizens in our diverse global society. The many character-building ideas found in these schools contribute to the formulation of the Blue Ribbon Schools' Comprehensive Model of Character Development discussed in Chapter 1.

AN EVALUATION MODEL
FOR CHARACTER EDUCATION PROGRAMS

How effective are the character education programs that the Blue Ribbon Schools have identified? If the current revival of character education is to succeed, it will have to successfully address the question of assessing program effectiveness (Leming, 1993a). Ralph Tyler (1949), considered by many as the founder of curriculum evaluation, defined evaluation as "essentially the process of determining to what extent the educational objectives are actually being realized by the program of curriculum and instruction" (p. 105). *Evaluation*, according to Webster's dictionary, means "to determine the worth of or to ascertain the value of, to appraise." By evaluating character education, we are attempting to ascertain the value of these programs or efforts. In order to assess their effectiveness in the Blue Ribbon Schools, we have to know what objectives schools hoped to meet by implementing these educational programs. Tyler's evaluation model consists of the following steps:

(*1*) Establish broad goals or objectives.
(*2*) Classify the goals or objectives.
(*3*) Define objectives in behavioral terms.
(*4*) Find situations in which achievement of objectives can be shown.
(*5*) Develop or select measurement techniques.
(*6*) Collect performance data.
(*7*) Compare performance data with behaviorally stated objectives.

It can be used as a basic model of evaluation upon which a specific evaluation of a character education program can be built.

In order to "establish," "classify," and "define" our objectives—Tyler's first three steps—a review of the character education paradigm presented in Chapter 1 may be helpful. If we understand "good character" as the intersection of moral knowing, moral feeling, and moral action, we will want to see (1) how well students have met the objective of "knowing" particular good actions that they should do; (2) how well they have grown in their attitude formation so that they "want and will" to do the good; and (3) to what extent they actually "do" acts of good character.

Moral knowledge is perhaps the easiest to evaluate. Moral knowledge includes knowing *that* certain things are right and others wrong and understanding *why* certain behaviors are right and others wrong (moral reasoning). The measurement of moral reasoning by Kohlberg and his followers has yielded innumerable studies showing that it is possible to raise a student's moral reasoning one-fourth to one-half of a stage when students are involved in the process of discussing moral dilemmas (Leming, 1993b). However, because none of the moral dilemma studies included any form of behavior as a dependent variable, such studies can only be said to assess one aspect of character—namely, moral knowing—rather than full character development. Various test formats (i.e., true-false, short-answer, multiple choice) can be used to assess students' knowledge of the definitions of virtues and their recognition of situations that call into play the living of these virtues. These tests also can be used as both pre-test and post-test measures to assess growth in knowledge in these areas after completion of a character education unit or program. In practice, even elaborate programs of inculcating virtue do not ensure later virtuous conduct by all participants. That is why virtues should be applied as well as studied in schools, giving students opportunities for displaying the desired character traits in good actions (Wynne 1993).

Evaluation of moral feeling is more difficult for several reasons: the field is much newer; the psychometrics are less sophisticated, accurate, and reliable; and it is more difficult to measure beliefs, attitudes, and feelings. Evaluation of the emotional or attitudinal side of character often makes use of self-report and protective measures such as sentence completion, picture interpretation, and rating scales. The validity and reliability of these measures is often not as great as for measures of moral knowing (Wiley, in press). In fact, one cannot reliably infer that internally good moral feelings and attitudes are necessarily the motivation behind observably "good" behavior; that is, one could be doing the action out of fear of punishment, for instance (Cline & Feldmesser, 1983).

Behavior is easier to measure than feelings, but in order to measure moral behavior programs, evaluators must agree concerning what behaviors show that students are living the specific character qualities that have been identified as important to the school implementing the character education program. Measurement of behaviors can be gathered through analysis of classroom conduct (e.g., attendance and discipline referrals) and anecdotal evidence (e.g., observations of students during small or large group activities, teacher journals or diaries). In addition, various survey instruments can be used to document behavior, such as the "School Character Survey" developed by Human Systems Development, 500 Evans Lane, Dayton, Ohio 45459; phone: 513-439-9315; or the "Hypothetical Scenarios" test developed by Stanley Weed of the Institute for Research and Evaluation, 6068 South Jordan Canal Road, Salt Lake City, Utah 84118; phone: 801-966-5644.

Continuing to the fifth step of the Tyler evaluation model outlined above: when the goals and objectives have been established, classified, and defined, and situations demonstrating achievement of character education objectives have been identified, measurement techniques must be developed or selected, and student performance data needs to be collected.

Two approaches can be used to collect data for an evaluation of contemporary character education programs: informal and formal. Informal evaluation methods rely on qualitative data, that is, data gathered by the evaluator in the natural setting of the school by using unobtrusive, multiple data-gathering methods, such as participant observations and interviews (Worthen & Sanders, 1987). These generate data from anecdotal evidence, surveys of teachers, parents, and students, and highly subjective perceptions. Formal evaluation of character education programs uses quantitative data, that is, data gathered using standardized, objective, and reliable measurements, instruments, or tests (i.e., both a pre-test and post-test). It must also utilize proper experimental design, that is, compare character education program students to non-program students, and attempt to control for potential sources of bias (Leming, 1993a). A number of evaluators have argued that quantitative and qualitative approaches should be utilized jointly as the two strategies have complementary strengths.

Formal evaluations are based on systematic efforts to define criteria and obtain accurate information about alternatives (Worthen & Sanders, 1987). It is very difficult to have a formal evaluation of a character education program with a true experimental design because of the subject matter: students in schools with many different teachers.

Even when students are randomly assigned to experimental and control classes, the "control breaks down" as the year progresses, that is, students come in, leave, or are absent; teachers differ in their teaching techniques even when using the same curriculum, and so forth. Additionally, there is a consensus that because character develops incrementally over time, it is unrealistic to expect an evaluation of a program after one year to prove anything definitively. Evaluation of a character education program needs to have a longitudinal component.

Most evaluators would therefore agree with Cline and Feldmesser (1983) that the quasi-experimental design of Campbell and Stanley (1966) is the most effective for the evaluation of character education programs. A quasi-experimental design uses two basic strategies: comparison groups and time-series analyses. Comparison groups are not strict "control groups" because it may not have been possible to assign the members randomly, or to control for newcomers or leavers. There may be other extraneous variables, such as, sex, race, age, or socioeconomic status, for which one cannot control. A school with limited funding cannot afford the cost of an experimental research evaluation with a control group. However, using the quasi-experimental design a school can gather data on its students before they begin the character education program and after they have experienced the program. This will be a valid evaluation. Time-series design means that measurements are taken before the program begins, during the program, and after the program ends. If both comparison groups and time-series can be combined in the same evaluation, the design is substantially strengthened. This is the preferred design for the evaluation of character education programs (Cline & Feldmesser, 1983).

EVALUATION OF CHARACTER EDUCATION IN THE BLUE RIBBON SCHOOL APPLICATIONS

The final step in the Tyler model of evaluation is to "compare performance data with behaviorally stated objectives." The Blue Ribbon Schools, in their applications, provided a large amount of qualitative data to show they were meeting the objective to foster "the development of sound character, democratic values, ethical judgment, and the ability to work in a self-disciplined and purposeful manner." Evaluation of the effectiveness of character education programs was sometimes mentioned in the actual schools' applications. For example, Dr. Cherry Jones, the principal at the Flanders Elementary School in Connecticut, explained how her school evaluates its effectiveness:

> We measure our effectiveness in motivating students to learn through their observable excitement and enthusiasm. They show themselves willing to take risks and participate in class. Former students return and reminisce about our programs. Because of the experience we have provided them in science and computers here, our students have become instrumental in establishing a telecommunications program at the middle school. They run the middle school newspaper, showing off their writing and computer skills. A high percentage of them make the honor roll.

The Burruss Elementary School, a large integrated school in Burris, Georgia, almost one fourth African-American, reports on how it evaluates the success of its total school character education program:

> Effectiveness indicators are positive parental feedback, the very small number of disciplinary infractions, and the high degree of on-task engaged student performance. Excellent test scores are another measure of effectiveness. The school climate is very positive and reflects student interest in learning. There are many visitors to the school and their comments almost always refer to busy children who are on task and show excellent behavior as well as a cheerful attitude.

EVALUATION OF CHARACTER EDUCATION BY U.S. DEPARTMENT OF EDUCATION SITE VISITORS

Most often the site visitors' reports were the largest source of documentation regarding the success of the character education efforts in the Blue Ribbon Schools. Under the section on "Student Environment," the site visitors made comments pointing to evidence of the character education outcomes the schools were seeking. In their comments they reported on observed student behaviors and overall school climate as a reflection of good character.

Student Behaviors Showing Character

Here are some examples of observations from site visitors regarding student behavior: At the Gesu School, a large K–8 school with an integrated student body in University Heights, Ohio, a site visitor reported: "Students help in the lunch room, the office, and the library without being paid."

"Students pick up papers in the hall even if they did not put them there themselves" at Green Trails School, another large, well-integrated school in Chesterfield, Missouri.

The site visitor to the Yakutat Elementary School in Arkansas reported: "Students can be in the library without adult supervision." Yakutat is a rural K–6 school with fifty-five percent African-American students, and 30% of the student body from families with low incomes.

At the Marion Street Elementary School in New York, a suburban school with a homogeneous student body of 382, the site visitor's report notes: "Students are given real responsibilities in the school; they operate a school store."

"Students pick up after themselves on the playground" at the Taper Avenue Elementary School, in California, a very large school of over 1000 very diverse students who are 16% Hispanic, 17% Asian, and 32% from lower-income families.

"Lost articles are returned" at the South Valley School, a small K–4 school in Moorestown, New Jersey with a heterogeneous student body.

The site visitor to the Robert Johnson Elementary School in Kentucky reported that "students stated that they had no money stolen or lost. A teacher said that three dollars stayed on her desk for two weeks, never being disturbed. This school has moral students." Robert Johnson is a large K–6 school with a homogeneous student body in Ft. Thomas, a large central city in Kentucky.

The site visitor to the Gulliver Academy, in Coral Cables, Florida, reported: "The teachers, administrators, and other staff all felt the students were exceptionally well-behaved. They cared about and were of good character. They felt that this was due to a large extent to the emphasis placed on these characteristics at Gulliver."

Gulliver Academy is a unique school. It is a for-profit independent K–8 school with a diverse student body of over 1000 students, 30% of whom are Hispanic, 3% African-American or Asian, and 10% from lower-income families.

The visitor to the Lewis Powell Magnet School in North Carolina noted these manifestations of good character:

> Students are polite to adults and each other. They hold doors for one another, they address adults with respect and you constantly hear "Thank

you." Character-building is integrated into the total school effort. A special education student found $2.00 and immediately turned it into the office saying "It may be someone's lunch money."

School Climate

Concerning climate: One visitor spoke to a third-grade student at the Kathryn Marklely School in Malvern, Pennsylvania, about the mentally-challenged children in the school and received the following response: "We don't treat people differently because they don't learn the same way; we treat them according to the way they act towards others." Kathryn Markely has a large homogeneous student body but also serves students with special educational needs.

The visitor to the Governor Bent School in New Mexico reported that at this school, "caring is the umbrella that supports students in their character and academic development."

A student told the visitor to the Ormand Beach Elementary School in Florida, "My teacher is understanding, honest, and she listens." Ormand Beach is a pre-K to fifth-grade integrated school that serves a student population that is 24% African-American, almost 50% from lower-income families, and 66% special education, as the school serves as the site for the exceptional student population of the eastern part of the Volusia County. The teachers at Ormand Beach continually try to recognize those students who exemplify good behavior and human kindness. They work together with the students to maintain a spirit of cooperation and mutual respect. The students feel that their teachers are doing a very good job at reaching this goal.

EVALUATIONS OF
CHARACTER EDUCATION PROGRAMS

Any district, school, or teacher that is serious about implementing a program of character education will want to evaluate the results of the program (Kirschenbaum, 1995). There are two kinds of evaluation that they will want to use: formative and summative (Bloom et al., 1971; Scriven, 1973). Formative evaluation is conducted during the operation of the program; it allows the evaluator to gather information (from participants, that is, the students and teachers, and from observers —

the parents) useful in improving a program that is underway. Formative evaluation is particularly helpful in determining whether or not teachers are implementing a particular character education curriculum effectively. Formative evaluation helps to improve the program by indicating areas that need to be modified, revised, or developed further.

Summative evaluations are conducted at the end of a program in order to assess the program's worth or merit—its overall impact. The data (qualitatively gathered from interviews or surveys, or quantitatively gathered from a formal research design) help the implementers of the program learn if they are accomplishing their stated goals, and can support a rationale for the continuance of the program (Kirschenbaum, 1995). Both formative and summative evaluation techniques should be used as schools seek to implement some of the programs mentioned in this book.

B. David Brooks and Mark Kahn (1993) state that the implementation of a character education program must include a pre-assessment of goals that involves articulating expectations clearly and explicitly detailing the various objectives to be accomplished. During the program implementation, periodic meetings among teachers help them to keep the goals in mind and to adapt classroom lessons accordingly. Finally, the program should have an assessment of the outcomes based on a post-evaluation of the results obtained from anecdotal reports from teachers and appropriate data on measurable changes in key variables.

Huffman (1994) concurs and suggests the following steps be followed in setting up a character education program evaluation:

(*1*) Design the evaluation component during the initial planning process. Identify the base line data to use.

(*2*) Review the character education evaluation literature early to get design ideas.

(*3*) Include an implementation assessment in the evaluation design. (As noted in some of the research cited in previous chapters, poor implementation of a curriculum is frequently the cause of disappointing results).

(*4*) Be prepared to answer questions about evaluating students.

(*5*) Involve parents, students, and all staff in developing the evaluation component.

(*6*) Conduct the program evaluation.

(*7*) Establish evaluation partnerships with colleges and universities.

Perhaps the most important thing that a school can do before it implements a particular character education program is to gather some base line data regarding student behavior, to which it can later compare data gathered after program intervention. If at all possible, it would be very valuable to choose randomly the groups of students (classes or schools) that will use the new character education program and the groups of students (different classes or different schools) that will not use it. These conditions, if they can be administratively actualized, will provide the school with a formal structure for evaluation. An evaluation conducted with an experimental or a quasi-experimental design can be added to the very small but growing research base on character education and provide a much needed resource for schools just beginning their character education programs.

EVALUATION OF BLUE RIBBON SCHOOLS' CHARACTER DEVELOPMENT PROGRAMS

Six of the character education programs found in the Blue Ribbon Schools have been evaluated, either "formally" or "informally." The evaluations used experimental and quasi-experimental or qualitative designs and were based on either quantitative or qualitative data. We will briefly report on these evaluations so that they may serve as a model for other schools that seek to implement and evaluate character education programs.

Teaching Children to Care

One of the best evaluations of a character education program is that done of the Child Development Project (CDP) in San Ramon, California (see Chapter 3 for a description of the project). Originally funded by the William and Flora Hewlett Foundation, the CDP had from its inception a clear focus on formal evaluation of results. The program was begun in 1982 in the San Ramon Valley Unified School District, a suburban middle-class community thirty miles east of San Francisco. The staff carefully matched two sets of three elementary schools in the district for size, socioeconomic status and degree of faculty and family interest in the program. Then one school in each matched pair was randomly chosen to receive the program. A cross-sectional preprogram assessment of a large random sample of students from program and comparison schools revealed no large or consistent differences between these two groups with respect to a variety of social attitudes, values, skills, and behaviors (Watson et al., 1989).

The basic design of the program intervention and evaluation was longitudinal; it began with groups of kindergarten students and followed these cohorts as they progressed through to the sixth grade. The evaluation involved both formative studies of teachers' implementation of the various program components—that is, cooperative learning, developmental discipline, the teaching of pro-social values through literature and the teaching of caring through opportunities to help schoolmates and family—and summative evaluation of the program effects on students both during the elementary school years when the program was in effect and in junior high school after it was over. The summative evaluation involved collecting data on students' interpersonal behavior, attitudes, academic, and interpersonal motivation, moral reasoning, and academic performance, using a variety of procedures such as classroom observation, experimental small-group activities, teacher and student questionnaires, interviews, and achievement tests (Developmental Studies Center, 1991, 1994).

The study showed that CDP students scored significantly higher on measures of sensitivity, consideration of others' needs, problem-solving skills, and use of conflict resolution strategies that were more pro-social. With regard to student behavior, the results were mixed depending upon grade level. No difference was detected between the comparison school and CDP school with regard to the incidence of negative behaviors. On the other behavior measures, a significant difference was detected favoring the CDP schools when the combined data was analyzed; however, the results were not as strong when analyzed by grade level. What the evaluation did show was that it was possible to teach pro-social behaviors to students and make some difference in their behavior outside of the classroom.

The evaluation of the CDP was one of the best examples of a formal evaluation study and as such was a significant contribution to the area of character education evaluation. It was rigorous in its research design, using random assignment of subjects to groups; it used control and test groups, gathered data using multiple measures both qualitative and quantitative, and was longitudinal in its scope. The design had both formative and summative evaluation components. The project and its evaluation have been replicated in various settings and the results have been significantly positive at each site.

The Success Through Accepting Responsibility (STAR) Program

The Jefferson Center for Character Education was founded in 1963 and has had its STAR program (Success Through Accepting Responsibility) implemented in approximately 6000 schools in virtually every state, in most major cities, and in Canada. The STAR curriculum includes short and easy-to-follow weekly lessons that can be integrated into the regular curriculum, as well as monthly character themes that are also featured on classroom posters. The key elements of the program include both content and process: (1) direct instruction in the teaching of character values, (2) a language-based curriculum using works of literature that exemplify the core character concepts in their characters, (3) positive language, (4) a *process* for making good character decisions (i.e., Stop, Think, Act, Review), (5) a school climate approach, (6) teacher-friendly materials that allow for flexibility and creativity, (7) student participation, and (8) parental involvement.

An informal evaluation of the STAR character education program's implementation in the Los Angeles elementary schools was conducted in the spring of 1991. Data were gathered by interviewing twenty-five administrators in schools where the program was implemented. Combining the data for all schools, the researchers found that after one year with the curriculum, all forms of discipline problems decreased (major discipline problems decreased by 25%, suspensions declined by 16%, the number of tardy students dropped by 40%, and unexcused absences fell by 18%). The median level of student participation in extracurricular activities increased slightly as did the median number of students on the principals' Honor Rolls; there was also an improvement in student morale and an increase in parental involvement in their children's education. The administrators said that the program achieved more than they anticipated: better student self-discipline, an opportunity to teach values in the classroom, and a common reference point for solving conflicts (Brooks and Goble, 1997; Franklin, 1996). The strengths of this evaluation include its pre- and post-comparisons on a number of measures, but its limitations were the lack of control groups and independent observers.

Impacting Student Behavior

The Character Education Curriculum from the American Institute of Character Education in San Antonio, Texas, has been producing character education curriculum materials for grades K–6 for over twenty-five years. The curriculum is in over 18,000 classrooms in 44 states. The Institute evaluates the effectiveness of its curriculum using survey data and anecdotal comments from persons interviewed who use the curriculum. It reports that a survey of a random sample of 269 elementary school teachers from across the nation showed that 96% noted improvement in their students' self-concept, 87% in students' oral language skills, 85% in behavior in the classroom, 71% in behavior in the lunchroom, and 69% in behavior on the playground. A survey of 57 elementary school principals from across the nation revealed that 84% reported improvement in the relationships between teachers and students; 77%, a decrease in discipline problems; 64%, a decrease in vandalism, and 68%, an increase in attendance.

Two formal evaluations have been conducted of the curriculum. The San Antonio Independent School District administered pre-tests of the Piers-Harris Children's Self-Concept Scale to three schools using the Character Education Curriculum, and three control schools not using the curriculum. A total of 507 students participated in the study. Four months later, a post-test was administered in the same schools and significant changes favoring the experimental schools were noted in many areas of self-concept.

Finally, a five-year evaluation (1991–1995) of the 15 schools in Spartanburg, South Carolina, using the Character Education Curriculum found that the faculty liked and supported teaching the curriculum. The students thought the topics discussed were important, felt that they learned something new, enjoyed the classes, and said they would like character education to be taught twice a week rather than just once a week (Character Education Institute, 1996).

The Quest Evaluation Kit

One of the most significant and valuable contributions to the evaluation of character programs is being made by Quest International. Its Evaluation Kit is designed for schools using positive youth development programs such as Quest in such areas as health education, prevention of at-risk behaviors, and family studies. The kit teaches the user how to implement tested evaluation methodologies such as a needs assessment and pre- and post-test measures, how to evaluate the data, and how to report the results to interested publics. The kit includes inventories, surveys, logs, observational checklists, data collection forms, and interview questions that can be used in conducting an evaluation. Of particular value are the Behavior Rating Tools that include "Observational Checklists for Pro-Social Behaviors" and the "Attitude and Projected Behavior Surveys." The Quest International Evaluation Kit can be obtained from Quest International, 537 Jones Road, P.O. Box 566, Granville, OH 43023-0566; phone: 800-837-2801.

Quest has also gathered a large amount of data regarding the effectiveness of its own programs on student performance in school settings. It has gathered its own surveys of participants in the Quest programs, and it has also used independent research agencies for more formal studies. For example, in 1991, Quest International conducted a study on the effects of the Skills for Adolescence curriculum as measured by attendance, school grades, California Achievement Test scores, and school attitude. A total of 497 students in grades 6–8 were selected for the study. A nonrandom assignment, pre-test/post-test design was used in which students from existing, intact classrooms were designated as either experimental or comparison groups. All students were pre- and post-tested with two instruments: the School Attitude Measure (SAM), a nationally normed measure of students' feelings and attitudes toward self and schools, and the California Achievement Test (CAT) for reading and mathematics. In addition to these two measures, student records were examined to compare school grade point average (GPA), subject area grades, school attendance, and citizenship marks. The School Attitude Measure revealed a slight but significant positive effect for students who received the Skills for Adolescence (SFA) program; language arts and mathematics grades were significantly higher for the SFA group; and the SFA group had significantly fewer days absent than the comparison group. However, California Achievement Test scores showed no difference between SFA and comparison groups. One can conclude that the SFA curriculum does help to increase student performance on some measures of school attitude, attendance, and academic knowledge (Quest International, 1991).

The Fort Washington Elementary School Evaluation

The character development program at the Fort Washington Elementary School in Clovis, California, has been described in previous chapters. Here we will report on its evaluation of the effectiveness of this award program. There are three major components of the Fort Washington character education program: (1) the co-curricular program, (2) the Exemplary Patriot Award Program, and (3) the Patriotic Classroom Award. The effectiveness of the Fort Washington character development program was evaluated after five years of implementation. Base line data were gathered on a number of key measures. The administration and faculty sought to examine the cause-and-effect relationship between the instructional program and its impact on student behaviors.

The total character development program was found to be effective in developing a positive, purposeful school climate; several key outcome variables were observed by evaluators. Specifically, scores on achievement tests improved and the number of students on the honor roll grew; daily attendance at school improved and incidents of school vandalism became non-existent; and the number of students who participated in school extracurricular activities increased greatly (Sparks, 1991).

Fort Washington found that the award program is instrumental in creating an effective and positive school climate for students as well as staff members and parents. More importantly, Fort Washington reported that the impact of this approach to character development appears to substantiate findings from ongoing "effective schools research" showing that quality schools are achieved when there is (1) a strong sense of mission; (2) high standards for all; (3) a high level of participation by staff, students, and parents; and (4) a well-planned student recognition structure that reinforces the behaviors desired and valued by the school and community.

Evaluation of the Heartwood Institute's Curriculum

James Leming and associates (1997) recently conducted an evaluation of the Heartwood Institute's Ethics Curriculum for Children. As described in Chapter 3, the Heartwood curriculum is a character education program that places its primary focus on children's literature as the vehicle for instruction in values and ethics.

The study was conducted in two school districts, one located in western Pennsylvania, and the other in southern Illinois, during the 1995–96 academic year. A total of 42 teachers in four schools along with their 965 students participated in the study. In each district, there were two other schools similar in size and economic make-up that agreed to be the comparison group. The Heartwood curriculum was implemented in a total of 20 classrooms. The program consisted of fourteen different lessons, each lasting 30–45 minutes, on seven different ethical attributes. The intention of the curriculum was to influence children's character development in three general areas: cognitive, affective, and behavioral.

This formal evaluation employed the quasi-experimental design advocated by Cline and Feldmesser (1983). There were comparison groups and pre- and post-tests; however, assignment to groups was not random but by volunteering. Instruments were developed to measure (1) the students' understanding of the vocabulary of the character traits taught by the Heartwood curriculum—*ethical understanding*; (2) the extent to which students expressed a preference for actions that exemplify the character attributes that serve as the objectives of the Heartwood curriculum—*ethical sensibility*; and (3) students' character-related behavior—*ethical conduct*. In addition to pre- and post-tests, interviews were conducted with teachers and students at the end of the academic year, and classroom observations were conducted at random intervals throughout the year. These instruments were administered in both the classrooms using the Heartwood curriculum and the comparison classrooms not using the curriculum.

It was found that program students at all grades demonstrated higher levels of ethical understanding of these attributes than did comparison students, and improved student conduct was also noted by teachers of students in the program as compared to reports given by teachers in the comparison classrooms. The findings on ethical sensibility showed that participation in the program did not make a significant difference in this area.

Leming states in his evaluation that "to be meaningful and to advance systematic thinking about knowledge in the field, research findings must be interpreted from some theoretical or conceptual frame of reference." Given the implicit teaching/learning model of the Heartwood curriculum, he feels that the social learning theory of Albert Bandura (1977) provides a coherent perspective as to how children's literature might facilitate moral growth by providing children with an opportunity for observational learning. Ideally, character education programs should be developed and evaluated from clear perspectives regarding the nature of character and how it is learned (Leming et al., 1997).

COMPONENTS OF EFFECTIVE
CHARACTER EDUCATION SCHOOLS

What, in conclusion, emerges as the profile of character education in the Blue Ribbon Schools? Our analysis of over 100 character education programs found in various Blue Ribbon Schools suggests that an effective character education program includes

(1) A strong school mission committed to developing a student's sense of morals, character, and good citizenship

(2) A high level of participation by the staff, students, and parents in the decision-making process by which they determine desired character qualities and subsequent activities that the school will use to foster good citizenship

(3) High standards for student academic performance that are realized throughout the curriculum by teaching methodologies that promote character (e.g., highlighting key character qualities in thematic, literature-based, and interdisciplinary units) and by teaching strategies, such as cooperative learning, learning styles instruction, and authentic assessment

(4) High standards for student behavior that are positively stated and understood by teachers, students, and community. All are involved in creating a caring school that is safe, nurturing, drug-free, and involved in community and global affairs

(5) A well-planned student recognition program that serves to communicate, encourage, and reinforce the character qualities, attitudes, and behaviors that are valued by the school and community

(6) A commitment to character education that is comprehensive, that is, all faculty, staff, administrators, and students are committed to good character. All teachers are involved in integrating character education into the various subjects they teach (math, science, social studies, literature, health, etc.) and all staff members (counselors, cafeteria and playground aides, secretaries, etc.) reinforce

the living of these good character traits. In addition, the community makes a commitment to reinforcing good character through the media and in the neighborhood.

SUMMARY

Before being recognized for the Blue Ribbon Award, schools showed in their application and during site visits that they did indeed foster the development of good character in their students. Ideas have been given on how each of the components of good character—moral knowing, moral feeling, and moral action—can be evaluated. A framework has been given for setting up a formal evaluation of a character education program. Finally, six character education program evaluations of varying breadth and rigor have been reviewed. The chapter concludes with a list of six recurring components of effective character education found in the Blue Ribbon schools. Given the facts that: (1) these components are repeatedly found in schools judged worthy of the highest national recognition, (2) some evaluations (such as that of the Child Development project) have experimentally demonstrated the effectiveness of at least some of these components, and (3) such components match the school qualities revealed by effective schools research, it seems reasonable to hypothesize that these six factors contribute to effective character education. However, many questions remain: Are all of these factors equally important? Are any of them dispensable? Are their effects interactive? Are they equally effective at all grade levels? Do the effects of these components on student character generalize beyond school and endure over time? These and similar questions must be answered by future research.

REFERENCES

Bandura, A. 1977. *Social Learning Theory.* Englewood Cliffs, NJ: Prentice Hall.

Bloom, B., J. T. Hasting and G. Madaus. 1971. *Handbook on Formative and Summative Evaluation of Student Learning.* New York: McGraw-Hill.

Brooks, B. D. and F. Goble. 1997. *The Case for Character Education: The Role of the School in Teaching Values and Virtue.* Northridge, CA: Studio 4 Publications.

Brooks, B. D. and M. Kahn. 1993. "What Makes Character Education Programs Work?" *Educational Leadership,* 51(3): 19–21.

Campbell, D. and Stanley, J. 1966. *Experimental and Quasi-Experimental Designs for Research*. Chicago, IL.: Rand-McNally.

Character Education Institute. 1996. *The Character Education Curriculum: Developing Responsible Citizens*. San Antonio, TX: Author, pp. 22–23.

Cline, H. and R. Feldmesser. 1983. *Program Evaluation in Moral Education*. Princeton, N.J.: Educational Testing Service.

Developmental Studies Center. 1991. *Evaluation of The Child Development Project: Summary of Findings to Date*. Oakland, CA.: Developmental Studies Center.

Developmental Studies Center. 1994. *The Child Development Project: Summary of Findings in Two Initial Districts and the First Phase of an Expansion to Six Additional Districts Nationally*. Oakland, CA: Developmental Studies Center.

Franklin, Z. 1996. "Jefferson Center for Character Education." [On line] available URL: http://www.netspce.org/~zaqix/jefferson.html

Huffman, H. 1994. *Developing a Character Education Program: One School District's Experience*. Alexandria, VA: ASCD.

Kirschenbaum, H. 1995. *100 Ways to Enhance Values and Morality in Schools and Youth Settings*. Boston, MA: Allyn & Bacon.

Laird, M. 1993. *Quest International Evaluation Kit*. Ohio: Quest International.

Leming, J. 1993a. *Character Education: Lessons from the Past, Models for the Future*. Maine: The Institute for Global Ethics.

Leming, J. 1993b. "In Search of Effective Character Education," *Educational Leadership*, 51(3): 63–71.

Leming, J., A. Hendricks-Smith, and J. Antis. 1997. *An Evaluation of the Heartwood Institute's An Ethics Curriculum for Children*. Chicago, IL: American Educational Research Association.

National Diffusion Network. 1993. *Educational Programs That Work*. Colorado: Sopris West Inc.

Quest International. 1991. "Analysis of Lions-Quest's Skills for Adolescence Program in Detroit Schools Using School Records, School Attitude Measure and California Achievement Test Data." Quest International Research and Evaluation Department.

Scriven, M. 1973. "The Methodology of Evaluation" in B.R. Worthen & J.R. Sanders eds. *Educational Evaluation: Theory and Practice*. Belmont, CA:Wadsworth.

Sparks, R. 1991. "Character Development at Fort Washington Elementary School." in *Moral, Character, and Civic Education*. J. S. Benninga, ed. New York: Teachers College Press, pp. 178–194.

Tyler, R. 1949. *Basic Principles of Curriculum and Evaluation*. Chicago, IL: University of Chicago Press.

Watson, M., D. Solomon, V. Battistich, E. Schaps, and J. Solomon. 1989. "The Child Development Projects: Combining Traditional And Developmental Approaches to Values Education," in *Moral Development and Character Education*. L. Nucci, ed. CA: McCutchan Publishing Corporation, pp. 51–92.

Wiley, L. In press. *Character Education*. New Hampshire: Character Development Foundation.

Worthen, B. and J. R. Sanders.1987. *Educational Evaluation*. New York: Longman.

Wynne, E. and K. Ryan. 1993. *Reclaiming Our Schools: A Handbook on Teaching Character, Academics, and Discipline*. New York: Macmillan Publishing Company.

THE BLUE RIBBON
AWARD PROGRAM

HISTORY OF THE ELEMENTARY
SCHOOL RECOGNITION PROGRAM

William Bennett, when he was the Secretary of Education, proclaimed 1985–86 as the "Year of the Elementary School" and, as part of that observance, began the Elementary School Recognition Program, also know as the "Blue Ribbon Award Program." The program was modeled after its successful predecessor, the Secondary School Recognition Program, which began three years before as a positive response to the criticisms made in the report *A Nation at Risk*. The purpose of the Blue Ribbon Award Program was to identify and give public recognition to outstanding public and private elementary schools across the United States, thereby focusing national attention on schools that were doing an exceptional job with all of their students in developing a solid foundation of basic skills, knowledge of subject matter, and fostering the development of character, moral values and ethical judgment.

Blue Ribbon Schools are identified on the basis of their effectiveness in meeting their particular goals, as well as the standards of quality applicable to elementary schools generally. An important consideration for recognition is the school's success in furthering the intellectual, social, and moral growth of all its students. In seeking successful schools, the program looks for schools with an established record of sustained high achievement and schools that have overcome obstacles and problems and are continuing to concentrate on improvement.

According to the criteria set up by the program, "for a school to be recognized, there must be clear evidence that its students are developing a solid foundation of skills in reading, writing, and mathematics. In addition, there must be evidence that school policies, programs, and practices are organized

203

to foster the development of sound character, a sense of self-worth, democratic values, ethical judgment, and self-discipline. Instructional programs should be organized to provide individual students with high-quality instruction appropriate to their age and grade in literature, history, geography, science, economics, the arts, and other subjects that the state, school system or school deems important" (U.S. Department of Education, 1993).

In 1985–86, special emphasis was given to schools which fostered the development of character, values, and ethical judgment in students while developing a solid foundation of basic skills and knowledge of subject matter. In 1987–88, emphasis was given to schools with unusually effective strategies for teaching math and science to their students; and in 1989-90, emphasis was given to schools with effective strategies for teaching geography to their students as well as to schools that had serious, content-rich programs in the visual and performing arts. The National Goals for Education were released in February of 1990 and thus became an important component in the National Recognition Program. In 1991–92, special attention was placed on schools with effective programs meeting the National Goals in history and math; and in 1993–94, the special emphasis was on schools with effective programs meeting the National Goals in science and, once again, mathematics.

The Blue Ribbon criteria state: "For any school to be judged deserving of recognition, there should be strong leadership and an effective working relationship among the school, the parents, and others in its community. The school should have an atmosphere that is orderly, purposeful, and conducive to learning and good character. The school should attend to the quality of instruction and the professionalism of its teachers. There must be a strong commitment to educational excellence for all students and a record of progress in sustaining the school's best features and solving its problems" (U.S. Department of Education, 1993).

In addition, in order to be eligible for nomination, schools had to meet "eligibility criteria," that included:

(*1*) The school had to be an elementary school (including some combination of grades from K–8) with its own administrator.
(2) Private schools must have been in operation for at least five years.
(3) The Office for Civil Rights must not have issued a letter of findings to the school district concluding that the nominated school has violated one or more of the civil rights statutes or that there was district-wide violation that might affect the nominated school. The Department of Justice must not have a pending suit against a school district alleging that the nominated school had violated one or more of the civil rights statutes or the

Constitution's equal protection clause.

(4) The school must also have met at least *one* of the following criteria with regard to student achievement during the last three years:

- 75% or more of the students must have achieved at or above grade level in mathematics and reading.
- The number of students who achieved at or above grade level in mathematics and reading must have increased an average of at least 5% annually; and, in the last year, 50% or more of the students must have achieved at or above grade level in both areas.
- The school must demonstrate exemplary progress and growth of students in math and reading individually or as a group as determined by a carefully worked out and fully documented system of evaluation.

THE BLUE RIBBON APPLICATION PROCESS

Once eligibility to apply is determined, a school that desires national recognition must complete an application form (see end of Appendix A) documenting how the school addresses the areas of

(*1*) Mission and goals

(*2*) Organizational vitality

(*3*) Leadership

(*4*) Teaching environment

(*5*) Curriculum and instruction

(*6*) Student environment

(*7*) Parent and community support

(*8*) Indicators of success

All applications are initially sent to the Chief State School Officers who nominate schools for consideration at the national level. Their applications are then reviewed by a National Review Panel that selects schools to recommend for site visits based on the quality of information in the nomination form. Two-day visits are conducted to each school so nominated. The site visit reports are forwarded to the Review Panel, which meets a second time to review all of the schools that received site visits. The panel recommends the final group of schools for recognition by the Secretary of Education. Representatives from each of the school are invited to Washington, D.C., for a recognition ceremony.

REFERENCES

Kerlinger, F. 1986. *Foundations of Behavioral Research, 3rd ed.* New York: Holt, Rinehart and Winston.

Krejcie, R. and D. Morgan. 1970. "Determining Sample Size for Research Activities," *Educational Psychological Measurement*, 30 (3):607–610.

Lickona, T. 1991. *Educating for Character: How Our Schools Can Teach Respect and Responsibility.* New York: Bantam Books.

U.S. Department of Education. 1993. Application for 1993–94 Elementary Blue Ribbon Schools Program. Washington, D.C.

CHECK ONE
_____ELEMENTARY SCHOOL
_____MIDDLE SCHOOL
_____JUNIOR HIGH SCHOOL

PREVIOUS BLUE RIBBON
SCHOOL _____YES _____NO
IF YES, YEAR(S)_____

Code_____
US DEPT OF ED USE ONLY

SPECIAL EMPHASIS CANDIDATE _____SCIENCE _____MATHEMATICS

1993-94 Elementary Blue Ribbon Schools Program   Cover Sheet

Congressional District_____   (All schools: Provide Congressional District as of 10/01/93)

Name of Principal_____
                 (Specify: Ms., Miss, Mrs., Dr., Mr., Other)   (As you wish it in the official records)

Official School Name_____
                      (As you wish it in the official records)

School Address_____   Tel. (   ) _____

_____   County_____

I have reviewed the information in this form, and to the best of my knowledge it is accurate.

_____   Date_____
        (Principal's Signature)

Private Schools: If the information requested is not applicable to you, write N/A in the space.

Name of Superintendent_____
                        (Specify: Ms., Miss, Mrs., Dr., Mr., Other)

District Name_____

District Address_____   Tel. (   )_____

_____

I have reviewed the information in this form, and to the best of my knowledge it is accurate.

_____   Date_____
        (Superintendent's Signature)

Name of School Board
President/Chairperson_____
                     (Specify: Ms., Miss, Mrs., Dr., Mr., Other)

I have reviewed the information in this form, and to the best of my knowledge it is accurate.

_____   Date_____
   (School Board President/Chairperson's signature)

207

PART I -- ELIGIBILITY

Please check the appropriate space for each of the statements below concerning your school's previous participation in the Blue Ribbon Schools Program and compliance with U.S. Office of Civil Rights requirements.

1. The school is an elementary school or a middle school including some combination of grades preK-8. Or the school is K-12 and the K-8 components are applying. Unless the school is K-12, the entire school is supplying for recognition.

    True_____   False_____

2. If a public school, the school has been in existence for three full years. If private, the school has been in existence for five full years.

    True_____   False_____

3. The school did not receive national recognition during the 1991-92 Elementary Blue Ribbon Schools Program.

    True_____   False_____

4. The Office of Civil Rights (OCR) has not issued a letter of findings to the school district concluding that the nominated school has violated one or more of the civil rights statutes or that there is a districtwide violation that may affect the nominated school. (A letter of findings should not be considered outstanding if the OCR has accepted a corrective action plan from the district to remedy the violation(s).)

    True_____   False_____

5. The nominated school or district is not refusing OCR access to information necessary to investigate a civil rights complaint or to conduct a districtwide compliance review.

    True_____   False_____

6. The Department of Justice does not have a pending suit alleging that the nominated school, or the school district as a whole, has violated one or more of the civil rights statues or the Constitution's equal protection clause.

    True_____   False_____

PART II -- DEMOGRAPHICS

DISTRICT   (Questions 1 and 2 not applicable to private schools)

1.   Total number of students (pre-K-12)* enrolled in the district _____

2.   Number of schools in the district:

     _____ Elementary schools
     _____ Middle schools
     _____ Junior high schools
     _____ High schools
     _____ TOTAL

SCHOOL   (To be completed by **all schools**)

3.   Population category that describes the public school district within which your school is located:

     _____ Large central city (in an SMSA** and population greater than or equal to 400,000)
     _____ Mid-size city (in an SMSA** and population less than 400,000 but greater than 50,000)
     _____ Suburban (not in an SMSA** and population greater than or equal to 25,000)
     _____ Small town (not in an SMSA** and population less than 25,000 and greater than or equal to 2,500)
     _____ Rural (population less than 2,500)

4.   _____ Number of years the principal has been in her/his position at this school?

     _____ If less than three years, how long was the previous principal at this school?

5.   Number of students enrolled at each grade level or its equivalent in your school:

     _____ preK*   _____ 2nd   _____ 5th   _____ 8th
     _____ K   _____ 3rd   _____ 6th   _____ Other
     _____ 1st   _____ 4th   _____ 7th
                                                               _____ TOTAL

6.   Racial/ethnic composition of   _____ % Native American or Native Alaskan
     the students in your school: _____ % Asian or Pacific Islander
                                           _____ % African American, not Hispanic origin
                                           _____ % Hispanic
                                           _____ % White, not Hispanic origin
                                           100.00% TOTAL

7.   Limited-English-proficient students in the school: _____ %   _____ Total Number
     Number of languages represented: _____   Specify which:

---

*   Include pre-kindergartners **only** if your school and/or district operates preK programs.
**   A standard metropolitan area (SMSA) includes a central city with a population of at least 50,000 or an urbanized area with a population of at least 50,000 with the neighboring area having a total of 100,000 or more inhabitants.

8. Students who qualify for free/reduced price lunch: _____% _____ Total Number
If this is not reasonably accurate estimate of the percentage of students from low-income families or your school does not participate in the federally-supported lunch program, specify a more accurate estimate and explain how you arrived at it.

9. Students receiving special education services: _____% _____Number Served
Indicate below the number of handicapped students according to handicapping conditions designated in the Individuals with Disabilities Education Act.

_____Deaf	_____Other Health Impaired
_____Deaf-Blind	_____Seriously Emotionally Disturbed
_____Hard of Hearing	_____Specific Learning Disability
_____Multihandicapped	_____Speech Impaired
_____Orthopedically Impaired	_____Visually Handicapped

10. Describe any significant changes in the data reported in items 4-8 that have occurred during the past five years.

11. Indicate the full-time equivalent (FTE) staff members in each of the below categories. (An FTE is one full-time position; if, for example, the school's regular work week is 40 hours, and two assistant principals spend a total of 60 hours per week as administrators and the rest in teaching, the assistant principal position is 1.5 FTE and .5 FTE's are assigned as teaching).

	FTE	Number of Staff	
Administrators	_____	_____	
Classroom teachers	_____	_____	
Special resource teachers	_____	_____	
Subject area specialist	_____	_____	
Paraprofessionals	_____	_____	
Library/media professionals	_____	_____	
Counselors, psychologists, nurses	_____	_____	
Clerical	_____	_____	
Custodial personnel	_____	_____	
Food service personnel	_____	_____	
Security officers	_____	_____	Total Number
Others	_____	_____	of Part-Time
			Staff Members
Total FTE's / Number of Staff	_____	_____	_____

Specify the types of special resource teachers and subject area specialists employed at your school, as well as the roles assigned to paraprofessionals.

12. **Context Statement:** Schools are judged within their own context rather than in direct comparison with all other schools. Describe the context of your school. Include, for example, the population it serves, socioeconomic conditions in the community, student mobility issues, historical milestones in the school's operation, school tradition, and the school's physical location and surroundings. Limit your statement to this one page.

13. **Nomination Abstract:** Summarize the strengths of your school, focusing on what it is that makes your school's unique and successful place worthy of national recognition. Highlight any innovative uses of time, space, staffing, organizational structures, and modern technology. Limit your abstract to this one page.

Part III: CONDITIONS OF EFFECTIVE SCHOOLING

A. LEADERSHIP

A1. What are the goals and priorities for the school and its students?

A2. How do the principal and other school leaders motivate staff, parents, and students to accomplish the school's goals?

A3. Who is the instructional leadership role carried out in your school?

B. TEACHING ENVIRONMENT

B1. What opportunities exist for teachers to be involved in decision making?

B2. What provisions are made to enable staff to engage in collegial planning and implementation of educational programs at your school?

B3 What are your school's formal procedures for supervising and evaluating teachers?

B4. How are beginning teachers and those new to your building supported and their skills strengthened?

B5. How does your school support and encourage the recognition of excellent teachers?

B6. What opportunities are provided to expand or alter teachers' roles to enhance their effectiveness with students and to improve job satisfaction?

B7. What is the process by which you ensure that staff development opportunities are congruent with the defined goals and priorities of your school?

C. CURRICULUM AND INSTRUCTION

C1. How is your school organized to reflect differing student needs and the school's goals and priorities?

C2. The National Goals call for strengthening subject-matter content in English, Mathematics, science, history, geography, art, and foreign languages. What is your curriculum in each of these subject areas?

212

C3. What other subject areas play essential roles in your schoolwide curriculum goals?

C4. What specific instructional strategies does your school employ to ensure that students learn to write effectively?

C5. How is your instructional program adapted to the needs of special populations, such as special education, Chapter 1, limited-English proficient, and students in needs of remediation?

C6. What special opportunities do you provide for advanced study, or enrichment for unusually talented or motivated students?

C7. What role does the school library/media center play in supporting instruction and enabling students to become information literate?

C8. What regular building-level procedures do you follow for evaluating your instructional programs?

D. STUDENT ENVIRONMENT

D1. What role does your school play in helping to ensure that children entering your school are prepared to participate successfully in formal schooling?

D2. What specific programs, procedures, or instructional strategies do you employ to develop students' interest in learning and to motivate them to study?

D3. What opportunities do students have to build sustained relationships with counselors, teachers, or other adults?

D4. What specific programs, procedures, or instructional strategies do you employ to identify, counsel, and assist potential dropouts or other at-risk or underachieving students?

D5. What extracurricular activities are available for students?

D6. What is your school's discipline policy?

D7. By what means does the school prevent the sale, possession, and use of drugs, including alcohol and tobacco, by its students on and off school premises?

D8. What opportunities exist for students to influence classroom and school policy?

D9. How do school programs, practices, policies, and staff foster the development of sound character, democratic values, ethical judgment, good behavior, and the ability to work in a self-disciplined and purposeful manner?

D10. How is your school preparing students to live effectively in a society that is culturally, ethnically, and economically diverse?

D11. How is your school preparing students to live effectively in a society that is globally competitive?

E. PARENT AND COMMUNITY SUPPORT

E1. How are parents encouraged to be involved with the schools?

E2. How does your school communicate student progress and overall school performance to parents and the broader community?

E3. What strategies does the school use to encourage parents to provide a supportive learning environment in the home and to inform parents about other learning opportunities?

E4. How does the school support the needs of families?

E5. What opportunities does your school provide for meaningful collaboration with other educational institutions and community groups?

F. INDICATORS OF SUCCESS

F1. What formal procedures does your school have for assessing and reporting student achievement?

F2. What performance-based measures or other assessments does your school use for assessing and reporting progress?

F3. What was your school's performance last year in the following areas:

Daily student attendance
Daily teacher attendance
Number of individual students involved
in serious disciplinary incidents

214

F4. Which awards received by your school, staff, or students during the last five years are most indicative of school success?

G. ORGANIZATIONAL VITALITY

G1. How does the climate of your school reflect its mission and provide an atmosphere that is orderly, purposeful, conducive to learning respectful of diversity, and open to change?

G2. What kind of school improvement process is in operation at your school?

G3. How has your school responded to recent educational research findings, national assessments of educational progress, efforts to establish national standards and curriculum frameworks, and the National Goals?

G4. As you look back over the last five years, what conditions and/or changes have contributed most to the overall success of your school?

G5. What do you consider the major educational challenges your school must face over the next five years?

BLUE RIBBON SCHOOLS
CITED IN THIS BOOK

The sample consisted of 350 schools selected at random from all the schools recognized by the Blue Ribbon Schools Recognition Program during the years 1985–86, 1987–88, 1989–90, 1991–92 and 1993–94. The list of schools below are the schools cited in the book. The contact name listed was the principal at the time the Blue Ribbon application was submitted. Many of these principal names have changed, but these are the official names listed with the Department of Education.

SCHOOL NAME AND AWARD YEAR
ADDRESS
CITY, STATE
PRINCIPAL
TELEPHONE

Aikahi Elementary School 1989–90
281 Ilihau Street
Kailua, HI 96734
Mrs. Roberta Tokumaru
808-254-3805

Argonaut Elementary School 1993–94
13200 Shadow Mountain Drive
Saratoga, CA 95070
Mrs. Sheri Hitchings
408-867-4773

Arroyo Elementary School 1989–90
11112 Coronel Road
Santa Ana, CA 92705
Mr. Gerald Aust
714-730-7381

Baker's Chapel Elementary School 1991–92
555 South Old Piedmont Highway
Greenville, SC 29611-6141
Mrs. Nancy J. Farnsworth
803-299-8320

Clara Barton Open School 1987–88
4237 Colfax Avenue South
Minneapolis, MN 55409
Mrs. Barbara Bellaire
612-627-2373

Bellerive Elementary School 1991–92
666 Rue de Fleur
Creve Coeur, MS 63141
Dr. Kenneth Russell
314-878-3314

Governor Bent Elementary School 1993–94
5700 Hendrix Road NE
Albuquerque, NM 87110
Mrs. Marilyn Davenport
505-880-3951

Caroline Bentley School 1991–92
511 Illinois Highway
New Lenox, IL 60451
Mr. Robert Gaines
815-485-4451

The Blake School 1989–90
110 Blake Road
Hopkins, MN 55343
Mrs. Beth Passi
612-935-6994

Blumfield Elementary School 1991–92
R.R. 3, Old Highway, 41 North
Princeton, IN 47670
Mr. James H. Kolb
812-386-1221

Brookridge Elementary School 1989–90
9920 Lowell
Shawnee Mission, KS 66212
Dr. Connie Welsh
913-381-3070

Bryant Ranch School 1993–94
24695 Paseo de Toronto
Yorba Linda, CA 92687
Dr. Bonita Drolet
714-692-8275

A. L. Burruss Elementary School 1991–92
325 Manning Road
Marietta, GA 30064
Mr. Jerry Locke
404-428-3417

Cedar Island Elementary School 1989–90
6777 Hemlock Lane
Maple Grove, MN 55369
Mrs. Kathleen B. Townsend
612-425-5855

Centennial Elementary School 1993–94
2200 W. Wetmore Road
Tucson, AZ 85705
Ms. Renate Krompasky
602-690-2291

Cherokee Elementary School 1987–88
8801 North 56th Street
Paradise Valley, AZ 85253
Dr. Bobbie Sfarra
602-996-0953

China Grove Elementary School 1989–90
514 South Franklin Street
China Grove, NC 28023
Mr. Alan D. King
704-857-7708

Como Park Elementary School 1991–92
1985 Como Park Boulevard
Lancaster, NY 14086
Ms. Andrea R. Stein
716-684-3235

Conder Elementary School 1985 – 86
8161 Brookfield Road
Columbia, SC 29223
Mrs. Pauline Bauguess
803-788-5944

Country Club Elementary School 1993 – 94
7534 Blue Fox Way
San Ramon, CA 94583
Mrs. Carol Rowley
510-828-7284

County Line Elementary School 1993 – 94
905 Mulberry Road
Winder, GA 30680
Ms. Phyllis Chastain
404-867-2902

Rodney B. Cox Elementary School 1993 – 94
201 West Martin Luther King Blvd
Dade City, FL 33525
Ms. Linda L. Rodrigues
904-567-5360

Crest Hill Elementary School 1991 – 92
4445 South Poplar
Casper, WY 82716
Mr. William Owen Jones
307-577-4512

Del Cerro Elementary School 1987 – 88
24382 Regina Street
Mission Viejo, CA 92691
Mr. Chuck Prince
714-830-5430

James L. Dennis Elementary School 1985 – 86
6501 Westbrook Drive
Oklahoma City, OK 73132
Dr. Sandy Wisley
405-722-6510

Diamond Elementary School 1989 – 90
4 Marquis Drive
Gaithersburg, MD 20878
Mrs. Jennie Fleming
301-840-7177

Dry Creek Elementary School 1993–94
8098 North Armstrong
Clovis, CA 93611
Mrs. Ann Lindsey
209-299-2161

East Elementary School 1989–90
893 East US 36
Pendleton, IN 46064
Mrs. Nancy S. Phenis
317-779-4445

Dr. James H. Eldridge Elementary School 1991–92
145 First Avenue
East Greenwich, RI 02818
Dr. Frances A. Gallo
401-885-3300

Elm Street School 1993–94
46 Elm Street
Newnan, GA 30263
Mrs. Carol P. Ploeger
404-254-2865

Everdale Elementary School 1987–88
2940 Glendale-Milford Road
Cincinnati, OH 45241
Mr. Bobby R. Cox
513-563-1040

Fairfield North Elementary School 1989–90
6116 Morris Road
Hamilton, OH 45011
Mr. Robert C. Fisher
513-868-0070

Flanders Elementary School 1993–94
Boston Post Road
East Lyme, CT 06333
Dr. Cherry Jones
203-739-8475

Forest Elementary School 1985–86
28963 Tudor Drive
North Olmsted, OH 44070
Mr. William Burkhardt
216-777-1149

Fort Washington Elementary School 1985–86
960 E. Teague
Fresno, CA 93710
Dr. Richard K. Sparks, Jr.
209-439-0520

Frankfort Junior High School 1993–94
22265 South 80th Avenue
Frankfort, IL 60423
Mr. John H. Loecke
815-469-4474

Benjamin Franklin Elementary School
262 Conklin Avenue
Binghamton, NY 13903
Mrs. Joyce Westgate
607-762-8340

Gesu Catholic School 1987–88
2450 Mirama Boulevard
University Heights, OH 44118
Sr. Mary Brendon
216-932-0620

Green Trails Elementary School 1987–88
170 Portico Drive
Chesterfield, MO 63017
Mr. Douglas Underwood
314-469-7400

Gulliver Academy 1991–92
12595 Red Road
Coral Gables, FL 33156
Mr. Joseph J. Krutulis
305-665-3593

Haines School 1993–94
155 W. Haines Avenue
New Lenox, IL 60451
Mr. Lee L. Fears
815-485-2115

Harrison Elementary School 1989–90
600 Broadway
Harrison, OH 45030
Mr. Robert W. Stoll
513-367-4161

Hedgcoxe Elementary School 1993–94
7701 Prescott Drive
Plano, TX 75075
Mrs. Sharon McAdams Gunn
214-517-1553

Highlands Elementary School 1989–90
27331 Catala Avenue
Saugus, CA 91350
Mr. Albert C. Nocciolo
805-297-0166

Hill Elementary School 1993–94
8601 Tallwood Drive
Austin, TX 78759
Ms. Glenda Adkinson
512-345-2213

Elvin Hill Elementary School 1987–88
201 Washington Street
Columbiana, AL 35051
Mrs. Ann B. Head
205-669-7165

Hillside School 1987–88
54 Orange Road
Montclair, NJ 07042
Mr. Robert J. Rosado
201-783-8952

Huffman Elementary School 1991–92
5510 Channel Isle Drive
Plano, TX 75093
Mrs. Vicki Halliday
214-248-1818

Independence Primary School 1993–94
7600 Hillside Road
Independence, OH 44131
Mrs. Judith Schultz
216-642-5870

Indian Trail School 1987–88
2075 St. Johns Avenue
Highland Park, IL 60035
Dr. Alan E. Simon
312-432-9257

Irwin School 1989–90
71 Racetrack Road
East Brunswick, NJ 08816
Mrs. Lucille Fisher
973-613-6841

Ivymount School 1993–94
11614 Seven Locks Road
Rockville, MD 20854
Mrs. Shari Gelman, M. Ed.
301-469-0223

Kilgour Elementary School 1991–92
1339 Herschel Avenue
Cincinnati, OH 45208
Dr. Catherine Swami
513-321-7840

Laurel Mountain Elementary School 1991–92
10111 D K Ranch Road
Austin, TX 78759
Mrs. Eleece Moffatt
512-258-1373

Susan Lindgren Elementary School 1991–92
4801 W. 41st St.
St. Louis Park, MN 55416-3245
Mr. Harry Hoff
612-922-1600

Livonia Primary School 1989–90
Puppy Lane
Livonia, NY 14487
Mr. David P. DeLoria
716-346-2323

Los Encinos Special Emphasis School 1987–88
1826 Frio
Corpus Christi, TX 78417
Mrs. Yolanda F. Gonzalez
512-853-6283

Lowell Elementary School 1993–94
1507 N. 28th Street
Boise, ID 83703
Mrs. Elaine Eichelberg
208-338-3478

Robert E. Lucas Intermediate School 1985–86
3900 Cottingham Drive
Cincinnati, OH 45241
Mr. Noel H. Taylor
513-563-4020

Manoa Elementary School 1985–86
3155 Manoa Road
Honolulu, HI 96822
Mr. James I. Tomita
808-988-3082

Marion Street Elementary School 1985–86
Marion Street
Lynbrook, NY 11563
Dr. Alfred Solomon
516-599-1394

Kathryn D. Markley School 1987–88
Church Road
Malvern, PA 19335
Mrs. Sally Winterton
215-644-1790

Mill Lake School 1991–92
Monmouth Road
Spotswood, NJ 08884
Mrs. Nancy Richmond
908-251-5336

Monte Cassino School 1993–94
2206 South Lewis
Tulsa, OK 74114
Sr. Mary Clare Buthod, O.S.B.
918-742-3364

Monte Gardens Elementary 1991–92
3841 Larkspur Drive
Concord, CA 94519
Mrs. Barbara Blankenship
510-685-3834

Moorestown Friends School 1991–92
110 E. Main Street
Moorestown, NJ 08075
Mrs. Larue Evans
609-235-2913

Moriches Elementary School 1993–94
Montauk Highway
Moriches, NY 11955
Dr. Paul Casciano
516-281-3020

Edward Morley Elementary School 1987–88
77 Bretton Road
West Hartford, CT 06119
Ms. Paulette Brading
203-233-8535

Mounds Park Academy—Lower School 1991–92
2051 East Larpenteur Avenue
St. Paul, MN 55109-4785
Ms. Joanne Y. Olson
612-777-2555

Mountain View Elementary School 1987–88
6001 Plantation Circle
Roanoke, VA 24019
Mr. Thompson H. Hall
703-563-4453

Mountain View Elementary School 1993–94
2002 East Alluvial
Fresno, CA 93720-0100
Mr. David M Derby
209-298-9781

Murdock Elementary School 1987–88
2320 Murdock Road
Marietta, GA 30062
Mr. W. E. Robertson
404-973-4545

Glenn E. Murdock Elementary School 1991–92
4354 Conrad Drive
La Mesa, CA 91941
Mrs. Kathie W. Dobberteen
619-461-9507

Kenneth E. Neubert Elementary School 1985–86
1100 Huntington Drive
Algonquin, IL 60102
Mrs. Donna Schuring
312-658-2540

New Canaan Country School 1993–94
P. O. Box 997
New Canaan, CT 06840
Mr. Nicholas Thacher
203-972-0771

Eric G. Norfeldt School 1991–92
35 Barksdale Road
West Hartford, CT 06117
Dr. Karen L. List
203-233-4421

Normandy Elementary School 1991–92
401 Normandy Ridge Road
Centerville, OH 45459
Mrs. Gloria R. Clouse
513-434-0917

Oakbrook Elementary School 1993–94
4700 Old Fort Road
Ladson, SC 29485
Mrs. Patsy Pye
803-821-1165

Ormand Beach Elementary 1993–94
100 Corbin Avenue
Ormand Beach, FL 32174
Mrs. Margaret Hyman
904-677-3611

Parkway School 1987–88
East 145 Ridgewood Avenue
Paramus, NJ 07652
Mr. Joseph M. Roma
201-262-7181

Perley Elementary School 1993–94
740 North Eddy Street
South Bend, IN 46617
Dr. Michelle Contreras
219-234-2722

Pine Grove School 1987–88
Main Street
Rowley, MA 01969
Ms. Susan King
617-948-2520

Pioneer Elementary School 1991–92
3663 Woodland Hills Drive
Colorado Springs, CO 80918
Mrs. Suzanne Loughran
719-598-8232

Lewis H. Powell Gifted and Talented 1991–92
Magnet Elementary School
1130 Marlborough Road
Raleigh, NC 27610
Mr. Patrick C. Kinlaw
919-856-7737

Quail Creek Elementary School 1991–92
11700 Thorn Ridge Road
Oklahoma City, OK 73120
Mr. Ancil Warren
405-751-3231

Quailwood Elementary School 1991–92
7301 Remington Ave.
Bakersfield, CA 93309
Mr. Steven L. Duke
305-832-6415

Red Bank Elementary School 1993–94
1454 Locan
Clovis, CA 93611
Sue Van Doren, Ed.D.
209-299-4135

Regnart Elementary School 1987–88
1170 Yorkshire Drive
Cupertino, CA 95014
Mrs. Dianne Brokaw
408-253-5250

Howard C. Reiche Community School 1991–92
166 Brackett Street
Portland, ME 04102
Mrs. Miriam L. Remar
207-874-8175

Anna M. Reynolds School 1993–94
85 Reservoir Road
Newington, CT 06111
Mr. Richard H. Frank
203-521-7830

Norbert Rillieux Elementary School 1985–86
7121 River Road
Waggaman, LA 70094
Mrs. Cynthia M. Lasserre
504-436-8336

Mary E. Roberts School 1989–90
Crescent and Williams Avenues
Moorestown, NJ 08057
Mr. Ralph J. Scazafabo
609-235-4000 x271

Saddle Rock Elementary School 1993–94
10 Hawthorne Lane
Great Neck, NY11023
Dr. Leslie Korant
516-773-1500

Russell Elementary School 1993–94
7350 Howdershell
Hazelwood, MO 63042
Mrs. Barbara Berry
314-839-9585

Saigling Elementary School 1991–92
3600 Matterhorn Drive
Plano, TX 75075
Mrs. Janie Miller
214-596-2300

St. Damian School 1991–92
5300 W. 155th Street
Oak Forest, IL 60452-335
Miss Barbara J. Wesolowski
708-687-4230

St. Isidore School 1993–94
435 La Gonda Way
Danville, CA 94526
Mrs. Kathleen Gannon-Briggs
510-837-2977

St. John Bosco School 1991–92
6460 Pearl Road
Parma Heights, OH 44130
Sr. Gretchen Rodenfels, O.S.U.
216-886-0061

St. Joseph Montessori School 1993–94
933 Hamlet Street
Columbus, OH 43201-3595
Ms. Donna Barton
614-291-8601

St. Luke School
519 Ashland Avenue
River Forest, IL 60305
Mrs. Judith Wynne
708-366-8587

St. Mark the Evangelist Catholic School 1991–92
1201 Alma Drive
Plano, TX 75075
Mrs. Suzanne Purtell
214-578-0610

St. Rocco School
931 Atwood Avenue
Johnston, RI 02919
Sr. Mary Carol Gentile
401-944-2993

Saint Rosalie School 1991–92
617 Second Avenue
Harvey, LA 70058
Sr. Mary Jeanne McLoughlin, OP
504-341-4342

Saint Stanislaus Bishop and Martyr School 1987–88
2318 N. Lorel Avenue
Chicago, IL 60639
Sr. Lora Ann Slavinski
312-622-3342

St. Thomas of Canterbury School 1987–88
336 Hudson Street
Cornell-on-Hudson, NY 12520
Sr. Helen R. Boyd
914-534-2019

St. Thomas More School 1993–94
4180 North Amber Drive
Brooklyn, OH 44144
Mrs. Monica M. Veto, M.S.,M.A.
216-749-1660

St. Thomas More Parish School 1993–94
5927 Wigton
Houston, TX 77096
Nadine Mouser
713-729-3434

Schuster Elementary School 1987–88
5515 Will Ruth
El Paso, TX 79924
Mrs. Nancy Archer
202-225-4831

Shelter Rock Elementary School 1991–92
Shelter Rock Road
Manhasset, NY 11030
Mr. Richard G. Koebele
516-365-4210

Dorothea H. Simmons School 1991–92
411 Babylon Road
Horsham, PA 19002
Mrs. Rita M. Klein
215-956-2929

Snug Harbor Community School 1993–94
333 Palmer Street
Quincy, MA 02169
Mr. Richard O'Brien
617-984-8763

South Valley School 1987–88
South Starwick Road
Moorestown, NJ 08057
Mrs. Violet R. Thompson
609-235-4000

Southwest Elementary School 1991–92
915 Gay Street
Howell, MI 48843
Mr. Fred Dobbs
517-548-6288

Spring Glen Elementary School 1991–92
2607 Jones Avenue South
Renton, WA 98055
Mr. Delbert D. Morton
206-859-7494

Stewart Elementary School 1993–94
11850 Conrey Road
Cincinnati, OH 45249
Mr. Barry S. Adamson
513-489-7133

Summerville Elementary School 1993–94
835 South Main Street
Summerville, SC 29483
Mr. Eugene Sives
803-873-2372

Taper Avenue Elementary School 1987–88
1824 Taper Avenue
San Pedro, CA 90731
Mr. Albert Fasani
213-832-3056

Booth Tarkington School 1993–94
310 South Scott Street
Wheeling, IL 60090
Mr. Avrum Poster
708-520-2775

Wm. Volker Applied Learning Magnet School 1993–94
3715 Wyoming
Kansas City, MO 64111
Dr. Rayna F. Levine
816-871-6200

W.H.L. Elementary School 1991–92
3427 Mission Ridge
Plano, TX 75023
Mrs. La Necia Nell Pearce
214-596-3618

Waiahole Elementary School 1989–90
48-215 Waiahole Valley Road
Kanoehe, HI 96744
Mrs. Linda Kamiyama
808-239-8395

Washington School 1991–92
122 S. Garfield
Mundelein, IL 60060
Ms. Shirley E. Anderson
708-949-2714

M.R. Weaver Elementary School 1985 – 86
520 St. Maurice Lane
Natchitoches, LA 71457
Mrs. Martha Wynn
318-353-3623

Weedsport Elementary School 1985 – 86
8954 Jackson Street
Weedsport, NY 13166
Mr. Howard P. Lapidus
315-834-6685

Westwood Elementary School 1993 – 94
435 Saratoga Ave
Santa Clara, CA 95050
Dr. Joya Chatterjee
408-983-2154

Whittier Elementary School 1987 – 88
1115 Laird
Lawton, OK 73507
Mrs. Marlene Jones
405-355-5238

Yakutat Elementary School 1985 – 86
P.O. Box 427
Yakutat, AK 99689
Mr. Jerry Schoenberger
907-784-3394

A BLUE RIBBON SCHOOL LIBRARY'S LIST OF CHARACTER EDUCATION BOOKS

GENERAL CHARACTER EDUCATION BOOKS

AUTHOR	TITLE
DePaola	Now One Foot, Now the Other
Heide	That's What Friends Are For
Heine	Friends
Sharmat	I'm Terrific
Sharmat	Frizzy the Fearful
Spier	People
Udry	Let's Be Enemies
Viorst	If I Were in Charge of the World and Other Worries
Yashima	Crow Boy
Videos:	The Most Important Person
	Jim Learns Responsibility
	Busy Bee
	Dr. Retriever's Surprise
	A Good Citizen Obeys Rules and Laws
	Responsibility
	Telling The Truth

COURAGE

Beatty	Little Owl Indian
Blos	Heroine of the Titanic
Brink	Caddie Woodlawn

AUTHOR	TITLE
Bulla	Lion to Guard Us
Bunting	Fly Away Home
Burnford	Incredible Journey
Calhoun	Night the Monster Came
Carlson	Harriet and the Roller Coaster
Christiansen	Calico and Tin Horns
Christopher	Catch That Pass
Church	Five Boys in Cave
Clymer	My Brother Stevie
Coles	The Story of Ruby Bridges
Cosgrove	Leo the Lop
Crofford	Matter of Pride
Crowe	Clyde Monster
Dalgliesh	Courage of Sarah Noble
DeJong	Wheel on the School
DePaola	Now One Foot, Now the Other
Eldridge	Salcott, the Indian Boy
Forbes	Johnny Tremain
Friskey	Seven Diving Ducks
Gates	Morgan for Melinda
George	Julie of the Wolves
Giff	Gift of the Pirate Queen
Gipson	Old Yeller
Greenberg	Bravest Babysitter
Johnson	Your Dad Was Just Like You
Little	Home from Far
Little	Jess Was the Brave One
Lydon	Birthday for Blue
Moncure	Courage
O'Dell	Island of the Blue Dolphin
Peet	Cowardly Clyde
Peterson	I Have a Sister, My Sister Is Deaf
Schwartz	Supergrandpa
Sperry	Call It Courage
Steel	Perilous Road
Steele	Wilderness Johnny
Uchida	Journey Home
Wallace	Shadow on the Snow
Wallace	Dog Called Kitty
Wilder	Little House on the Prairie

COURTESY

AUTHOR	TITLE
Brown	Perfect Pigs
Crume	What Do You Say?
Hoban	Little Brute Family
Joslin	What Do You Do, Dear?
Peturcelli	Learn Value of Consideration
Riehecky	Sharing

CULTURAL AWARENESS (GENERAL)

Albyn	Multicultural Cookbook for Students
Allen	Cultural Awareness for Children
Aurelio	Skipping Stones
Demi	The Magic Boat (China)
Dorros	This Is My House
Girard	We Adopted You, Benjamin Koo (Korea)
Goode	Diane Goode's Book of Silly Stories and Songs
Hamilton	All Jahdu Storybook
Heide	Day of Almed's Secret (Africa)
Hirsh	Dictionary of Cultural Literacy
Hodges	The Magic Boat (China)
Kennedy	Culturgrams '92
Knight	Talking Walls
Kuklin	How My Family Lives in America
Lankford	Hopscotch around the World
Lattimore	The Winged Cat (Egypt)
Miles	Annie and the Old One (Native Americans)
Morris	Bread, Bread, Bread
Oughton	How the Stars Fell into the Sky (Native Americans)

DISCIPLINE/DEPENDABILITY

Cosgrove	Little Mouse on the Prairie
Hall	Ox-Cart Man
Locker	Family Farm
Moncure	Saying Please
Ziegler	Manners

HONESTY

AUTHOR	TITLE
Arnold	The Signmaker's Assistant
Berenstain	Berenstain Bears and the Truth
Blume	Otherwise Known as Sheila the Great
Brink	Bad Times of Irma Baumlein
Brown	The True Francine
Calmenson	Principal's New Clothes
Demi	The Empty Pot
Duvoisin	Petunia, I Love You
Elliott	Ernie's Little Lie
Estes	The Hundred Dresses
Fitzgerald	Great Brain Reforms
Giff	Fish Face
Holmes	Charlotte Cheetham, Master of Disaster
Hurwitz	Cold and Hot Winter
Matsuno	A Pair of Red Clogs
Ness	Sam, Bangs, and Moonshine
Spencer	Value of Honesty: Story of Confucius
Wilhelm	Tryone the Double Dirty Rotten Cheater
Yacowitz	The Jade Stone

HUMAN WORTH AND DIGNITY

Andersen	The Ugly Duckling
Bradman	Michael
Carlson	Annie and the New Kid
Cohen	Best Friends
Graff	Helen Keller: Toward the Light
Johnson	One of Three
Lester	Tacky the Penguin
Newman	It's Me, Claudia
Pio	The Magic Donkey
Rylant	Angel for Solomon Singer
Sharmat	329th Friend

JUSTICE

Hutchins	Tale of Thomas Mead
Sharmat	Bartholomew the Bossy

AUTHOR	TITLE
Troll	Ball, the Book, and the Drum
Wood	Tugford Wanted to Be Bad
Ziegler	Fairness

PATRIOTISM

Benchley	Sam the Minuteman
Bunting	The Wall
Bunting	How Many Days to America?
Dalgliesh	Thanksgiving Story
Fritz	What's the Big Idea, Ben Franklin?
Fritz	Where Was Patrick Henry on 29th of May?
Jezek	Miloli's Orchids
Lawson	Mr. Revere and I
Lippman	Peter Lippman's America
Miller	Story of the Star Spangled Banner
Mitchell	Cornstalks and Cannonballs
Parlin	Patriot's Day
Roop	Buttons for General Washington
Scott	Memorial Day
Swanson	I Pledge Allegiance

PERSONAL OBLIGATION FOR PUBLIC GOOD

Brenner	Mr. Tall and Mr. Small
Hirsh	Hannibal and His 37 Elephants
Houston	My Great-Aunt Arizona
Javernick	What If Everybody Did That?
Levinson	Snowshoe Thompson
Peet	Pamela Camel
Rand	Prince William
Willard	Nightgown of the Sullen Moon

RESPECT FOR AUTHORITY

Allard	Miss Nelson Is Missing
Arnold	Who Keeps Us Safe?

AUTHOR	TITLE
Oppenheim	Mrs. Peloki's Substitute
Potter	The Tale of Peter Rabbit

RESPECT FOR SELF AND OTHERS

Airello	Secrets Aren't Always for Keeps
Alexander	My Outrageous Friend, Charlie
Berenstain	Berenstain Bears and the In-Crowd
Carrick	Some Friend
Caseley	Harry and Willy Carrothead
Crowdy	Pride
DeLuise	Charlie the Caterpillar
Fiday	Respect
Henkes	Chrysanthemum
Hoffman	Henry's Baby
Howe	I Wish I Were a Butterfly
Lionni	Six Crows
Sadler	It's Not Easy Being a Bunny
Sharmat	I'm Terrific
Sharmat	What Are We Going to Do about Andrew?
Sharmat	I Am Not a Pest
Spinelli	Somebody Loves You, Mr. Hatch
Tompert	Charlotte and Charles
Waber	Ira Says Goodbye
Waber	Lovable Lyle
Washima	Crow Boy
Yolen	Sleeping Ugly

RESPONSIBILITY

Blake	Mystery of the Lost Letter
Day	Frank and Ernest
Delton	Angel in Charge
Duncan	Janet Reachfar and Chickabird
Hargreaves	Hippo, Potto, and Mouse
Johnson	Value of Responsibility—Bunche
Pemberton	Responsibility
Riehecky	Carefulness
Waddell	Farmer Duck

TOLERANCE

AUTHOR	TITLE
Burnhoff	Isabelle's New Friend
Doherty	Paddiwack and Cozy
Glen	Ruby
Goldenbock	Teammates
Hughes	The Snow Lady
Jin	My First American Friend
Kibbey	My Grammy
Kuklin	How My Family Lives in America
Lester	Tacky the Penguin
Ormsby	What's Wrong with Julio?
Otey	Daddy Has a Pair of Striped Shorts
Rosenberg	My Friend, Leslie
Rylant	Miss Maggie
Schotter	Capt. Snap and the Children of Vinegar Lane

A Nation at Risk, 14, 21
Adams, John, 157
administrators, 189
Adolescent Family Life Act, 77
Adopt a Family Program, 174
advisor/advisee program, 53
Aikahi Elementary School, 145
American Association of School
    Administrators, 48
animal care, 172
announcement, P. A., 51
Apacki, Carol, 70
Argonaut Elementary School, 93, 145,
    171
Aristotle
    on becoming virtuous, 117
    definition of virtue, 2,4
    end of all activity, 181
    Nichomachean Ethics, 2, 117, 181,
        187
art, 177
assemblies, 7, 50–51, 160
assessment
    authentic, 129–130, 199
    implementation, 191
    multiple alternative modes of, 118,
        121
    needs, 195

Association for Moral Education, 50
Association for Supervision and
    Curriculum Development, 21
Attitude and Projected Behavior
    Survey, 195
awards, 7, 88–90, 96, 160
    good citizenship, 167–169

Babes, 71
Baker's Chapel Elementary School,
    172
Bandura, Albert, 198
bank accounts, 137
Barton School, Clara, 152
Barton, Donna, 120
behavior
    at-risk, 195
    interpersonal, 193
    moral, 185
    rating tools, 196
Bellerive Elementary School, 41, 94,
    162
Bennett, William, ix, 15, 46
Bentley School, Caroline, 147
bike-a-thon, 174
Blake School, 151
Blanchard, Ken, 142
blind, 104

Bloom, Benjamin, 105
Blue Ribbon Award Program
　purpose, ix – x
　selection, xi
Blue Ribbon School, 7, 10, 11
　comprehensive model, 8 – 10
　evaluations of schools, 182 – 183,
　　188 – 190, 192 – 199
Blumfield Elementary School, 51
Brain, right and left, 125
Brookridge Elementary School, 135
Brooks, David B., 42, 191
Bryant Ranch School, 150
buddy programs, 166 – 167
bulletin boards, 51, 91, 160
Burruss, A. L. Elementary School, 127,
　188

cafeteria aides, 199
California Achievement Test, 196
caring, 162, 177, 193
　beyond the classroom, 165
　for others, 173
　school, 199
　within the classroom, 165
caroling, 174
Catholic schools, 30, 32
Cedar Island Elementary School, 148
Centennial Elementary School, 128, 145
Center for Civil Education, 161
ceremonies, 88, 91, 96
Chance, Paul, 94
Character
　defined, 5 – 7, 29 – 30
　developed, 119
　heart side of, 105
　private traits of, 159
　public traits of, 159
　themes, 194
Character Counts
　Coalition, 22
　Week, 22 – 23
Character education, 27 – 29
　comprehensive school-wide
　　approach, 8, 182
　core values, 15, 33, 101
　curriculum, 38 – 39, 195

defined, 6 – 11, 159
evaluation, 191
six pillars of, 22
teaching
　direct approach, 17, 29
　indirect approach, 17
Character Education Conference,
　National, 50
Character Education Forum, 50
Character Education Institute, 40 – 41
Character Education Partnership, 22, 50
Chatterjee, Dr. Joyce, 129
Cherokee Elementary School, 102
Child Development Project, 42
　evaluation, 192 – 193
children's literature, 198
Children's Morality Code, 16
China Grove Elementary School, 72
citation, 154
citizenship, 140, 147, 157
　education, 158
　Council for the Advancement of
　　Citizenship, 161
　good citizenship, 88, 199
　　award, 167 – 169
　National Task Force of Citizenship
　　Education, 163
civic
　civic-mindedness, 159
　education, 158 – 164
　virtues, 157
civility, 159
CIVITAS, 161
CLASS — Community Leadership
　　Activities for Students, 53
class meetings, 101, 161
classroom poster, 194
climate, 90, 190
Clinton, William, ix, xv
Combs, Arthur, 106
Come in from the Storm, 80
communitarian network, 159
community service, 160, 172
　projects, 129, 174 – 175
Como Park Elementary School, 51, 71
comparison groups, 187
Conder Elementary School, 149

conflict management, 140, 143–145
  mediators, 101
conflict resolution
  activities, 69, 162
  defined, 146, 152, 153, 155
  skills, 193
control groups, 193
Control Theory in the Classroom, 149
controversial issues, 163
cooperation, 92, 162, 177
Cooperative Integrated Reading
  Composition, 123
cooperative learning, 41, 199
  CDP Program, 193
  Character Education Institute
    Curriculum, 41
  promotes character, 118, 127, 161
  special techniques of, 121–124
core programs, 173
Council for the Advancement of
  Citizenship, 161
counselors, 28, 52, 199
Country Club Elementary School, 43,
  173, 176
County Line Elementary School, 37,
  63, 66, 149
courage, 119
Crest Hill Elementary School, 51, 172
current events, 163, 172
curriculum
  academic, 28
  formal, 8
  hidden, 8
  informal, 8
  integrated, 123
  language-based, 177, 194
  programs, 7

DARE, 63
data
  base-line, 197
  collection forms, 196
  qualitative, 186, 192
  quantitative, 186, 192
deaf, 104
decision making, 171
  in drug education, 63, 65

  process, 199
  skills, 69
Declaration of Independence, 16
Del Carro Elementary School, 40
democratic
  ethics, 15
  qualities, 178
  values, 123
Dennis, James L. Elementary School,
  174
Denoyer, Richard, 36
Developing Character in Student, 124
Dewey, John, 17, 18
dilemmas, 185
diligence, 106, 119
Dinkmeyer, Don, 109
discipline
  affective, 149
  cooperative, 140, 145
  developmental, 193
  moral, 140, 148
  positive, 140, 148–149
  problems decreased, 194, 195
  process, parental involvement, 137
Discipline with Dignity, 153
Discipline with Love and Logic, 140,
  146
Discovery textbook, 71
drivers license, 154
drives, food and clothing, 174–175
drug education, 59–75
  as character education, 61
  comprehensive approach, 67
  core moral values, 81
  develops coping skills, 65
  influence of T.V. and movies, 67
  parental involvement, 74
  programs, 74
Drug Free School Recognition
  Program, 59
  Anti-Drug Abuse Act of 1986, 59
  drug-free schools, 199
Durkheim, Emile, 133
Dutiful Child's Promise, 16

Earth Day, 174
East Elementary School, 154, 162

Easter egg hunt, 174
Educating for Character, 49
effective schools research, 197
Elementary School Recognition
     Program — see Blue Ribbon
     Award Program, ix
Elm Street School, 38
Elvin Hill Elementary School, 163
Emotional Intelligence, 75, 87, 98–99
emotional well-being, 173
emotions, 98
empathy, 158, 159, 177
encouragement, 94
environmental awareness, 174
Escriva, de Balaguer, 33–34, 120
ethically literate, 153
ethics of society, 159
ethics, 90, 198
     social, 172
ethical
     conduct, 198
     understanding, 198
evaluation, 66–67, 184
     design, 191
     evaluation of effectiveness, 65
     formal, 186
     formative, 190–191, 193
     informal, 186
     summative, 190–191, 193
Everdale Elementary School, 37
Everdale School, 37
Exemplary Bear Award, 168
Exemplary Patriot Award Program,
     167–168, 197
expectations, high, 120, 125
expertise oriented, 153
Expressions, 128
extracurricular activity participation, 194

fair play, 152
Fairchild, Milton, 16
Fairfield North Elementary School, 92,
     103
fairness, 177
faith, 128
family studies, 195
flags, 177

Flanders Elementary School, 54, 125,
     188
foreign languages, 177
Forest Elementary School, 98
Fort Washington Elementary School, 167
     evaluation, 197
fortitude, 120
4MAT, 125
*Frames of Mind: The Theory of
     Multiple Intelliegences,* 125
Frankfort Junior High School, 138–139
Franklin Elementary School, Benjamin,
     161, 178
friendship, 175
fund raisers, 174

Gallup Poll, 33
games, 160
Gardner, Howard, 125–126
Georgia School District, 37–38
Gesu Catholic School, 188
Glasser, William, 149
global
     citizens, 177
     society, 161
Goals 2000, 66
Goleman, Daniel, 75, 87, 98–99
Governor Bent Elementary School, 39,
     137, 153, 190
Grant, W. T. Foundation — sex
     education research, 76
Green Trails Elementary School, 189
Growing Healthy, 71, 78
Gulliver Academy, 189

habits of the heart, 157
hall, 189
Handbook, 140, 150
handicapped, 104
Harrison Elementary School, 39
Harthshorn & May, 18
health education, 195
Heart Smart, 174
Heartwood Institute Ethics curriculum,
     43–44, 177, 197
     in-service, 49
Hedgcoxe Elementary School, 35

helpfulness, 162
helping hands, 175
Here's Looking at You, 64–66
Hewlett Foundation, William and Flora,
    192
Highlands Elementary School,
    147–148
Hill Elementary School, 67, 176
Hillside School, 79
homework, 74
honesty, 162, 167
honor roll, 154, 194
Hornbook, 15
Huffman Elementary School, 34–35,
    110
Huffman, Henry, 47, 191
human dignity, 142
humanists, 106–107
humility, 119

Independence Primary School, 98, 162
Indian Trail School, 175
intelligence, emotional, 87
interdisciplinary, 128
interviews, 193
    questions, 196
inventories, 196
Irwin School, 40
Ivymount School, 110

Jefferson Center for Character
    Education, 41, 42
    evaluation, 194
    in-service, 49
    STAR Program, 95
Jefferson, Thomas, 16, 157
Johnson, Ann Donegan, 45
Johnson Elementary School, Robert,
    189
Johnson, Spenser, 142
Jones, Dr. Cherry, 125, 188
Josephson Institute, 22
judgment, good 136
Jurs, Stephen, 70
Just community, 20
Just Say No, 66–67
justice, 120, 128, 177

Kahn, Mark, 191
Keystone Kids, 154
Kids on the Block, 104
Kids Teach Kids, 72
Kilgour Elementary School, 52
Kilpatrick, William, 14, 34
    criticizes Quest, 69–70, 72
    on ethos, 90
Kohlberg, Lawrence, 18–20, 185
    theory, 163
Kohn, Alfie
    on awards, 96
    good citizenship awards, 168
    intrinsic motivation, 94
    Punished by Rewards, 91
Kolb, James, 51–52

language arts, integrated, 126
Laurel Mountain Elementary School,
    176–177
laws, 160
leadership, 123, 162
    conferences, 53
    programs, 166
learnball, 154
learning disabled, 104
learning styles, 118, 121–122, 199
    modalities, 124–126
learning, profound, 119
Leming, James, 18, 198
Lets Talk Turkey, 72
library, 189
Lickona, Thomas, 2, 6, 8, 14
    author of *Educating for Character,*
        2–3
    character based sex education, 76, 78
    Comprehensive Model of Character
        Education, 8
    cooperative learning, 159
    defines moral values, 2
    effective drug education, 61
    model of good character, 6, 85
    moral discipline, 148
    multiple intelligences, 126
    respect and responsibility, 153, 164
    summer institute, 49
    value of work, 120

life
  sacredness of, 61
  skills program, 69
Lindgren Elementary School, Susan, 140
literacy
  cultural and moral, 119
  emotional, 98–99
literature
  classical, 127
  exemplifying core character concepts, 194
litter control, 174
Livonia Primary School, 153
logs, 196
longitudinal, 187, 193
Los Angeles Elementary Schools, 194
Los Encinos Special Emphasis School, 99
love, 128
Lowell Elementary School, 166, 177

Madison, James, 157
Magnet Elementary School, 160, 189
Manoa Elementary School, 99
Marion Street Elementary School, 189
Markley School, Kathryn, 190
Martin, Nancy, 149
Maslow, Abraham, 106
McClellan, B. E., 15, 17
McGruff the Crime Dog, 67
McGuffey Readers, 16
Me-ology "values clarification technique", 72
media, 200
Medical Institute for Sexual Health, 76
meeting, classroom, 69
Memphis State University researchers, 97
Mender, Allen, 153
meter maid, 154
Mill Lake School, 160
mini-lessons, 38, 166, 167
mission statement, 7, 28, 31
Monse, Nadine, 126
Monte Cassino School, 102

Monte Gardens Elementary, 53, 136
Montessori materials, 93
Moorestown Friends School, 145, 177
moral
  action, 7, 200
    in citizenship education, 159
  code, 159
  dilemma discussions, 163–164
  education program, 172
  experts, 21
  feeling, 7, 86, 105, 185, 200
    in citizenship education, 159
  knowing, 6, 200
    in citizenship education, 159
    evaluated, 185
  reasoning, 193
    levels, 163
  relativism, 111
  responsibility, 159, 177
  values education, program of, 61
Moral Education in the Life of the School, 21
Morally Mature Person
  six characteristics, 21
  sound, 160
Moriches Elementary School, 169
morning announcements, 91
motivation, 93
  intrinsic, 93, 154
  programs, 86
mottos, 95, 96
Mountain View Elementary School, 89, 92, 101, 168
multicultural
  literature, 177
  studies, 177
  units, 161
multimodal, 73
multiple intelligences, 118, 125
Murdock Elementary School, 73–74
Murphy, Madonna, vii, 50
music, 177

National Association of Christian Education, 111

National Association of State Boards of
Education, 75
National Guidelines for Sexuality in
Character Education, 76, 77
Native American, 177
neatness, 120
Neubert Elementary School, Kenneth,
154
New Canaan Country School, 136
New England Primer, 15
New England Town School, 15
New York Times, 13
newsletter, 91
Norfeldt School, Eric, 142
Normandy Elementary School, 160
Nucci, Larry
  director of the Center for the Study
    of Moral Development, 3
  drug education program, 61
  editor of *Moral Development and
    Character Education,* 3
  summer institute, 50
nursing homes, 161, 174
nutrition awareness, 174

Oakbrook Elementary School, 168
observational
  checklists, 196
  learning, 199
One Minute Manager, 142
Ormand Beach Elementary, 190

parents, 28, 30, 199
  parental involvement, 194
    in discipline process, 137
    in drug education, 74
Parkway School, 95, 100
participatory process, 141
Patriotic Classroom Award, 197
Peer outreach, 72
Perley Elementary School, 97, 135
perseverance, 92, 159, 177
petitions, 172
PEW Charitable Trust, 161
Phi Delta Kappa, 33
philosophy, 105, 106

Piers-Harris Children's Self-Concept
Scale, 195
Pine Grove School, 151
Pioneer Elementary School, 144, 146,
173–174
Plano School District, 34
playground, 189, 199
Pledge of Allegiance, 162
Powell Gifted and Talented Magnet
School, Lewis, 189
portfolio, 118, 122, 129–130
posters, 51
Preamble to the Constitution, 16
Prevention is Primary, 71
PRIDE—Positive Reinforcement of
Individual Discipline, 152
Princeton School District, 36–37
principal, 28, 150
  letter home, 54
  principal's corner, 51
problem solving, 162
Project Charlie, 67–68
prosocial behaviors, 96, 102, 107, 124,
193
  Observational Checklist, 195
  skills, 102, 154
  values in CDP, 193
protest letters, 163
prudence, 119, 120
punishment, 140–141
Puppets with a Purpose, 40

Quail Creek Elementary School, 125
Quailwood Elementary School, 31, 63
Quality Schools, 140, 149
Quest
  curriculum, 68–69
  evaluation, 195–196
  International Non-Profit
    Organization, 68
questionnaires, 193

reading, 177
realists, 106
reality therapy, 149
recycling, 161, 174

Red Bank Elementary School, 121
Regnart Elementary School, 55
Reiche Community School, Howard
    51, 79
reinforcement, positive, 94
Remar, Miriam, 51
research design
    quasi-experimental, 187, 192, 198
respect, 159, 177
    for authority, 162
    for property, 162
responsibility, 162
    responsibility model, 154
rewards, 94, 140–141
    intrinsic and extrinsic, 94
Reynolds School, Anna, 170–171
Riley, Richard, secretary of education,
    54
Rillieux Elementary School, Norbert,
    174
Roberts School, Mary E., 102
Rogers, Carl, 72–83, 106
role-playing, 69, 160
Roma, Joseph, 100
rubric, 130
rules, 160
Russell Elementary School in Missouri,
    152, 161
Ryan, Kevin
    definition of character, 5
    Director of the Center for the
        Advancement of Ethics and
        Character, 5
    summer institute, 49

Saddle Rock Elementary School, 29–30
safety awareness, 174
Saigling Elementary School, 80, 129,
    135, 160
San Antonio Independent School
    District, 195
San Ramon Valley Unified School
    District, 192
Schlafly, Phyllis, 109
school
    attitude, measure, 196
    climate, 188, 194

Schuster Elementary School, 91
science, 166, 167
self-esteem, achievement, 121
senior citizens, 175
sensitivity training, 109
service:
    activities, 174–175
    learning, 173
    projects, 177
Sewickley Academy, 43–44
sex education
    abstinence only programs, 75–77
    character based, 76
    comprehensive health and sex
        education, 81
    research on, 76
Simmons School, Dorothea, 65
simulations, 160
situation ethics, 111
Skills for Adolescents, 196
skills
    social, 123
    proactive, 123
Smokey the Bear, 174
Snug Harbor Community School, 143
social learning theory, 198
social studies class, 161, 166, 167, 177
social well-being, 173
socially aware, 160
Socrates, 1, 85, 117
South Valley School, 189
Southwest Elementary School, 161
Spartanburg, South Carolina, 195
sports, 177
Spring Glen Elementary School, 123,
    146
St. Damian School, 71, 103
St. Isidore School, 150, 175–176
St. John Bosco School, 171
St. Joseph Montessori School, 93, 120
St. Luke's, 30
St. Mark the Evangelist Catholic
    School, 141
St. Rocco School, 175
St. Thomas More School, 13, 98, 126
St. Thomas of Canterbury School, 112
staff, 189, 199

STAR Success Through Accepting
  Responsibility (see Jefferson
  Curriculum)
Statue of Liberty renovation, 174
Stein, Andrea, 51
Stewart Elementary School, 37, 109
St. Rosalie School, 142, 163
St. Stanislaus Bishop and Martyr
  School, 138
standards, academic, 117
standards, high, 117, 199
structured learning approach, 102
student council, 161, 171
student motivation program, 87
Student Recognition Program, 199
student suggestion box, 172
students, 118–119
  morale, 194
study buddy, 166
substance abuse program, 59–60
summer institute for teachers, 49–50
Summerville Elementary School, 130
surveys, 196
  data, 195
Sylvester, Robert, 9

Tarkington School, Booth, 89
teachable moments, 101
teacher, 28, 46, 189, 190
teacher-friendly materials, 194
teaching methodologies, 199
Team Assisted Individualization — TAI,
  122–123
team building techniques, 123
technology, 122, 128
temperance, 120
tests, achievement, 193
Thanksgiving food baskets, 174
thematic instruction, 119, 121,
  128–129
thinking
  process, higher order, 122, 128–129
  skills, developing, 129
Time-to-Think Room, 141
Time-out, 141
time-series analysis, 187
Tocqueville, Alexis, 157

town meeting, 164
trust, 162
truth, 106, 128
tutoring, 173
Tyler, Ralph, 184–187

U. S. Department of Education — drug
  education act, 59–60
UNICEF, 174
Urban Institute, 75

Value Tales, 45
values
  core, 39
  cultural, 4
  moral, 3
  social, 3
  three pronged approach to teaching,
    100
  traditional, 60–61
values clarification, 19
  in drug education, 68
vandalism, 195
virtue, 1, 2
  cardinal, 34
  lives of, 181
  teachers of, 117
Volker Applied Learning Magnet
  School, 39, 145

Waiahole Elementary School, 102
Washington School, 141–142
Watchman Expositor, 68
Weaver, M. R. Elementary School, 174
We Help Ourselves, 80
Weedsport Elementary School, 175
Weekly Reader, 45–46
Wells Elementary School, 35
Westwood Elementary School, 69, 101,
  129, 166, 177
What Works — Schools Without Drugs,
  61, 67
White House Conference on Character
  Education, 50
Whittier Elementary School, 128
whole language, 119, 121, 126–128
Wilt-Berry, Joy, 45

Wynne, Edward
  author of *Reclaiming Our Schools,*
    31, 88
  on awards, 88
  on ceremonies, 91
  defines character, 3, 106, 136

moral education methodology, 48
  on moral literacy, 47
Wynne, Judith, 30

Yakutat Elementary School, 189

Dr. Madonna M. Murphy received her bachelor's degree in philosophy from the University of Chicago and her master's and doctorate from Loyola University Chicago in Educational Leadership and Policy Studies. She has taught at the elementary, high school, and college level. For the past 15 years, she has taught philosophy, ethics, and character education to college students. Recently, she has specialized in teaching Philosophy of Education and Character Education for Teachers. She is a member of the Philosophy of Education Society, the Character Education Partnership, the Association of Moral Educators, Association for Supervision and Curriculum Development, and Phi Delta Kappa. She has served as a site visitor for the U.S. Department of Education Blue Ribbon Schools Panel. She has presented her research on the Blue Ribbon Schools at the American Educational Research Association, the Character Education Partnership Forum, the Association for Moral Education's Annual Meeting, the National Character Education Conference, and the Summer Institute on Character Education in Cortland, New York. She has conducted several in-services at schools interested in beginning character education programs. She works at the College of St. Francis as an associate professor of Education.